Social Informatics

Social Informatics: Past, Present and Future

Edited by

Pnina Fichman and Howard Rosenbaum

CAMBRIDGE SCHOLARS

PUBLISHING

Social Informatics: Past, Present and Future
Edited by Pnina Fichman and Howard Rosenbaum

This book first published 2014

Cambridge Scholars Publishing

12 Back Chapman Street, Newcastle upon Tyne, NE6 2XX, UK

British Library Cataloguing in Publication Data
A catalogue record for this book is available from the British Library

ISBN (10): 1-4438-5576-6, ISBN (13): 978-1-4438-5576-1

TABLE OF CONTENTS

CONTRIBUTOR LIST

Editors

Pnina Fichman is an Associate Professor and the Director of the Rob Kling Center of Social Informatics in the School of Informatics and Computing at Indiana University, Bloomington. Her work focuses on social informatics; she published the books, *Global Wikipedia* and *Multiculturalism and ICT*.

Howard Rosenbaum is an Associate Dean in the School of Informatics and Computing at Indiana University. He has been involved in social informatics since 1997, writing a book (with Kling and Sawyer) and numerous articles about SI and working with collaborators to raise the profile of SI in the information sciences.

Authors

J.P. Allen is an Associate Professor in the School of Management, University of San Francisco.

Andrew Cox is a Lecturer at The Information School, University of Sheffield, UK.

Gary Burnett is a Professor in the School of Information within the College of Communication of Information at Florida State University.

Kathleen Burnett is a Professor and Director in the School of Information within the College of Communication of Information at Florida State University.

Kristin Eschenfelder is a Professor and Director in the School of Library and Information Studies at the iSchool, University of Wisconsin-Madison.

Pnina Fichman is an Associate Professor and the Director of the Rob Kling Center of Social Informatics in the School of Informatics and Computing at Indiana University, Bloomington. Her work focuses on social informatics; she published the books, *Global Wikipedia* and *Multiculturalism and ICT*.

Kenneth R. Fleischmann is an Associate Professor in the School of Information at the University of Texas at Austin. His research focuses on the role of human values in the design and use of information technologies. He is the author of *Information and Human Values*.

Noriko Hara is an Associate Professor in the School of Informatics and Computing at Indiana University Bloomington. Her research examines the means by which collective behaviors – including knowledge sharing, online mobilization, and communities of practice – are enabled and/or impeded by information technology, and is rooted in the social informatics perspective.

Mark Hartswood is a Research Associate at Oxford University who has worked within Social Informatics for more than 15 years, now focusing on Responsible Research and Innovation and ICTs. Mark curates a highly interdisciplinary Social Informatics seminar series in the School of Informatics in Edinburgh featuring local and international scholars.

Charles C. Hinnant is an Assistant Professor in the School of Information at Florida State University. His research interests include social and organizational informatics, digital government, information management and policy, technological innovation, and public management. He is currently on the editorial board of *Government Information Quarterly*.

Michelle M. Kazmer is an Associate Professor in the School of Information within the College of Communication of Information at Florida State University. Her research on distributed knowledge processes is focused on dementia caregivers, scientists, and e-learners.

Brian Knop is a doctoral student in the Department of Sociology at Florida State University.

Lysanne Lessard is an Assistant Professor in the Telfer School of Management at the University of Ottawa. Her research takes a socio-technical perspective on the design and modeling of knowledge-intensive business services and knowledge infrastructures.

Paul F. Marty is an Associate Professor in the School of Information within the College of Communication of Information at Florida State University. His research and teaching interests include museum informatics, information behavior, and user-centered design.

Eric T. Meyer is a Senior Research Fellow at the Oxford Internet Institute, University of Oxford, UK. He is an active social informatics researcher, particularly focusing on changes in research across the sciences, social sciences, and humanities as digital tools and data become inextricably intertwined with everyday scholarly practices.

Howard Rosenbaum is Associate Dean of Graduate Studies in the School of Informatics and Computing at Indiana University. He has been involved in social informatics since 1997, writing a book (with Kling and Sawyer) and numerous articles about SI and working with collaborators to raise the profile of SI in the information sciences.

Madelyn Sanfilippo is a doctoral student in Information Science at the School of Informatics and Computing at Indiana University.

Steve Sawyer is professor in the School of Information Studies at Syracuse University. He has been involved in social informatics since the 1990s, writing a book (with Kling and Rosenbaum) and a series of articles about advancing social informatics and sociotechnical approaches.

Besiki Stvilia is an Associate Professor in the School of Information within the College of Communication of Information at Florida State University.

Grant Leyton Simpson is a doctoral student in Information Science and English at Indiana University. His dissertation investigates sociotechnical aspects of digital humanities research from the 1960s to the present, with specific focus on medieval studies projects.

Adam Worrall is a Doctoral Candidate in the School of Information within the College of Communication of Information at Florida State University. He studies information and information behavior within and around sociotechnical contexts of ICT, including research in social informatics, digital libraries, scientific collaboration, social media, and online communities.

Shuheng Wu is a Doctoral Candidate in the School of Information within the College of Communication of Information at the Florida State University. Her research interests include knowledge organization, scientific data management, social informatics, image indexing, and information and data quality.

INTRODUCTION

The study of people, technologies and the contexts in which these technologies are designed, implemented and used has long interested scholars in a wide range of disciplines, including the social study of computing, science and technology studies, the sociology of technology, and management information systems. Driven initially by a growing awareness that the integration of information and communication technologies (ICT) into organizations was changing organizational structures and processes, researchers began to ponder how the routinization of ICT in the workplace was also changing workers' practices. As ICT use has now spread from organizations, various networked devices have become routine information appliances in people's social lives, and the web has become an increasingly pervasive and important source of information, communication and connection, researchers have begun to ask deeper and more profound questions about how our lives have become bound up with technologies. A common theme running through this research is that the relationships among people, technology and context are dynamic, complex, and critically important to understand. Beginning in the early 1980s, scholars have been peering into and attempting to untangle the complexities of these relationships; many of these investigations were undertaken using the rubric of social informatics (SI). Since the mid 1990s, research and theorizing in SI has picked up in pace, even as the breadth and depth of the work has inspired a new generation of scholars.

We believe that this volume will be useful for scholars and researchers intrigued by the questions and issues that characterize this critical approach to the study of the complex relationships among people, technology and context and who want to assess the current state of SI. The work presented here will be especially useful for students and new researchers who are beginning to ask questions about the impacts of our technologies and digital services on our lives. In fact, the organization of the book fits well into an academic course covering SI. Students can begin reading about the intellectual history of SI, follow up with exemplars of contemporary research that uses an SI approach and finish by exploring speculations about the future of SI, a future in which these students can play an important role.

Since 2005, SI researchers have gathered every fall at the Annual Social Informatics Research Symposium, organized by the Special Interest Group in Social Informatics (SIG-SI) of the Association for Information Science and Technology (ASIS&T). The Symposium, which has been held in conjunction with the ASIS&T annual meetings, is now a meeting place for people interested in exploring the social aspects of computerization. Over the years, it has attracted a vibrant mix of established scholars, newcomers to SI and, importantly for the future of this field, many doctoral students from a broad range of disciplines. Some of the symposia papers have been empirical and others conceptual; some authors have presented research in progress or posters, while others have presented fully developed papers. Not surprisingly, the topics and approaches in these papers have varied widely over the years, but the common thread has been the focus on people, technologies, and contexts of ICT design and use. At recent Symposia, SIG-SI and the Rob Kling Center for Social Informatics at Indiana University have presented two awards, one for the best SI paper published in the preceding year and one for the best SI paper published by a student in the preceding year.

This book grew out of the 8th Social Informatics Symposium, which was held in Baltimore in the fall of 2012. A series of very interesting papers were presented that focused on the past, present, and future of social informatics, exploring a wide range of topics relevant to the field. Cambridge Scholarly Publishers approached the Symposium organizers, Pnina Fichman and Howard Rosenbaum, to develop the Symposium theme into what has become this edited volume. Seven of the papers presented at the 2012 Symposium have been expanded into full length chapters and are included in this book along with five papers that were solicited by the editors from presenters at previous SI symposia. The result is a volume with 12 chapters that provides a look backward to the origin of SI, several examples of current research by SI scholars and several chapters that offer different visions of the future of SI.

The first two chapters in this book, which make up the section on the past of SI, provide new perspectives that trace and assess the evolution of SI and speculate on its future as a discipline. Rosenbaum's critical historical narrative of the evolution of SI as a scientific and intellectual movement draws on social movement theory. He focuses on early developments in SI and traces them back to Europe, the USSR and Japan, challenging the conventional belief that the origin of SI was in a 1996 US workshop where Rob Kling and colleagues sought to gather their disparate research in the social aspects of computing under a common conceptual umbrella. Rosenbaum's story concludes in 2005. Sanfilippo and Fichman review three decades of SI literature and identify four distinct periods. They also trace the origin of SI to the 1980s, before the term was used by North American scholars who conducted what might now be considered SI research. Sanfilippo and Fichman identify a period of foundational work, followed by development and expansion prior to 2000. Two periods that contribute to SI research follow afterward: a robust period of coherence that was influenced by Rob Kling and a period of diversification that started shortly after his death and continues today. They conclude by raising questions about the possible future expansion or extinction of SI research.

Five chapters provide a sense of the variety in current SI research and exemplify what Sanfillipo and Fichman call its period of diversification. Diversification in SI goes well beyond these examples and includes research in the history of computing, network science, some science and technology studies, information technology in organization and society, and more. Each of these chapters describes work that pushes SI into a different direction and suggests new paths for SI researchers. Meyer is concerned that SI may become irrelevant if it cannot be more deeply integrated into mainstream sociotechnical research and theory. He claims that although we understand the complexities of socio-technical configurations better today than we did 15 years ago, the volume of SI in curricula and gray literature rather than in the published and peer-reviewed journal literature is both encouraging and troubling. Meyer – like Sawyer and Hartswood, who write on the future of SI later in this volume – suggests that SI focus on the hyphen in socio-technical, affording equal importance to the "socio" and the "technical" and differentiate itself from other socio-technical approaches that typically privilege one over the other. He finds much of value in the socio-technical interaction network (STIN) strategy which, he argues, is a contribution that comes from the SI literature and is an alternative to the social construction of technology (SCOT) approach and actor-network theory (ANT). The STIN strategy allows us to draw on the useful insights of SCOT and ANT but does not wholly embrace a relativist perspective and is skeptical of the possibility that non-human actants can exert agency in social situations.

Fleischman seeks to bring the concept of value closer to the core of SI, arguing that a concern for human values was present implicitly, as a key element of the essential institutional and cultural contexts, in Kling and colleagues' definition. Fleischman finds in pioneering SI work insights about values and value conflicts in computerization that laid the groundwork for what he calls "value sensitive design." The concept of values and instances of value conflict have been investigated in a wide variety of disciplines and he carefully builds a case that these should be studied in SI as well because of the clear entanglement of values and value conflict in the design, implementation and use of ICTs. To illustrate the utility of this approach, he describes several cases of "design interventions" that forge connections between the design of ICTs and the values of users and speculates about the future of values and design and how they are transforming and will continue to transform SI.

Hara and Fichman take a conceptual approach and apply an SI lens to social media, focusing particularly on knowledge sharing in online communities and the concepts of boundaries and boundary crossing. This is interesting and important, they argue, because knowledge sharing in online communities is an integral part of the social web and, unlike the organizational context of most early research in SI, is occurring outside of organizations, therefore challenging taken-for-granted assumptions and prior research findings about ICT, people, and context. Drawing on insights from the research literature on boundaries, boundary crossing, boundary spanning, and boundary objects, they propose a typology of frameworks for the analysis of boundary types and properties, distinguished by the presence or absence of physical, cognitive, social, and political components. With this typology, they suggest, SI researchers may have the conceptual tools to examine knowledge sharing in online communities that exist outside of traditional organizations and to test and modify these early conceptualizations in light of their usefulness in and fit with new and different socio-technical contexts.

Eschenfelder introduces a theoretical framework called "use regimes" that focuses on a particular area of inquiry – the practices through which people arrange and carry out the transfer of intellectual and cultural works. More specifically, use regimes are temporary stabilizations of networks of associations related to the practices of transferring or distributing creative and intellectual works. The use regimes framework reflects many of the tensions currently felt in SI. On one hand, it embodies the core principles of SI (e.g., ICT are interpreted and used in different ways by different people; ICT enable and constrain social actions and relationships, etc.). On the other hand, the framework expands what is commonly understood to be SI research in several ways detailed in her chapter.

In the last chapter in this section, Burnett and colleagues describe a site-specific empirical study of scientists at work that demonstrates the utility of an SI perspective for untangling the complexities of the uses of ICT in scientific practice. Their case study focuses on the collaborative work done by distributed teams of scientists who work remotely on long-term projects and gather periodically at the National High Magnetic Field

Laboratory in Florida for brief, intensive periods of work. Using a theory of information worlds that foregrounds the uses of a range of ICT both to enable and to hinder communication among researchers, they study the impacts of social, technical, institutional and disciplinary factors on the conduct of complex, multidisciplinary scientific research over time.

After these exemplars of contemporary SI research, the concluding section of the book addresses a critically important question: what is the future of SI? It is clear that a growing cohort of scholars and researchers have a deep and abiding interest in understanding the tangled web of connections and interactions among people, technology, and context and it is also clear that these researchers are approaching this domain from a variety of perspectives and with an impressive range of theories and methods. It is also worth mentioning that many more scholars around the globe conduct work, which has not been included here, that looks at the same problems and asks similar questions about the relationships between people, technology, and context. The diversity is evident in the previous section is a good indication that SI as an approach to research is thriving and helping to generate useful insights; the themes running throughout the work have become a part of a common intellectual tradition that forms the core of knowledge characterizing contemporary SI. Interestingly, many of the chapters that address the past and present state of SI also make reference to future directions of SI in research, teaching and institutional infrastructure.

The five scholars who explicitly take up the question of what should happen next describe different futures for SI, grounded in their disparate visions of the trajectory of the discipline. SI researchers, in their opinions, should revive concepts and approaches already known in socio-technical research and renovate them conceptually with an eye on cognate disciplines and methods, as well as utilize some of the unique insights and concepts of SI. These include the potential of the socio-technical interaction network (STIN) as a sensitizing concept, a rehabilitation of the critical impulse of SI, a serious exploration of a philosophical approach, critical realism, and a practice approach to ground SI conceptually and extend its utility. Moreover, these chapters call for collaborative large-scale research and for a synergy between micro and macro research as ways to develop SI. Taken together, the authors in this section raise several pertinent questions about the scope and boundaries of SI.

In the first of the chapters reflecting on the future of SI, Lessard argues that one way forward is to foreground critical realism as a philosophical basis for studying and theorizing the relationships at the core of the field. Arguing that SI research has been criticized for a reductionist approach to the relationship of mutual shaping between ICT and the people who design, manage, and use them, she suggests approaching mutual shaping as a problem of the relationship between structure and action. One key insight from critical realism with significance for SI is that socio-technical interactions are ontologically distinct from the structures and generative forces that cause them. This distinction, she argues, will allow research to consider analytically the role of structure in shaping but not determining action and provide a stronger basis for mid-range theories of ICTs and people in organizations, and in particular, of the information infrastructures that should be the focus of SI research.

Simpson argues that SI, taken as a critical approach to the study of the sociotechnological production and use of artifacts, can be enriched by drawing on the material semiotics of ANT and, from the humanities, textual studies. Humanistic inquiry has a place in SI, he contends, particularly as SI recovers its critical impulse. Carefully developing an argument for the relevance of bibliography and textual criticism in SI, he describes an expansive conception of text that includes technologies of inscription, material artifacts, and the social practices that are bound up in them. He calls for researchers in SI and the humanities to take up this critical approach, using digital humanities as an example of the fruitful cross-pollination that can occur from such boundary-spanning activities.

Cox investigates the implications for SI of a shift in research and theorizing from current concerns to a focus on practice, arguing that the resulting attention paid to the concepts of materiality and embodiment show much promise when studying people's uses of ICT in a wide range of settings. Tracing the rise of what he calls "practice thinking" in different social sciences from foundational thinkers including Wittgenstein, Giddens, and Bourdieu, he argues that concepts such as communities of practice and sociomateriality began to appear in information science, information systems, and science and technology studies at the turn of the twentieth century. Describing four main assumptions of this approach, Cox uses the example of food blogging to illustrate how SI research can be deepened and enriched with these concepts and assumptions.

Allen suggests that SI return to its roots and explore the impacts of the cultural and institutional contexts of formal organizations, specifically business organizations. In doing so, he positions SI as a critical alternative to conventional approaches for studying the complexities of global business, thus reinvigorating SI research and theorizing and also laying the groundwork for business reform. He argues that SI can explain the new productivity paradox – the inability of the digital economy to generate prosperity and opportunity in sustainable ways – and in doing so, the approach will have demonstrated its value and ensured its continued existence in the academy.

In the final chapter, Sawyer and Hartswood make a case for the continuing relevance of SI by arguing that its focus on the complex interconnections among technology, people, their interactions with each other and with ICTs, and the setting in which this all takes place provides a needed corrective to studies of computerization. To conceptualize the socio-technical nature of computing in society, it is necessary for SI researchers to have a shared sense of what to investigate and how to investigate it. They suggest that the materiality, meaning the form and function of the computing artifact, and performative nature of computing are useful grounds from which to begin this work.

The collection of papers in this volume presents a view of SI that emphasizes the core relationships among people, ICT, and organizational and social life from perspectives that integrate aspects of social theory. Reading these chapters reveals that SI is, in fact, a lively and dynamic problem-centered approach to the study of computerization and society that provides researchers with organizing principles, insights, and concepts that drive critical, theoretical, and empirical research. Social analyses of computing have been at the core of SI for almost four decades and it has never been a more necessary research endeavor than it is now. Ubiquitous computing, the internet of things, the social web, the pervasiveness of big data – all indicate the extent to which computerization and ICT have become deeply entangled and routinized in our lives in taken-for-granted and uncritical ways. SI is therefore an increasingly important perspective through which the invisible can be made visible and its hidden assumptions brought to light for careful critical examination. This is an important and necessary endeavor as the speed of technological change increases, challenging our abilities to reflect on its development and impacts. Because the future of SI depends on its continued institutionalization and its take-up by a new generation of scholars and researchers, we hope that this volume entices and intrigues researchers and theoreticians to engage with the challenge SI poses.

Of course, the approach presented in these papers is not the only standpoint from which to view SI but we hope it will be considered, adopted, criticized, and perhaps modified by others. Many scholars working in and around the domain of SI define their research more narrowly and identify themselves with specific societies and groups (e.g., Internet Research, Human Computer Interaction). However, a continued, productive, and recognized scholarship that self-identifies as SI is clearly critical; any intellectual movement needs a coherent and shared core body of knowledge, but this by itself, is not sufficient. The diversity of philosophical and methodological perspectives described in the chapters that follow demonstrate that the domain of SI is one of active debate where scholars from a wide range of backgrounds are thinking clearly and deeply about the foundations of SI; it is the churn of ideas makes SI of contemporary interest. For SI to thrive, it needs an institutional infrastructure of departments, research centers, degree programs, conferences and publishing venues that support SI research and teaching. There is evidence that such institutionalization is progressing, but the question remains whether the current state of SI is helping or hindering its growth and development. We believe that these issues need to be thought through and hope that this volume is an early contribution to the discourse.

ACKNOWLEDGEMENTS

We would like to thank each of our colleagues who made contributions to this volume. We acknowledge Debora Shaw and thank her for her valuable suggestions. We are also very grateful for the assistance from Clinton McKay and we are in debt to Carol Koulikourdi from Cambridge Scholars Publishing for her initiative to publish this book.

PART I

PAST

CHAPTER ONE

THE PAST: SOCIAL INFORMATICS AS A SCIENTIFIC AND INTELLECTUAL MOVEMENT

HOWARD ROSENBAUM

> Most movements have inconspicuous beginnings. The significant elements of their origins are usually forgotten or distorted by the time a trained observer seeks to trace them out. Perhaps this is why so much theoretical literature on social movements concentrated on causes (Gurr 1970; Davies 1962; Oberschall 1973) and motivations (Toch 1965; Cantril 1941; Hoffer 1951; Adorno et al. 1950), while the 'spark of life' by which the 'mass is to cross the threshold of organizational life' (Lowi 1971, 41) has received scant attention. (Freeman 1999, 7)

> In 1996, some participants in this research community agreed that the scattering of related research in a wide array of journals and the use of different nomenclatures was impeding both the research and the abilities of 'research consumers' to find important work. They decided that a common name for the field would be helpful. After significant deliberation, they selected 'social informatics.' (Kling, Rosenbaum and Sawyer 2005, 30)

Introduction

This chapter explores the emergence and rise of Social Informatics (SI) using a framework based on a social movement theory that views such domains of scientific activity as scientific and intellectual movements (SIMs). Based on a powerful analogy that will be explained below, this approach is useful because it employs conceptual and methodological tools of social movement research to provide an interesting perspective on the rise and fall of scientific disciplines. It will be used here to examine the trajectory of SI between the early 1980s and mid 2000s and will provide a corrective to the conventional origin story about SI that pinpoints its creation in a discussion that took place at a 1996 workshop in the US.

What, then is a social movement? Tilly (1984, 306) describes social movements as

> … a sustained series of interactions between power holders and persons successfully claiming to speak on behalf of a constituency lacking formal representation, in the course of which those persons make publicly visible demands for changes in the distribution or exercise of power, and back those demands with public demonstrations of support.

According to Snow, Soule and Kriesi (2004, 11), social movements are

> … collectivities acting with some degree of organization and continuity outside of institutional or organizational channels for the purpose of challenging or defending extant authority, whether it is institutionally or culturally based, in the group, organization, society, culture, or world order of which they are a part.

Why do social movements emerge when they do? Are they brought into being by an influential person whose presence and activities provide the impetus for a movement to begin? Can a movement be touched off by the publication of a seminal paper or monograph? Can a critical incident be the point of origin of a movement? Could the process be more complex and nuanced, rooted, for example, in particular social, organizational, and historical contexts? Although the significant individual, publication, and incident certainly have roles to play in the histories and development of social movements, many researchers have moved past the great person explanation, the myth of the "big book," and other similar origin stories when studying the emergence of social movements. Meyer and Rohlinger (2012, 137) explain that, like the great person claim, the "big book myth is a variant of an 'immaculate conception' … story of movement origins, in which mobilization occurs suddenly, without apparent antecedent, through a few dedicated individuals, and produces relatively quick political response." The problem, they argue (2012, 145), is that this type of explanation "encourages a fundamental misunderstanding of the process of social change" and ignores the hard work and participation of many individuals and groups who are typically written out of the history of the movement by this approach. In contrast, much more attention should be paid to the role of social, cultural, political, and other macro-level factors as key components in enabling and constraining social movements.

One assumption that underlies the argument in this chapter is that the rise and fall of scientific worldviews, which include such components as epistemologies, ontologies, key concepts and ideas, theories, perspectives, frameworks, research, methods, and findings, can be more clearly understood when framed as social movements. This assumption is drawn from Frickel and Gross (2005), who propose a theory of scientific and intellectual movements (SIMs), which, they suggest, can better account for the central mechanisms of social change in the world of science, knowledge, and ideas. Anticipating the rejection of what would come to be called the "immaculate conception" explanation of social change (Meyer and Rohlinger 2012, 137), Frickel and Gross (2005, 204) argue that when considering the social and historical trajectories of SIMs,

> … an adequate sociohistorical understanding … cannot be had by focusing exclusively on the actions or contributions of any one individual (e.g., the intellectual leader of the movement) except insofar as those actions affect the web of social relationships that comprises the SIM.

Further, they assume that many of the insights that have come from contemporary social movement research can be used to explain the trajectories of SIMs and claim that (2005, 204)

> … the history of almost every field of study … is a history of new scientific or intellectual movements that rose up to challenge established patterns of inquiry, became the subject of controversy, won or failed to win a large number of adherents, and either became institutionalized for a time, until the next movement came along, or faded into oblivion.

Following their lead, SI is seen here as a SIM, meaning that it is a collective effort "to pursue research programs or projects for thought in the face of resistance from others in the scientific or intellectual community" (Frickel and Gross 2005, 206). Because of the assumption that a SIM is analogous to a social movement, its emergence and development involve collective action, recruitment, training, strategic decision making, and collective action frames intended to mobilize members, acquire and use resources, and raise the movement's profile in a relevant academic community. To be considered a SIM, a movement must develop around a "knowledge core" towards which "participants are consciously oriented, regardless of their understanding of it" (Frickel and Gross 2005, 207). The movement's early leaders tend to be high status academics who are able to articulate the essential elements of its knowledge core and engage in network and institution building. At least initially, the expression of the SIM's intellectual scope involves the assertion that some part of the conventionally accepted worldview in a discipline is in need of reformulation, or has not been sufficiently theorized or researched. In some cases the claim may be advanced that an entirely novel theoretical approach is being proposed that challenges the fundamental assumptions of the status quo in a discipline. In general, however, when a SIM is forming, the set of practices, insights, beliefs, findings and other components of the knowledge core are typically formulated in opposition to the conventional worldview of the field into which the movement is emerging. Although this assertion echoes a Kuhnian (1970) approach, it does not have to be triggered by mounting instances of stubborn research anomalies nor does it have to lead to instances of paradigm change.

Once the scientific and intellectual movement has emerged, its early members begin to develop internal social structures and routine scientific practices, refine its knowledge core, and engage in the work of research, publication, and presentation. This is critically important because, as Frickel and Gross (2005, 213) explain, "(l)ike social movements, SIMs do not just happen, but once their key ideas are formulated, they must be orchestrated, coordinated, and collectively produced." These early members make use of their social networks to publicize the movement to external audiences and attract new members, both established academics and, equally importantly, new students. As the movement attempts to take its place in its corner of the academic environment, pressures emanating from the larger web of academic, institutional and exogenous stakeholders in which it is enmeshed will enable and hinder its progress. Some of the factors that play a role in shaping the trajectory of a SIM include the ability of members to access and mobilize organizational and institutional resources to build, maintain, and extend the basic social and intellectual structures of the movement, the extent to which they are able to demonstrate the impact of their research through funding, publication and citation, the ability of new and established members to compete for and obtain positions in appropriate research universities and funding institutions, and the extent to which they develop a shared scientific and intellectual identity. Frickel and Gross (2005, 225) point out that:

> Like social movements, SIMs represent contentious challenges to normative practices and institutions and, as such, are inherently political. Requiring ongoing coordination at various levels of organization, SIMs are episodic creatures that eventually and inevitably disappear, either through failure and disintegration, or through success and institutional stabilization.

The framework they propose to explain the rise and fall of SIMs will be used here to help explain developments in the emergence and evolution of SI. It is useful because it focuses on "the ways in which social processes and events shape the internal content of intellectual and scientific inquiry" and establishes conditions under which a movement may "gain control, if only for a limited time, of what Collins (1998) calls the 'intellectual attention space.'" (Frickel and Gross 2005, 204). It can account for the processes through which SI has emerged, attracted scholars' interest and support, attempted to gain prestige and influence in the landscape of socio-technical studies of computerization in society, and sought some degree of institutional stability. In brief, the earliest use of the term to describe a research domain was in Norway in the early 1980s. Degree-granting academic programs in SI were established in Norwegian and Slovenian universities in the mid to late 1980s. Around the same time, scholars in the former Soviet Union also established an ambitious program in SI research and education. A few years later, in the early 1990s, Japanese scholars began to engage in institution building and publish SI research. At this time in the UK, several programs and centers devoted to investigating computerization from an SI perspective were established at leading universities. In the mid 1990s, American researchers began to describe studies of the social aspects of computing as SI research. In the past two and a half decades, SI research, researchers and programs emerged in at least six different regions of the world with the American version seeming to have had the greatest impact in terms of the numbers of publications, conference papers, workshops, and research centers.

This chapter explores the emergence and development of SI as a preliminary step in untangling the complex background of the concept and the discipline and sketching the boundaries of the research domain the concept is intended to cover. The SIM framework will be used to illustrate the ways in which various factors helped and hindered the emergence and development of SI in its current form. Some basic assumptions that underlie SI research are described after which the chapter concludes with comments about the potential of SI as a SIM. A caveat in what follows is that all source materials are published in English, so it is possible that nuances in discussions of SI in other languages may be lost in translation.

A Brief History of Social Informatics

What constellation of factors led to the emergence of SI as a scientific and intellectual movement? When did it first appear? What type of trajectory has it had since its emergence? There is a tradition of studying technology and society theoretically and empirically in a range of disciplines including but certainly not limited to history, sociology, communications, anthropology, management information systems and, more recently, science and technology studies. With so much activity in so many disciplines, what need was SI intended to fill and where would its intellectual home be?

The history of informatics (without the modifier) stretches across much of the 20th century. Brookes (1984, 221) notes that in 1917, the term was part of the political and academic discourse in the Soviet Union, arguing that Lenin's "role as the founder … of Russian *informatics* is not as well known in the West as it deserves to be." This version of informatics was defined as "the study of the general properties of scientific information processes" which was distinct from the "science of information" (Brookes 1984, 223). According to Brookes (1984, 222), although "the information technology of the early 1920's was of course limited," Lenin "sought to exploit all that was then available" and oversaw the development of information systems in Russia intended to manage the flood of scientific and technical information occurring in the world following the first World War. One example (Brookes 1984, 222) was the Foreign Science and Technology Bureau, established in 1920 to

> … collect foreign patents, note new discoveries, acquire, translate and publish selected books and journals, notify Western Europe about developments in Russia and buy foreign exhibitions displaying scientific and technical advances for display in Russia.

After this early use of the term, there was not much intellectual activity around the concept until 1957, when a German computer scientist, Steinbuch, "coined the word *Informatik* by publishing a paper called *Informatik: Automatische Informationsverarbeitung"* translated as "Informatics: Automatic Information Processing" (Absolute Astronomy 2013). Although associated with computer science, the concept became broadened in the mid 1960s by a Russian information scientist, Mikhailov, who (Le Roux 2009, 4)

> … worked at the Russian Scientific and Technical Information Institute of Russian Academy of Sciences … [and] redefined "informatika' as an independent discipline that refers to the "theory of scientific information", and not merely applied information technology, that investigates the structure, properties and specific content of scientific information, as well as the regularities of scientific information activity, its theory, history, methodology and organization.

In the 1960s the term was used in proceedings of a 1965 UCLA symposium on on-line information systems. As early as 1971, the Organization for Economic Cooperation and Development gave the term prominence in a set of publications titled "OECD Informatics Studies" with informatics defined as "the study of information content, representation, technology, and the methods and strategies associated with its use" (Niblett 1971; Kimbel 1973). Brookes (1980, 20) argues that in the late 1970s, informatics was at the core of information science and since this time, the term has been used to describe "the study of information content, representation, technology, and the methods and strategies associated with its use" (Sawyer and Eschenfelder 2002, 431). In 1989, the first UNESCO Congress on "Education and Informatics" was held in Paris with a goal of "using collective experience and joint exploitation of limited resources in the sphere of new information technologies in education" (UNESCO, nd). The second Congress was held in Moscow in 1994, and, according to UNESCO (nd) "Russia represented not only the country-organizer … but also one of the most advanced countries in the field of education and application of new technologies for education development." Aspray (2011, 233) recently offered a clear definition of the term

> The field of informatics is about the application of information concepts and technology to an application domain, but it studies these issues from the information perspective; it foregrounds the information concepts and methods and backgrounds the specific application, whether it concerns health, engineering, biology, or real estate.

However, tracing the history of the term "informatics" is beyond the scope of this chapter. More important for the matter at hand is that throughout the 1980s, the term "informatics" began to acquire modifiers describing the varied domains in which computerization was beginning to have an impact; early examples include medical and legal informatics. For this chapter, the most important modifier appeared in early 1980s when Norwegian social scientists whose work focused on the intersections among technology, organizations, and work began to describe what they did as "social informatics." Roggen (2005) claims that "social informatics, the interdisciplinary field of informatics, … [was] established as a science in 1982 by Stein Bråten" at the University of Oslo. Originally called "socio-informatics," Bråten saw it as a "scientific domain between psychology, sociology and informatics" (Roggen 1998). At this time, Bråten and colleagues, including Jahren, Jansen, and Roggen, began researching, publishing, and teaching SI. Soon after, the Ministry of Education established an academic program in SI at the University of Oslo in 1985 (Vehovar 2013a). A notable pedagogical contribution was provided by Roggen, who, in 1996, introduced "the Sociology of the World Wide Web … as a web science, based on the principles of social informatics" (Vehovar 2006).

Similar activity was occurring simultaneously to the east where the Faculty of Social Sciences at University of Ljubljana, Slovenia established a program in SI in 1985 (Vehovar 2013b). In their version, the term "relates to interaction between society and information-communication technologies" at macro and micro levels of analysis. As a consequence of all of this activity, according to Robbin and Day (2006), SI was beginning to achieve status as a discipline. The collective actions of these researchers and academics set the stage for the development of SI as a SIM, particularly the collective action frames intended to recruit, train and mobilize members, acquire and use resources, and that would, as a result, raise the movement's profile in their countries.

Around the same time that scholars in Norway and Slovenia were forming academic units around SI similar efforts were underway in the Soviet Union. The oldest scientific paper in ISI's Web of Science explicitly related to SI is "On the shaping of Social Informatics," published in 1989 by Russian philosopher A.D. Ursal, affiliated with the USSR Academy of Science (Vehovar 2006, 76). This is an important paper because Ursal (1989, 12; 15) describes the emergence of SI as a consequence of the increasing pervasiveness of information technologies in scientific activity and argues for its centrality among forms of inquiry focusing on the study of information, information technologies, and society:

> The increasing interaction between social sciences and informatics not only manifests itself in particular aspects of this interaction, but also causes new systemic (or, in other words, synergistic) effects that testify to integrative processes in this field moving to a qualitatively new level. First of all, we mean here the line in scientific research that is called "social informatics" or "socioinformatics."
>
> Social informatics is supposed to integrate social and natural-technical knowledge, hence it should belong to the family of complex or even general-scientific discipline ... As an integrative and general-scientific form of knowledge, social informatics must thus serve as a connective and consolidating link between all major branches of modern science (along with philosophy and other general-scientific means).

In this paper, he articulated several of the themes that would become central to the version of SI popularized by Kling and colleagues in the mid 1990s. For example, Ursal (1989, 10) argues that SI is a new scientific discipline uniquely positioned to study the impacts of what he called "informatisation," a "socio-technological" process "based on the production and implementation of electronic computing technology," the purpose of which is to employ information technologies to gather and use information to improve the human condition. In a prescient insight, Ursal (1989, 10) describes the relationship between society and informatics as being characterized by mutual shaping because "informatisation constitutes only one characteristic of the interaction between society and informatics; another is the reciprocal impact of society on informatics development."

Unpacking this insight, Ursal sees SI as having two main precursors that he describes (1989, 10) as "the informatisation of society and the socialization of informatics" First, he (1989, 10) points to the increasing pervasiveness of informatisation, as a "process of gaining information with the help of informatics means to secure the survival of mankind and a further acceleration of its progress." Second, he argues that SI arises from the interactions between informatics, a scientific and technical discipline, and the social sciences, which focus on humans and society. In more practical terms, he believes that SI has been deeply influenced by the spread of computerization into the social sciences which has given "rise to a new type of research and, in general, mental activity marked by a higher accuracy, logical strictness, analytical and constructive advantages over the conventional level (Ursal 1989, 12)." Further, Ursal (1989, 12) explains

> The personal computer does not serve as a mere tool for computations, but as a new means of intellectual activity helping to shape a new "informational" world-outlook and methodology. New information technology changes the methodology of scientific research proper and hence, the understanding of scientific activity.

Therefore, SI, in his view (1989, 10; 13) provides "in-depth studies of actual trends and patterns in the interaction between society and informatics;" it earned its modifier because "science is much closer to such humanities as psychology or sociology, which deal with the complexity of human existence with its unclear essence." In another prescient insight, he (1989, 11) also sees in SI a deeply critical impulse, claiming that

> Practical information activity in our society demonstrates dangerous deformations. These include an almost complete disregard of public opinion, exaggerated optimistic presentation of the current state and silence over errors, wide-spread deliberate disinformation by giving false (higher) figures, etc. Social (including scientific) information being an important characteristic of society, bears its imprint, since it immediately reflects the state and dynamics of the social system within which it functions.

> To our regret, the above-mentioned task of informatics humanization is recognized with a certain delay, namely, at those stages of informatisation when many negative consequences of this process have clearly manifested themselves. First of all, we mean here an extremely dangerous combination of militaristic and other authoritarian trends with informatisation, as well as economic losses resulting from unauthorized access to computer memories (information thefts, virus-programs, the hecker (sic) movement, etc.).

Subsequently, according to Kolin (2011, 460),

> Russian scientists set out the approach to the study of Social Informatics in the education system in the time of substantial upgrading in terms of becoming an information society…
>
> A legitimate reaction of science to this new social need was the establishment of a new research direction in the field of informatics that appeared in Russia in the mid-1980s and became known as Social Informatics.

Ursal clearly influenced the development of SI in Russia, arguing that "socialized" informatics was the appropriate approach to use to study society because it operated at the intersection of the natural and the human sciences. A fundamental assumption of this version of SI was that there was a co-evolution between society and its information characterized by "unity and mutual indissociability" (Kolin 2011, 460). By moving towards a position embracing a concept of mutual shaping early in its emergence, Russian SI became an independent scientific discipline at the core of which was the problem of "global informatization" (Kolin 1994, 22). Interestingly, Russian SI assumed that this relation of mutual shaping ("bilateral" in Kolin's terminology) was entwined with the process of informatization, which has (Kolin 2011, 461)

> … impact on social structures, as well as the role and position of the individual in society" while the social structure of society and people's attitude to the process of informatization, in turn, have a significant impact on the nature and pace of the development of this process.

Russian SI was teleological and utopian, with stated goals of identifying and studying opportunities for human and societal development while being cognizant of the threats and challenges of living in a new information society. The epistemological grounds on which SI was based were that "the world around us has the property of information, and, therefore, the unity of the regularities of the phenomenon of information in nature and society is due to a common origin" (Kolin 2011,

461). To know this world, therefore, is to proceed philosophically. In more operational terms, however, SI was cast in a more practical light, focusing on "the problem of the formation and development of the Information Society, new opportunities and challenges of democratization, freedom of information and security rights, etc." (Kolin 2011, 461).

During the 1990s there was considerable activity in Russia as the SI agenda was advanced nationally and internationally. Within the country, SI took hold in Russian educational institutions (Kolin 2011, 463)

> … in the late 1980s, when we came to realize the social significance of the information society. Therefore, a number of Russian universities have established specialized departments of Social Informatics. Russia also chairs the Association of Social Informatics, which continues its work to date.
>
> In the mid 1990s, Moscow State Social University … established the Institute of Informatics Problems of the Russian Academy of Sciences … which has successfully operated for five years and produced a significant number of professionals with sociologist-informatics expertise.

Internationally, Russian SI scholars participated in the 2nd UNESCO International Congress "Education and Informatics" held in 1994, presenting their report "Social Informatics" which was incorporated into the curriculum of a proposed course "Fundamentals of Informatics." This activity contributed to the trajectory of the SIM by articulating elements of the knowledge core that was subsequently integrated into local and international curricula. However, Ursal's work has been little noticed outside of Russia, was not cited by Kling and colleagues, and has not been cited by contemporary SI researchers, despite the fact that his 1989 paper was published in English in a volume of the International Forum on Information and Documentation.

Yet another version of SI emerged in Japan in the mid 1990s. Although the term "information society" has had currency in Japan since the early 1960s (Kumon 2008, 6), Japanese scholars, affiliated with the Japan Association for Social Informatics (JASI) and the Japan Society for Socio-Information Studies (JSIS), both founded in 1996, developed an approach, "socio-informatics, which treats information interdisciplinarily and synthetically" (Endo and Abe 2008, 3). Since 2004, these organizations have held combined conferences and, beginning in 2008, have published the English language "Journal of Socio-Informatics" (Kurosu 2010, 70). According to Kurosu (2010, 73), the President of the JASI recently explained that

> Socio-informatics is, in its essence, a discipline of interdisciplinary and field-crossing nature which is related to cultural sciences, social sciences and to the field of engineering and that of medicine. Based on this, we are aiming at the construction of a new academism which deals with the Japanese society and the world in the future by integrating theory and practice.

Between 1990 and 1998, academic programs in socio-informatics were established at six Japanese universities: the Faculty of Social Information at Sappro Gakuin University (1990), the School of Social Information Studies at Otsuma Women's University (1992), the Faculty of Social and Information Studies at Gunma University (1994), the Faculty of Social Information Science at Hiroshima Bunka Gakuin University (1996), the Faculty of Social Information at Jumonji Women's University (1998), and the Department of Social Informatics in the Graduate School of Informatics at Kyoto University (1998). Since then, a School of Social Informatics has been established at Aoyama Gakuin University. Addressing issues including the fundamental nature of the concept of information, the effects of ICT on social life, and structures and the design of a "good" information society, scholars and researchers in socio-informatics have sought (Endo and Abe 2008, 3-4)

> 1. To solve various aspects of production, circulation, accumulation, and use or consumption of information in society.
>
> 2. To reconstruct a theoretical framework about a social system from the viewpoint of "Information."
>
> 3. To search for a relationship between the new information/ communication network and social system.

Socio-informatics in Japan has proceeded along several different paths. According to Yoshida (2008, 35), one type, the earliest and initially most influential, emerged from the discipline of journalism, focusing on the development of mass communication theory and the analysis of various forms of mass communication media including the internet and mobile phones; the second, for which he (2008, 37) takes credit

> … focuses on the biological revolution that started as an elucidation of DNA information by Watson-Crick, spreading to all areas of life science and bioscience, and which began to develop in biotechnology or bioengineering based upon this spread.

More specifically, Yoshida's goal for socio-informatics is to "clarify 'modern characteristics of self organization,' dealing with the information society into which information and information processing permeate" based on "general theories concerning self organization of informatics of social systems" (Kusosu 2010, 72). Nishigaki and Takenouchi (2009, 81) propose a third type, "fundamental informatics," that focuses on the philosophical foundations of information and seeks "radical insights into various informational phenomena in biological, mechanical and social fields, rather … basic knowledge of information and communication engineering." These versions of socio-informatics, however, seem to converge on three insights: the importance of studying "social phenomena from the viewpoint of 'information'," the centrality of the assumption that "information is a basic factor" on which and through which human society is constituted, and the imperative that information should not be studied by "extracting it independently" because it is generated through the actions of humans and the society in which they live. Here too, the basic characteristics of a SIM are present; the core body of knowledge has been developed and articulated through the collective actions of members of the Japanese SI community and there has been considerable institutionalization with the development of academic programs at multiple locations, professional organizations, and specialized publications. This indicates a successful trajectory, although, because of language barriers, the research work has not been widely disseminated outside of Japan.

The emergence of SI in the United Kingdom followed a different path than has been seen in Norway, Slovenia, Russia and Japan. There has been a long and ongoing tradition of research in the UK reaching back into the 1950s that has examined relations among technology, people, work, and organizations. This sociotechnical approach predates the emergence of SI by three decades; a description of this tradition is provided by Davenport (2008, 519) who explains that SI research in the United States and sociotechnical research in the United Kingdom "share a common interest in the production of technology, and work with complementary concepts and methods, formal links between the two have not been strong for much of the historical period under review." Despite the lack of formal interaction between representatives of these two traditions, there has been considerable activity in the UK focused on SI. The University of Edinburgh, Scotland, where "socially oriented studies of science, technology and innovation were supported … from the mid 1960s" (Davenport 2008, 523), established a School of Informatics in 1998. It is now the largest such School in the UK and one of the largest in Europe, with over 500 research staff and more than 700 students. The version of informatics that developed was influenced by the fact that the School was an amalgam of five units: the Department of Artificial Intelligence, the Centre for Cognitive Science, the Department of Computer Science, the Artificial Intelligence Applications Institute, and the Human Communication Research Centre. Informatics is (School of Informatics 2012)

> … the study of the structure, the behaviour, and the interactions of natural and engineered computational systems.
>
> The central focus of Informatics is the transformation of information – whether by computation or communication, whether by organisms or artefacts. Understanding informational phenomena – such as computation, cognition, and communication – enables technological advances.
>
> Informatics has many aspects, and encompasses a number of existing academic disciplines – Artificial Intelligence, Cognitive Science and Computer Science. Each takes part of Informatics as its natural domain.

Within the School is the Social Informatics Cluster, which (Social Informatics Cluster 2012)

> … works at the intersection of technologies, work practices and organisations, by studying information technologies in their organisational contexts. A multi-disciplinary group that draws on insights from HCI, CSCW, participatory design, organisational sociology and ethnomethodological studies of work, the cluster's activities aim to go beyond traditional ways of developing IT systems, by engaging with IT professionals and breaking down the barriers between IT systems design and use.

At Edinburgh Napier University, Scotland, a Center for Social Informatics has been established in the Institute for Informatics and Digital Innovation. One of five centers in the Institute, its mission is to (Center for Social Informatics 2012) "to develop a distinctive body of work that reflects a shared interest in socio-technical interaction at different levels of organisation, and at different stages in the system life cycle." In contrast to the more computationally oriented version of informatics at the University of Edinburgh, the Center has adopted a working definition of SI and a research focus on organizations both of which are closely allied with the American version, which will be discussed next.

The latest and arguably most influential version of SI emerged in the mid 1990s in the United States. For reasons that will be made clear below, the trajectory of SI in the US followed a different path, transcending national boundaries and achieving international reach. The story is somewhat complicated because the decision to describe an approach to studying the social aspects of computing as SI was made in 1996, labeling a stream of research and theorizing about computerization that began some two decades earlier, largely among computer scientists. A group of scholars at the University of California at Irvine, including Kling, had been studying computerization and society since the late 1970s, but their research, loosely gathered under the umbrella of the social study of computing was published in a wide range of journals and presented at conferences in different disciplines. According to Sawyer and Tapia (2007, 264)

> … members of the faculty at the University of California at Irvine (UCI) came together out of common interests in the social aspects of computing. In evolving and expanding discussions, they involved their professional social networks in examining approaches, principles, and venues for showcasing social analyses of computing. This network of social relations centered on the UCI group played a central role in the spread of social informatics – both in the United States and internationally.
>
> This group of like-minded colleagues … began working together on a series of courses, studies and projects regarding the design, take up and uses of ICT. The membership … varied as faculty and students came and went from UCI. However, the discussions continued, and the network of colleagues who were involved at UCI and at other places grew through the 1980s and into the 1990s. The UCI group came to include scholars such as Mark Ackerman, Lisa Covi, James Danziger, Bill Dutton, Margaret Elliott, Les Gasser, Jonathan Grudin, Suzi Iacono, John King, Kenneth Kraemer, Roberta Lamb, Walt Scacchi, and many others.

As has been described above, there was considerable activity among scholars and researchers in Scandinavia, the UK, Russia, and Japan who worked in departments and schools of social informatics established many years prior to the American version. It seems likely that their work, particularly their publications available in English or in translation, would have influenced the American version of SI. As is well known, Kling was a key figure in the rise of SI in the US, however, SI did not emerge sui generis from either Kling or from the UCI group alone. Sawyer and Tapia (2007, 264) explain that Kling and colleagues at UCI and information systems researchers in "the United Kingdom, and in Scandinavia were known to each other and involved in collaborative projects, conferences, and scholarly debate." Exploring the ties between Kling and colleagues and the European information systems research community is beyond the scope of this chapter. What is more relevant is the influence of SI scholars in Europe on Kling and his colleagues' thinking; more to the point, there was interaction between Kling and SI researchers in Scandinavia.

A key event in the coalescence of SI as a SIM occurred in 1989, when Kling visited the University of Oslo in Norway and met with Bråten and Roggen and learned about their new discipline, SI, and "its terms, concepts, theories, models, and research projects carried out by Bråten and his collaborators" (Roggen 2005). One outcome of this interaction was apparent in 1996, at a workshop on digital libraries funded by the National Science Foundation. Kling and colleagues were discussing a problem: although their research focused on a common domain, the complex relationships between computerization and society, they were publishing their work in diverse journals and describing it as falling with different domains including the "social analysis of computing," "human-centered computing," the "social study of information technology," and the "sociology of computing." According to Kling, Rosenbaum, and Sawyer (2005, 30), at this workshop

> … participants in this research community agreed that the scattering of related research in a wide array of journals and the use of different nomenclatures was impeding both the research and the abilities of 'research consumers' to find important work. They decided that a common name for the field would be helpful. After significant deliberation, they selected 'social informatics.'

This discussion was followed in 1997 by another National Science Foundation funded workshop held at Indiana University in Bloomington where many of the same people gathered, under Kling's direction, to set a research agenda for SI. One outcome of their work was the definition of SI that has become a taken for granted and fundamental assumption of the discipline's core of knowledge, as initially outlined in Kling (1999) and Kling, Rosenbaum, Sawyer, Weisband and Crawford (2001). According to Sawyer and Tapia (2007, 264), Kling reflected in 2004 "that the conceptualization of 'social informatics' arose in part as a means to help convey the broad sweep of activities regarding social analyses of computing and to help convey central concepts in this work to computer scientists."

The 1996 and 1997 workshops marked the beginning of a decade and a half of activity in American SI. Upon joining the School of Library and Information Science at Indiana University in 1996, Kling established the first Center for Social Informatics in the United States; now renamed the

Rob Kling Center for Social Informatics, it continues to be a meeting place for scholars and students interested in SI research. In 1996, Kling and colleagues created a Social Informatics minitrack at the Association for Information Systems annual conference that is still active as the Social Theory in Information Systems Research minitrack. A Special Interest Group for Social Informatics in the Association for Information Science and Technology held its ninth annual research symposium at the society's annual meeting in 2013. Meyer (this volume) discusses in greater detail the contours of the intellectual community that has arisen around the core body of knowledge of SI. As of this writing, according to the website "Social Informatics," maintained by the University of Ljubljana, there are ten universities in the United States and twenty three universities and institutes in fourteen countries with programs, doctoral or masters minors, or tracks within degrees focused on SI; there are seven universities that have schools, departments, or faculties of SI, all outside the United States; and there are many more that offer one or more courses about SI (Vehovar 2013).

There has also been considerable publishing activity, a careful analysis of which has been done by Sanfilippo and Fichman (this volume). One outcome of the flurry of publications and presentations given between 1996 and 2005 that were gathered under the conceptual umbrella of SI was that a core body of knowledge emerged, often articulated as key insights or principles from SI research. This occurred despite the fact that as it has evolved, SI has become an approach influenced by social science theories and methods that cuts across many academic disciplines. Researchers working in information systems, library and information science, sociology, anthropology, communications, journalism, management, and other disciplines use the concepts and tools of SI to study technology and society (Sawyer and Rosenbaum 2000, 89). Despite this heterogeneity, SI research converges on a problem, understanding "the complex relationships between the design and use of advanced information and communication technologies and the character of real social life in settings where people use them," (Robbin, Lamb, King, and Berleur 2007, 17). In 2005, Kling's last manuscript, co-authored with Rosenbaum and Sawyer, was published summarizing the state of the art of SI research and theorizing and outlining the core body of knowledge. This book also presented the conventional history of SI, effectively writing out of the story the developments that occurred in Norway, Slovenia, Russia, Japan and the UK. It offered an origin story for SI, reinforced by Kling's articles defining the term and the discipline. This chapter is intended to be a corrective to this origin story.

Kling (1999; 2003), Sawyer and Rosenbaum (2000), Sawyer and Eschenfelder (2002), Lamb and Kling, (2003), Davenport (2005), Sawyer (2005), Kling, Rosenbaum and Sawyer (2005), Rosenbaum (2009), and Sanfilippo and Fichman (this volume) all discuss key insights and principles of SI that are important components that have come to define the knowledge core of American version of SI; five major assumptions underlying SI research in the US are described here.

The first assumption is that ICTs are parts of sociotechnical systems that include technical artifacts (software, hardware, and infrastructure) and social components (people, organizations, norms and values, policies, social practices, etc.). A second and closely related assumption is that ICTs do not exist in social or technical isolation and are embedded in complex and dynamic networks of social, cultural, organizational, and institutional contexts (Kling 2003, 2656; Kling, Rosenbaum, and Sawyer 2005, 16). These systems therefore have historical trajectories (Kling, Rosenbaum, and Sawyer 2005, 54). Further, the people who design and use ICTs are also parts of the sociotechnical system and must be seen as social actors (Lamb and Kling 2003) meaning that they "are not simply users of ICT, but are socially-complex individuals who are engaging [in] uses of ICT as members of one or more organizations that make use of ICTs to engage in mediated social interactions" (Sawyer and Tyworth 2006, 54). Kling and Scacchi (1982) described this assumption as the "web of computing," a metaphor that predates both the World Wide Web and SI. This concern for embeddedness also points to the theoretical and empirical significance of the context in SI analyses.

A third assumption is that the components of sociotechnical systems are in relationships of mutual shaping, an insight that has been important in the work of Orlikowski (1992). In any given system, "the social contexts and technological artefacts are perpetually interacting and shaping each other" (Sawyer and Tyworth 2006, 51). Mutual shaping stands in contrast to assumptions of technological and social determinism by charting a middle path, acknowledging that at different moments in the trajectory of a sociotechnical system, the direction of the shaping may move toward either the technological or the social, resulting in intended and unintended consequences with no expectation of symmetry. This means, for example, that the design, implementation, use and management of ICTs are always socially situated in ways that enable and constrain these processes (Sawyer and Tyworth 2006, 52) but not necessarily with equal impact. On the one hand, the context of ICT use directly affects the meanings and roles the technologies have for the people using them; on the other, the interpretations that people develop to help them grasp ICTs shape their adoption and uses of these technologies. Sawyer (2005, 10) argues that an implication of mutual shaping is that "the situated nature and uses of computing mean that context and use are bound up through practice: to report on use is to report on the situations of that use." Accepting this assumption, SI researchers seek to "uncover and explain the coupling of technology and social order." (Davenport 2005, 17).

A fourth assumption is that ICTs are configurable, meaning that they are flexible, can be used in different social and organizational contexts in different ways, and evolve over time in use and sometimes in ways not anticipated by their designers. This recognizes the research finding that "many 'systems' are composed of unique configurations and assemblages of components" (Kling et al. 2000, 28). ICTs are parts of larger assemblages of technical components that may be drawn from different off the shelf products, developed in house, or customized in ways not intended by designers so that "the result is a particular configuration – a complex array of standardised and customised automation elements" (Williams and Edge 1996, 861). The goal of such a configuration is to meet the needs of the various stakeholders in the system ranging from the IT professionals who design and build it to the top managers who simply need output from the system to aid in their decision making. This process has been called "technology-use mediation" and describes the efforts to align the structure and functioning of the ICTs with existing work and other organizational practices (Orlikowski et al. 1995, 423). Recently, as more technologies have moved out of organizational and into larger social contexts, configurability has taken on a new meaning where individuals customize and configure technologies to meet their own needs. By acknowledging that configurability implies temporality, it is clear that sociotechnical systems have trajectories that begin with their design and continue until they are no longer in use. SI researchers can therefore follow the evolution of an ICT configuration focusing on its history and future; its trajectory includes a social history and a trail of technological and social progress, obstacles, challenges, successes and failures. Trajectories can be traced and studied and although ICTs have the potential to be influential in social and organizational change, their trajectories often favor the status quo (Kling, Rosenbaum, and Sawyer 2005, 95). Configurability is a useful assumption because it can help "make some of the contradictory uses and consequences of computerization more intelligible" (Kling et al. 2000, 29).

A fifth assumption underlying SI research is the significance of a critical approach (Sawyer and Tyworth 2006), focusing on "disjunctions between popular and professional claims about the social values and uses of [ICT] and the empirical reality of such" (Day 2007, 575). Day (2007,

576) argues that this critical impulse is at the heart of SI and, developed more deeply, can move SI in novel and rewarding directions because its "empirical objects ... can be as much conceptual constructs as empirical entities, and [its] central concern [can be] the examination of the notion of information as a culturally and historically specific conception of knowledge." According to Kling et al. (2000, 19), this type of critical orientation

> ... encourages information professionals and researchers to examine ICTs from multiple perspectives (such as those of the various people who use them in different contexts, as well as those of the people who pay for, design, implement or maintain them), and to examine possible failure modes and service losses, as well as ideal or routine ICT operations.

This approach easily incorporates genre and discourse analyses into the SI researcher's methodological tool kit as it becomes "ultimately, a discursive and cultural examination of the construction of meaning and concepts related to ICTs," (Day 2007, 578). This leads to a focus on the "value choices and social conflicts regarding the uses of ICTs" (Sawyer and Tapia 2007, 263).

Researchers adopting this approach call into question the conventional wisdom and assumptions about technology, people, work and play and, in doing so, employ "perspectives that do not automatically and uncritically adopt the goals and beliefs of the groups that commission, design, or implement specific ICTs" (Sawyer and Eschenfelder 2002, 437). This approach aligns well with an assumption from the social construction of technology concerning the role of values and ideology in the design, development and use of technologies; ICT use has moral and ethical aspects that have social and political consequences. This insight is developed in great detail and precision on Fleischman's discussion of SI, values and design (this volume). In some cases, "IT applications can ... shift the balance of influence and power in organizations by restructuring access to information, technical staff, and the kind of authority that informational resources can bring" (Kling 2003, 2658). Consequently, the implementation and use of ICTs typically produce winners and losers.

Conclusion

The goal of this chapter has been to sketch the background of SI by exploring its history through the lens of Frickel and Gross's (2005) framework of SIMs. By drawing on social movement theories, their approach offers a way to explain change in science and examine the trajectory of disciplines by treating the emergence and development of a discipline as the result of collective action and not as a consequence of a "great person," "seminal paper," or "critical incident." This is not to deny the influence that a person, article, or incident may have on a movement, but this influence must be placed in the larger context of "the web of social relationships that comprises the SIM" (Frickel and Gross 2005, 204). Their framework allows the complexity of disciplinary history to be foregrounded, providing a useful way to account for the trajectory of SI.

As a SIM, SI has had a trajectory characterized by fits and starts as research programs, curricula, and academic units have emerged in different countries between early 1980s and the late 1990s. As has been described above, SI emerged at six different locations; beginning in Norway, then in Slovenia, Russia, Japan, the United States, and the UK. While sharing a common interest in the relationship between technology and society, the versions of SI have been somewhat different in each location, reflecting the sociotechnical, cultural, political and other factors that influenced the scholars involved. In all six cases, researchers with shared interests in the study of technology and society engaged in collective action over a number of years to create and establish SI programs, curricula, research centers, and, in some cases, journals and professional organizations in their countries. This is similar to the development of social movements because "SIMs do not just happen, but once their key ideas are formulated, they must be orchestrated, coordinated, and collectively produced" (Frickel and Gross 2005, 213). Of the six, the American version initiated by Kling and colleagues in 1996 has arguably become the most influential; Frickel and Gross's (2005) framework allows speculation about why this has been the case.

Several factor have impacted the trajectory of SI in these different countries including language of publication, presentation, and pedagogy, the development and articulation of a core body of knowledge, use of digital information and communications networks, and the mobilization of resources to raise the movement's profile in a relevant academic community. The versions of SI that were in languages other than English (Norwegian, Slovenian, Russian, and Japanese) have been and continue to be at a disadvantage in an international intellectual arena. The published research is difficult to find and must be translated to be of widespread use outside the countries of origin.

The work of the early members of the SIM includes developing internal social structures and routine scientific practices and engaging in the work of research, teaching, publication, and presentation. One outcome of this work is to create and refine the knowledge core of the movement.

Equally important, however, is the articulation of this body of knowledge to internal and external audiences. Kling and colleagues put considerable effort into this activity with a series of articles beginning in 1999 about the intellectual core of SI (Kling 1999) culminating in a book which gathered together the assumptions, insights and significant findings of SI research (Kling, Rosenbaum, and Sawyer 2005). This stream of work also played another important role in the development of the SIM because it was typically organized around the criticism of what was called the "standard" or "direct effects" model of the effects of technology on society (Kling 1999; Kling et al. 2000). By pitting SI against various forms of technological determinism in a manner more explicit than any of the other versions of SI, the American version was positioned as a research program that posed a challenge to some sort of conventional wisdom or knowledge in the discipline and stood "in the face of resistance from others in the scientific or intellectual community" (Frickel and Gross 2005, 206). The result has been to popularize the American version in the international academic community, spreading it far more widely than any of the other groups have been able to do. This effort was aided in no small part by the rise of the web as a significant channel for scholarly communication. For example, a working paper series on the web site of the Center for Social Informatics at Indiana University (now the Rob Kling Center for Social Informatics) begun in the late 1900s made writings about the knowledge core of the American version of SI available to the global academic community interested in the study of technology and society. Only the SI researchers in the UK have come close in their ability to make use of the web.

The ability to acquire and make use of organizational and institutional resources is another way in which SI researchers have attempted to move the discipline forward. This insight is explored in much greater detail by Sawyer and Hartswood (this volume). Frickel and Gross (2005, 207) argue that early leaders of a SIM tend to be high status academics who use their networks for institution building and resource mobilization. These resources are used to build, maintain and extend the basic social and intellectual structures of the movement, to enroll new members into the movement, both established scholars and, equally as important, students, and to seek some degree of institutional stability. In addition, members demonstrate the impact of their research through funding, publication and citation, through competing for and obtaining positions in appropriate research universities and funding institutions, and developing a shared scientific and intellectual identity. In all six cases, early leaders and their colleagues have been able to effectively mobilize resources to engage in institution building. Braten and colleagues were able to establish the first program in SI at the University of Oslo; a program soon after began at the University of Lubjanika in Slovenia, an institute and academic programs were established in Russia, programs and professional organizations were established in Japan, research centers remain active in the UK, and programs and centers have been established in the US. In terms of institution building, as of this writing, there are ten schools in the US with programs, minors or tracks in SI. There are seven schools with faculty, schools or departments of SI twenty-three schools and institutes in the world with programs, minors or tracks in SI. There are many more offering coursework in SI. There are research centers where scholars are discovering their common interested in the core problem SI. There are tracks in conferences and workshops devoted to SI research.

What then of the future of SI as a scientific and intellectual movement? Its trajectory seems to be moving forward with considerable activity in many different parts of the world. Although language barriers still exist, an interesting consequence of the pervasiveness of digital scholarly communication is that SI researchers throughout the world now have an easier time than ever finding out about each other's work and communicating with each other; one hope that the cross-pollination if ideas will lead to new collaborations and new advances in the discipline. As a SIM, SI seems healthy. Later in this volume, there will be other analyses of what the future holds for SI.

References

Absolute Astronomy. 2013. Informatics. http://www.absoluteastronomy.com/topics/Informatics_%28academic_field%29.

Aspray, William. 2011. "The History of Information Science and Other Traditional Information Domains: Models for Future Research." *Libraries & the Cultural Record*, 46(2): 230-248.

Brookes, Bertram C. 1980. "Informatics as the Fundamental Social Science." In *New Trends in Documentation and Information: Proceedings of the 39th FID Congress,* Sept. 1978, edited by Peter J. Taylor, 25-28 FID Publication 566. London: ASLIB, 20.

—. 1984. "Lenin: The Founder of Informatics." *Journal of Information Science*, 8: 221-223.

Center for Social Informatics. 2012. Institute for Informatics and Digital Innovation. Napier University. About Us https://wiki.inf.ed.ac.uk/Main/SIC.

Davenport, Elisabeth. 2005. "Social Informatics in Practice: A Guide for the Perplexed." *Bulletin of the American Society for Information Science and Technology I,* 31(5): 17. Accessed July 2007. http://www.asis.org/Bulletin/Jun-05/davenport.html.

—. 2008. "Social Informatics and Sociotechnical Research – A View from the UK." *Journal of Information Science*, 34: 519.

Day, Ronald E. 2007. "Kling and the 'Critical': Social Informatics and Critical Informatics." *Journal Of The American Society For Information Science And Technology*, 58(4): 575.

Endo, Kaoru, and Keiichi Abe. 2008. "On the Occasion of Publication of the Journal of Socio-Informatics." *Journal of Socio-Informatics*, 1(1): 3-4.

Freeman, Jo. 1999. "On the Origins of Social Movements." In *Waves of Protest: Social Movements Since the Sixties*, by Victoria Johnson and Jo Freeman, 7-24. Lanham: Rowman and Littlefield.

Frickel, Scott, and Neil Gross. 2005. "A General Theory of Scientific/Intellectual Movements." *American Sociological Review*, 70(2): 204-233.

Halavais, Alex. 2005. "Social Informatics: Beyond Emergence." *Bulletin of the American Society for Information Science and Technology,* 31(5). Accessed July 2007. http://www.asis.org/Bulletin/Jun-05/helavais.html.

Horton, Keith, Elisabeth A. Davenport, and Trevor Wood-Harper. 2005. "Exploring Sociotechnical Interaction with Rob Kling: Five 'BIG' Ideas." *Information Technology & People*, 18(1): 51.

Kimbel, Dieter. 1973. "Computers and Telecommunications; Economic, Technical and Organisational Issues." OECD Informatics Studies, #3.

Kling, Rob. 2003. "Social Informatics." *Encyclopedia of Library and Information Science*. New York, New York: Marcel Dekker, Inc., 2656-2661.

—. 1999. "What is Social Informatics and Why Does it Matter?" *D-Lib Magazine* 5 (1). http://www.dlib.org/dlib/january99/kling/01kling.html.

Kling, Rob, Holly Crawford, Howard Rosenbaum, Steve Sawyer, and Suzanne Weisband. 2000. "Learning from Social Informatics: Information and Communication Technologies in Human Contexts." Report to the National Science Foundation.

Kling, Rob, Howard Rosenbaum, and Steve Sawyer. 2005. *Understanding and Communicating Social Informatics: A Framework for Studying and Teaching the Human Contexts of Information and Communication Technologies*. Medford, NJ: Information Today.

Kling, Rob, Howard Rosenbaum, Steve Sawyer, Suzanne Weisband, and Holly Crawford. 2001. "Information Technologies in Human Contexts: Learning from Organizational and Social Informatics." Report to the National Foundation on the Workshop on Social Informatics (1997).

Kling, Rob, and Walt Scacchi. 1982. "The Web of Computing: Computer Technology as Social Organization." *Advances in Computers*, 21: 1-90.

Kolin, Konstantin. 1994. "Social Informatics – Scientific Basis of Postindustrial Society." *Social Informatics*, 94: 4-23.

—. 2011. "Social Informatics Today and Tomorrow: Status, Problems and Prospects of Development of Complex Lines in the Field of Science and Education." *Triple C: Cognition, Communication, Co-operation*, 9(2): 460-465. http://www.triple-c.at.

Kuhn, Thomas S. 1970. *The Structure of Scientific Revolutions*. Chicago: Chicago University Press.

Kumon, Shumpei. 2008. "An Infosocionomist's View." *Journal of Socio-Informatics*, 1(1): 6-20.

Kurosu, Toshio. 2010. "In Search of a Paradigm of Socio-Informatics: On Socio-Informatics and Social Informatics." *Journal of Socio-Informatics*, 3(1): 69-81.

Lamb, Roberta, and Rob Kling. 2003. "Reconceptualizing Users as Social Actors in Information Systems Research." *MIS Quarterly,* 27(2): 197-235.

Lamb, Roberta, and Steve Sawyer. 2005. "On Extending Social Informatics from a Rich Legacy of Networks and Conceptual Resources." *Information Technology and People*, 18(1): 9-20.

Le Roux, C.J.B. 2009. "Social and Community Informatics Past, Present and Future: An Historic Overview." 10th Annual DIS Conference 10-11 September.

Meyer, David S., and Deana A. Rohlinger. 2012. "Big Books and Social Movements: A Myth of Ideas and Social Change." *Social Problems*, 59(1): 136-153.

Niblett, G.B.F. 1971. Informatics Studies: No 2: Digital Information and the Privacy Problem. Organization for Economic Development and Cooperation Informatics Studies, #2.

Nishigaki, Toru, and Tadashi Takenouchi. 2009. "The Informatic Turn-Who Observes the "Infosphere"?" *Journal of Socio-Informatics*, 2(1): 81-90.

Orlikowski, Wanda J. 1992. "The Duality of Technology: Rethinking the Concept of Technology in Organizations." *Organizational Science*. 3(3): 398-427.

Orlikowski, Wanda J., JoAnne Yates, Kazuo Okamura, and Masayo Fujimoto. 1995. "Shaping Electronic Communication: The Metastructuring of Technology in the Context of Use." *Organization Science*, 6(4) 423-444.

Robbin, Alice, and Ron Day. 2006. "On Rob Kling: The Theoretical, the Methodological, and the Critical." September 21-23. Seventh International Conference "Human Choice and Computers" (HCC7), Maribar, Slovenia.

Robbin, Alice, Roberta Lamb, John Leslie King, and Jacques Berleur. 2007. "As we may remember." In *Social Informatics: An Information Society for all? In Remembrance of Rob Kling*, edited by Jacques Berleur, MarkkuI Nurminen and John Impagliazzo, 17-21. Boston: Springer.

Roggen, Ingar. 2007. Home Page. Accessed July 2007. http://www.iss.uio.no/websociology/.

—. 2005. Personal communication, email, October 17.

—. 1998. Specialization Course in Web Sociology and Social Informatics. http://folk.uio.no/iroggen/WEBsociologyINFOeng.html.

Rosenbaum, Howard. 2009. "Social Informatics." *Encyclopedia of Library and Information Science*. New York, New York: Marcel Dekker, Inc., 2656-2661.

Sawyer, Steve. 2005. Social Informatics: Overview, Principles and Opportunities." *Bulletin of the American Society for Information Science and Technology*, 31(5): 10. Accessed July 2007. http://www.asis.org/Bulletin/Jun-05/sawyer.html.

Sawyer, Steve, and Kristin Eschenfelder. 2002. "Social Informatics: Perspectives, Examples, and Trends." *Annual Review of Information Science and Technology*. 427-465. Information Today.

Sawyer, Steve, and Howard Rosenbaum. 2000. "Social Informatics in the Information Sciences: Current Activities and Emerging Directions." *Informing Science*, 3(2): 89. Accessed July 2007. http://inform.nu/Articles/Vol3/indexv3n2.htm.

Sawyer, Steve, and Andrea Tapia. 2007. "From Findings to Theories: Institutionalizing Social Informatics." *The Information Society: An International Journal*, 23(4): 263-275.

Sawyer, Steve, and Michael Tyworth. 2006. "Social Informatics: Principles, Theory, and Practice." In *Social Informatics: An Information Society for all? In Remembrance of Rob Kling*, edited by Jacques Berleur, MarkkuI Nurminen and John Impagliazzo, 49-62. Boston: Springer.

School of Informatics, Edinburgh University. 2012. Vision. Overview. http://www.ed.ac.uk/schools-departments/informatics/about/vision/overview.

Snow, David A., Sarah A. Soule, and Hanspeter Kriesi (eds). 2004. The Blackwell Companion to Social Movements, Blackwell Companions to Sociology. Malden, Mass.: Blackwell.

Social Informatics Cluster. School of Informatics. Edinburgh University. 2012. Social Informatics Cluster. https://wiki.inf.ed.ac.uk/Main/SIC.

The Faculty of Social Sciences, University of Ljubljana, Slovenia. Social Informatics. 2007. Accessed July 2007. http://www.social-informatics.org/index.php?fl=0&p1=181&p2=5&p3=&id=197.

Tilly, Charles. 1984. "Social Movements and National Politics." In *Statemaking and Social Movements*, edited by Charles Bright and Susan Harding, 297–317. Ann Arbor, Mich.: University of Michigan Press.

UNESCO. Institute for Information Technologies in Education (nd). 2nd International Congress on Education and Informatics. http://iite.unesco.org/publications/3214575/.

Ursul, A.D. 1989. "On the Shaping of Social Informatics." *International Forum on Information and Documentation*, 14(4): 10-18.

Vehovar, Vasja. 2013a. History. Social-Informatics.org University of Ljubljana, Faculty of Social Sciences http://www.social-informatics.org/c/133/History?preid=197.

—. 2013b. Study Programs. Social-Informatics.org University of Ljubljana, Faculty of Social Sciences http://www.social-informatics.org/index.php?fl=2&p1=181&p2=151&lact=3&bid=5.

—. 2006. "Social Informatics: An emerging discipline?" In *Social Informatics: An Information Society for all? In Remembrance of Rob Kling*, edited by Jacques Berleur, MarkkuI Nurminen and John Impagliazzo, 73-85. Boston: Springer.

Williams, Robin, and David Edge. 1996. "The Social Shaping of Technology." *Research Policy*, 25(6): 865-899.

Yoshida, Tamito. 2008. "Supertemporal and Temporal-constrained Characters of Socioinformatics." *Journal of Socio-Informatics*, 1(1): 37-45.

CHAPTER TWO

THE EVOLUTION OF SOCIAL INFORMATICS RESEARCH (1984-2013): CHALLENGES AND OPPORTUNITIES

MADELYN SANFILIPPO
AND PNINA FICHMAN

Introduction

Social informatics (SI) is "the interdisciplinary study of the design, uses and consequences of information technology that takes into account their interaction with institutional and cultural contexts" (Kling 1998, p.52; 1999). SI provides flexible frameworks to explore complex and dynamic sociotechnical interactions. As a domain of study related largely by common vocabulary and conclusions, SI critically examines common conceptions of and expectations for technology, by providing contextual evidence.

This chapter describes the evolution of SI research in the US and UK and identifies challenges and opportunities for future research. We divided SI research into four major periods: an early period of *foundational work* which grounds SI (Pre-1990s), a period of *development and expansion* (1990s), a robust period of *coherence* and influence by Rob Kling (2000-2005)[1], and a period of *diversification* (2006-Present).[2]

Each of the four periods is divided into four sections: principles, concepts, approaches, and findings. *Principles* refer to the overarching motivations and labels employed to describe scholarly work. *Approaches*

[1] This time period extends 2 years after Rob Kling's death because some of his publications appeared later, and many publications that appeared immediately after his death were not only strongly inspired by him but also a tribute to him and his SI research.

[2] Due to space limitations, not all relevant publications or scholars are covered.

describe the theories, frameworks, and models employed in analysis, emphasizing the multi-disciplinary and interdisciplinary nature of SI. *Concepts* include specific processes, entities, themes, and elements of discourse within a given context, revealing a shared SI language surrounding change, complexity, consequences, and social elements of technology. *Findings* from seminal SI works illustrate growing insights over time and demonstrate how repeatable explanations unify SI. In the concluding remarks, we raise questions as to the possible future expansion or extinction of SI research.

Period of Foundational Work (pre-1990s)

Our review begins with early critical studies by Rob Kling and colleagues; Kling and Iacono (1984a; 1984b; 1988; 1989) empirically tested and challenged deterministic discourse surrounding computerization in work and educational settings. These inquiries revealed findings and concepts, which later became central to SI research. This early research was not clearly labeled by the authors as a coherent body of SI work.

Principles

Kling and Iacono (1984b) challenged deterministic narratives surrounding information system implementation; their findings did not support either socially or technologically deterministic discourses. Instead, the evidence supported economically rational arguments explained through metaphors of organizational politics (Kling and Iacono 1984b). They demonstrated that critical analysis provided more accurate explanations of computerization outcomes than simplistic determinisms.

Collaborations between Kling and Iacono produced a definite sociotechnical principle (1989) to explain the complex interrelationship between social and technical variables (1988). Social theorization, grounded in case studies, described the sociotechnical nature of computer-based information systems embedded in social, organizational contexts. Social and technical choices lead to the development, implementation, and adoption of technology, thereby integrating them in context. The sociotechnical nature of computerization served as a guiding principle within developing the interdisciplinary notion of SI research.

Approaches

As a socio-technical approach without definite overarching principles, early research represents the varied, deeply interdisciplinary approaches that continue to be emblematic of SI research. Kling and Iacono employed institutional social shaping approaches, political analysis, and discussed both a computerization movement framework and sociotechnical studies (1984a; 1984b; 1988; 1989) to emphasize specific topics of analysis, such as technology in education and bureaucratic information systems. These diverse approaches represent the indefinite theoretical boundaries of SI.

In order to understand information and communication technologies (ICTs) in context, an institutional social shaping approach was developed to characterize boundaries, controls, information flows, actors, and rules, which situate computerization (Kling and Iacono 1984a; 1989). This approach was developed from:

- Institutional Theory (Kling and Iacono 1984a);
- Social Control Models from Sociology (Kling and Iacono 1984a);
- Organizational Theory (Kling and Iacono 1989).

The theoretical frameworks employed by Kling and Iacono (1984a; 1984b; 1988; 1989) represent the value of SI approaches to business, political, and social problems traditionally addressed by individual scholarly domains. SI, from the beginning, was not bounded by one overarching theory. Kling and Iacono drew on social theories from other disciplines in order to theoretically contextualize ICTs. First, social control and leverage were analyzed by using political theories of coalition formation, ideologies and preferences, mobilization of support, and legitimacy (Kling and Iacono 1984b). Second, sociotechnical theories were used to explain unanticipated changes or stasis and consider information systems and technologies in context (Kling and Iacono 1989). Third, computerization movement analysis was developed (Kling and Iacono 1988) to characterize beliefs, practices, and discourse surrounding ICT, as well as to differentiate between attributes of computerization movements. Value laden arguments made by computerization movement advocates often establish unrealizable expectations for technology given a context (Kling and Iacono 1988).

Concepts

Through these interdisciplinary approaches, Kling and Iacono articulated what would become key SI concepts to discuss findings, including: change (1988), complexity (1989), context (1984a), control (1984a; 1984b; 1989), efficiency (1989), institutions (1984a; 1989), management (1984a; 1989), organizational politics (1984b; 1989), power relationships (1984b; 1989), and values (1988). From these concepts, the language of SI developed.

Social context is significant in evaluating technological outcomes (Kling and Iacono 1984a). Institutional and organizational contexts are especially complex, as they designed to achieve efficiency, productivity, and profitability through technology and change (Kling and Iacono 1984a; 1988; 1989). Institutions are of particular importance because of their scale and early-mover role in adopting new technologies (Kling and Iacono 1984a; 1989).

Management and control create unequal distributions of authority, information, and access to technologies (Kling and Iacono 1984a; 1984b; 1989). From these disparities stem conflict within organizational and institutional contexts, for which common resolution is ICT change or stasis; often ICT implementation favors the status quo because powerful actors advocate for their personal benefit and attempt to control change, yet stasis might be the resolution even when ICT does not favor the statue quo (Kling and Iacono 1984a; 1984b; 1988).

Organizational politics and power relationships elegantly reveal the impact of ideologies and interests on ICT outcomes (Kling and Iacono 1984b; 1989), just as social values create norms and barriers to the compromise of those norms, which impact ICT outcomes (Kling and Iacono 1988). Values, in addition to establishing contexts, which may or may not be amenable to ICT change, are also embedded in ICTs themselves (Kling and Iacono 1988).

Findings

In this emerging stage, SI findings were iterated as descriptive accounts of the realities computerization in primarily organizational settings, rather than as prescriptive and technologically optimistic computerization goals. Kling and Iacono discovered that:

- Politics and interests impact ICT outcomes (1984b; 1988; 1989);
- ICT use is situated and context dependent (1988; 1989);
- Context is complex (1984a);
- ICTs favor the status quo (1984a; 1984b);
- ICTs are not value neutral (1988); and
- ICTs have multiple and paradoxical impacts (1989).

These findings explained not only why popular narratives about and expectations for positive organizational technology outcomes were often problematic, but also why contextual assessment and theorization, considering a spectrum of details, was necessary (Kling and Iacono 1984a; 1989).

Kling and Iacono (1984a; 1984b; 1988; 1989) argued that ICTs were not used in vacuums and could not be isolated from the variables surrounding use when planning for, designing, and implementing them.

Period of Development and Expansion (1990s)

Throughout the 1990s, SI developed as an interdisciplinary perspective, forming a relatively cohesive set of principles, clearly labeled by the authors as SI. SI was employed to evaluate social aspects of technologies in diverse contexts, ranging from computerization (Iacono 1996; Kling 1994; 1998; Kling and Star 1997) to the information society (Iacono 1996; Kling 1998).

In addition to new applications, new SI specific approaches were proposed. Lamb described and evaluated informational context as a theoretical construct (1996) and distinct critical and analytical orientations of SI emerged (Kling 1994; 1998). Core concepts were supported and supplemented as SI expanded to include additional collaborators (i.e. Kling and Lamb 1996; 1999).

Principles

From the onset, scholars doing SI research have disagreed about what to call it and what overarching intellectual principles have guided their inquiries. While the 1990s saw a rise in the use of the terms Social Informatics (e.g. Kling 1998; Kling, Rosenbaum, and Hert 1998) and organizational informatics (e.g. Kling and Star 1997; Kling and Tillquist 1998), other work was simply guided by a sociotechnical perspective (e.g. Kling and Lamb 1996; 1999). Diversity of principles abounded, ranging from social aspects of ICT (e.g. Iacono 1996; Kling 1994; 1996) to human centered approaches to computing (Kling and Star 1997).

SI defined principles within itself as a domain during the 1990s (Kling 1998; Kling, Rosenbaum, and Hert 1998). An interdisciplinary focus on interactions between ICTs and context was important because ICTs were increasingly tied to social practice, yet primarily viewed as tools, isolated from creators and users, without embedded social properties (e.g. Iacono 1996; Kling, Rosenbaum, and Hert 1998). Kling (1994; 1996) stressed the need to explore social possibilities of computerization, rather than functional computing efficiency and productivity alone. Kling and his colleagues worked to better understand sociotechnical interactions (Kling and Lamb 1996; 1999; Kling, Rosenbaum, and Hert 1998) and social aspects of ICT (e.g. Kling 1994; 1996; 1998), in part to explain rapid technological change and in part to define SI (Kling, Rosenbaum, and Hert 1998).

Organizational informatics examined sociotechnical interactions in organizational contexts in order to understand economic outcomes and consequences (Kling and Lamb 1999). The rise of organizational informatics paralleled increasing computerization in business and growth of e-business; the digital economy was studied to explain viability, processes, and advantages of online business in different industries (Kling and Lamb 1999).

While guiding principles varied, additional scholars were drawn to the issues that Kling and Iacono had earlier considered. Not only was the conversation and focus developing, but also by the end of the 1990s, scholarship evolved around specific SI principles.

Approaches

To develop these principles, a variety of theoretical constructs were employed including newly proposed SI approaches, involving critical (Kling 1994; 1996) and analytical orientations (Kling 1996), and informational context (Lamb 1996). The institutional social shaping approach continued to be employed (Iacono 1996), while structuration and systems theory constructs were also transferred to SI work (Contractor and Seibold 1993; Kling and Star 1997).

The introduction of specific orientations in SI was significant because it structured and legitimated SI approaches and motivations. The critical orientation developed from the earliest SI impulses to challenge thin arguments about technology and computerization through robust empirically supported arguments (i.e. Kling 1994; 1996). The analytical orientation deconstructed specific sociotechnical interactions to characterize social and organizational changes as they occurred (Kling 1996).

For example, Lamb (1996) developed one of the earliest sociotechnical theories within SI: informational context. Lamb (1996) conceptually reframed ICT's social potential as technological mediation, effective interpersonal interaction, and access to power.

The introduction of structuration into SI work was also significant, supporting the social shaping of technology (Contractor and Seibold 1993). Systems theory supported SI insights through the development of human-centered systems (HCS) theory as: social and technical analysis; continued, longitudinal, and iterative development; complex human-machine interactions; and focus on users in development, design, evaluation, and use (Kling and Star 1997).

Theories from other disciplines and new SI theorization increasingly bolstered SI objectives to improve design and understand actual ICT uses and consequences, rather than prescribe design or narrowly explain outcomes through particular disciplinary theories.

Concepts

Growing interests and concerns with all possible variables affecting outcomes in diversifying domains shaped conceptual analysis. Understanding the complex reality of change in sociotechnical environments continued to be a major concern (e.g. Iacono 1996; Kling, Rosenbaum and Hert 1998) and was reflected in the specific language of complexity (Kling 1996; Kling and Star 1997; Kling and Tilquist 1998), and context (e.g. Kling 1998; Lamb 1996).

New concepts and variables – including legitimacy (Kling and Tilquist 1998), externalities (Kling and Star 1997), and social structure (e.g. Contractor and Seibold 1993) were considered as additional scholars identified factors relevant to the use, context, and adoption outcomes of new technologies. Practice-oriented efforts articulated areas of concern for policy makers, information professionals, and educators; however, impact was limited as SI scholarship was not yet very visible.

Findings

Common, repeatable findings continue to unify SI research. Significant work throughout the 1990s reinforced early conclusions, yet identified many more facets of sociotechnical interactions than values (Kling 1996), power balances (Contractor and Seibold 1993), and situatedness (Iacono 1996), which were previously evaluated. These findings illustrated the nuance of situated social and technical interaction. SI findings in this period begin to explain more precisely and under different conditions the role of ICTs in social and organizational change.

Additional findings included:

- Context impacts implementation and use (e.g Contractor and Seibold 1993; Kling and Tilquist 1998; Lamb 1996);
- Social shaping and context of technology matter (Iacono 1996; Kling 1998; Kling and Star 1997);
- Change is constant (Kling 1996);
- There are unintended consequences of ICTs (Kling and Lamb 1996);
- There is a productivity paradox associated with ICTs (Kling 1998; Kling and Star 1997);
- Outcome distributions are unequal (Kling and Star 1997);
- There are moral and ethical aspects of ICTs (Kling 1996);
- Articulation work is important to avoid consequences (Kling and Lamb 1999);
- External factors affect sociotechnical interaction (Kling and Lamb 1996); and
- ICT users are social actors (Iacono 1996).

Period of Coherence (2000-2005)

During this time SI was most cohesive, yet there was also foreshadowing of diversification and disagreements as early findings began to be questioned (Agre 2002). SI grew more robust and integrated compared to either before 2000 or after Kling's lingering hold on the domain faded. Kling's influence was most explicit during the early 2000s. During this period, Kling defined SI more concretely (Kling 2000a; 2000b) and collaborated prodigiously (i.e Kling, McKim, and King 2003; Kling, Rosenbaum, and Sawyer 2005). His unexpected passing brought an outpouring of reflective pieces on his impact on scholarship, as well as on the significance of SI (Iacono, King, and Kraemer 2003; Lamb 2003; Lamb and Sawyer 2005; Mansell 2005; Wood-Harper and Wood 2005).

Principles

Labels employed for this kind of work continued to vary; SI principles were refined and diversified at this time. The sociotechnical construct (e.g. Kling 2000a; 2000b; Sawyer and Rosenbaum 2000) and opposition to determinism (Agre 2002; Meyer and Kling 2002; Lamb and Sawyer 2005) still described SI research. These fundamental constructs continued to be useful in explaining ICT design, uses, and consequences, despite the persistence of determinism and the separate treatment of social and technical variables in other disciplines.

Many SI researchers described the dichotomy between standard deterministic models and sociotechnical models (Kling 2000b; Kling and

Callahan 2003; Kling, McKim, and King 2003), as identified by Meyer and Kling (2002). Sociotechnical models served practically oriented SI, through which strategies for sociotechnical change could be successfully identified and executed (Kling and Callahan 2003). These models also allowed for differentiation between parallel developments in similar setting with divergent implementation outcomes (Kling and McKim 2000).

Sociotechnical principles were used to identify social and technical facets of context and interaction in various settings (Courtright 2004; Hara and Kling 2002; Kling and Courtright 2003; Sawyer and Tapia 2005). Complex overlapping socially-constructed contexts of culture, organizations, and relationships also frame and influence technology by situating use and iteratively interacting with users and technologies (Kling 2000a; 2000b); Lamb and Davidson argue further that ICTs are socially embedded (2005). Kling provides and expands upon a specific sociotechnical model in which social infrastructure supports or undermines the potential of information technology, based on core SI findings surrounding conceptions of ICT in organizations and society (Kling 2000b).

SI, in principle, has constantly been redefined; Lamb and Sawyer defined SI in terms of its history of opposition to simplistic, deterministic arguments, as well as its sociotechnical orientation (2005). Lamb and Kling emphasize the sociotechnical construct as grounded in the SI findings that ICT users are primarily social actors (2003).

A number of articles, chapters, and entire books have been devoted to specifically explaining SI, including a series of articles in which Kling described SI as the "interdisciplinary study of the design, uses, and consequences of information technologies that takes into account their interaction with institutional and cultural contexts" (2000a, p.218). Some version of Kling's definition has guided a variety of publications (e.g. Kling 2000b; Kling and Hara 2004; Kling, Rosenbaum, and Sawyer 2005).

However other approaches to explaining SI as a research domain have been developed. Davenport described SI as contextual "practice-based research" to frame work in organizations in terms of stakeholders, unintended consequences, costs and benefits, interactions, externalities, environmental variables, barriers, and boundaries (2005). Also prevalent at this time was the conception of SI as research grounded in specific principles, rather than common motivations. Sawyer and Rosenbaum stated that "SI researchers focus on the social consequences of the design, implementation, and use of ICTs over a wide range of social and organizational settings" (2000, p.89). Kling, Rosenbaum, and Sawyer (2005) argued that SI was an interdisciplinary space for inquiry on similar problems, rather than a new discipline with shared methods and theories; their book first published the SI triangle of technology, institutions, and culture.

Within SI, sub-domains were carved out during this period and specific informatics-centered labels were established, including: critical informatics (Iacono, King, and Kraemer 2003; Kling 2003; Lamb and Sawyer 2005), organizational informatics (e.g. Kling 2000a; Sawyer and Eschenfelder 2002; Sawyer and Rosenbaum 2000), and educational informatics (Kling and Hara 2004). SI was applied enough during this period to necessitate further sub-differentiation.

Furthermore, discussions of the social aspects of ICT not only persisted, but were pervasive (e.g. Davenport 2001; Iacono, King, and Kraemer 2003). There were arguments that social variables are not obfuscated by technology, but rather social and technical environments co-evolve before and after implementation (Kling, Rosenbaum, and Sawyer 2005). Deconstructing practice through SI principles allows social (e.g. Hara and Kling 2002; Kling and McKim 2000), political (Mansell 2005), and economic (Ekbia and Kling 2005; Mansell 2005) boundaries and limitations to be co-examined, rather than be seen as footnotes to study of function.

In fostering socially-rich dialogue surrounding ICT, analysis became more nuanced; what began as a critical orientation became something guided more by principles as the critical perspective (Lamb and Sawyer 2005) and human-centered principles (e.g. Lamb and Kling 2003; Sawyer 2005) expanded to include usability concerns (Kling, Rosenbaum, and Sawyer 2005; Lamb and Kling 2003). For example, acknowledgement of the people who design and use ICTs provides better design and policy solutions for social users (Kling, Rosenbaum, and Sawyer 2005).

SI was guided by clear principles during this period. The development of specific principles particularly indicated the impact and level of participation in this area of scholarship, perhaps foreshadowing the establishment of SI as a scholarly institution. Momentum developed for research attention to sociotechnical problems and changes.

Approaches

Between 2000 and 2005, focus on political and economic aspects of sociotechnical interactions was a major trend (Agre 2000b; Ekbia and Kling 2005; Mansell 2005).

Institutional theory (Lamb and Davidson 2005) and the institutional social shaping approaches (Agre 2000a) continued to ground research. The social shaping of technology (SST), arguably a socially deterministic approach, became a more concrete theoretical approach in SI (Kling and McKim 2000; Sawyer and Tapia 2005). Sociotechnical theory provided a more balanced perspective on social and technical interactions than social shaping theory (Lamb and Kling 2003; Sawyer and Tapia 2005), and synthesized sociotechnical studies (Lamb and Sawyer 2005) of earlier work.

Emphasis on economic and political issues complemented SI's traditional emphasis on design and policy implications (Kling 2000a; 2000b). Economic theory (Agre 2000b; Ekbia and Kling 2005; Mansell 2005) – specifically as a theory of economies of scale (Agre 2000b), the theory of networked society with respect to production relationships (Ekbia and Kling 2005), and rationality through theories of political economy (Mansell 2005) – explained behaviors and interests involved in investment in technology and the benefits of ICT innovation and adoption. By explaining informational, global, and networked attributes of ICTs, economic theory can explain complexity and predictively model for strategic ICT planning (Ekbia and Kling 2005). Political analysis supplemented explanations of resistance to and enforcement of institutional and organizational norms, including strategic practices (Mansell 2005).

A second major trend focused on networks, which was in some ways correlated with the economic theory of networked society (Ekbia and Kling 2005), as well as an understanding of ICT users as social actors (Lamb and Davidson 2005; Lamb and Kling 2003). Network theory, emphasizing relationships and interactions between actors, institutions, and information resources, deconstructed ICT use for collaboration and coordination to a conceptual level (Lamb and Davidson 2005). Actor-network theory facilitated egocentric analysis to understand important nodes and specific interactions (e.g. Hara and Kling 2002; Sawyer and Tapia 2005). Network analysis provided a modeling mechanism to characterize types of relationships and central importance of specific nodes within communities (Courtright 2005).

The sociotechnical interaction network (STIN) explicitly applied network theory to sociotechnical contexts by including technologies as nodes that interact with actors, groups, and resources (e.g. Kling 2000a; Kling, McKim, and King 2003; Lamb 2003). This contextual application established sociotechnical network models, including the social actor model, to account for the mutually shaping interactions between social and technical factors (e.g. Kling and Callahan 2003; Meyer and Kling 2002).

Other SI-specific approaches developed recognizing: 1) the importance of empirically grounded discourse for successful outcomes through technical action frames (Iacono and Kling 2001); 2) institutional and technical dimensions of workplaces as ICT interaction contexts in information environments (Lamb, King, and Kling 2003); and 3) the idea that the complexity of sociotechnical innovation, introduction, and change can only be explained through multivariate theoretical combinations as a multiview approach (Wood-Harper and Wood 2005).

Analysis of SI research has revealed critical, normative, and analytical orientations (e.g. Lamb and Sawyer 2005; Sawyer and Rosenbaum 2000). The second orientation – normative – practically and tangibly translates SI into implications for design, policy, or use alternatives (Lamb and Sawyer 2005).

Diverse theoretical approaches resulted in part from the increased visibility of SI and its central scholars, drawing in communication and media scholars, as well as scholars of the political economy. Increased theorization in SI was also important to validate SI discussions.

Concepts

Concepts analyzed during this period included many of the earlier constructs, as well as a new emphasis on coordination (Lamb and Davidson 2005), cooperation (Ekbia and Kling 2005), uncertainty (Courtright 2004), and governance (Agre 2000a), each of which is fundamentally linked to respective theoretical trends: network theory; economic theory; political theory, information environments; and political theory. The concept of sociotechnical systems evolved due to the networked properties of ICTs in use (Kling 2000a; Sawyer and Rosenbaum 2000).

Context – with specific emphasis on social context (e.g. Kling and McKim 2000; Mansell 2005; Sawyer and Eschenfelder 2002), as opposed to sociotechnical, institutional, and organizational variations – continued to be examined (Iacono, King, and Kraemer 2003; Sawyer 2005). Institutions conceptualized social arrangements, including norms and practices (e.g. Agre 2002; Kling 2003; Lamb and Kling 2003). Organizational environments provided another context in which to examine interactions (Agre 2000b; Ekbia and Kling 2005; Lamb, King, and Kling 2003). These contexts and arrangements of relationships were studied as networks (e.g. Agre 2000b; Ekbia and Kling 2005) and communities (e.g. Kling and Courtright 2003). Attention was also paid to the infrastructure that supports these arrangements (Courtright 2005; Davenport 2001; Kling 2000a).

Interactions were examined as coordination (Lamb and Davidson 2005), cooperation (Ekbia and Kling 2005), collaboration (e.g. Agre 2000a; Kling, McKim, and King 2003), and communication (e.g. Hara and Kling 2002; Lamb 2003; Mansell 2005). By examining these interactions, researchers theorized about power relationships (Agre 2000a; 2002; Ekbia and Kling 2003), organizational politics (Sawyer and Tapia 2005), identity (Lamb and Davidson 2005; Lamb and Kling 2003), management (e.g. Davenport 2001; Kling and Hara 2004; Sawyer and Tapia 2005), control (Ekbia and Kling 2003), complexity (e.g. Iacono, King and Kraemer 2003; Kling, McKim, and King 2003), and dynamics (Courtright 2004).

The introduction of additional political, economic, and network science concepts was important in broadening the scope of the discussion to include larger scale social issues. These themes also reflected research trends in other distinct and tangential areas of study, allowing SI discourse to be accessible and easily integrated with current conversations.

Findings

Findings surrounding social context were verified, and, taken together, reinforced the principle that there is a social shaping of technology (e.g. Kling 2000a; 2000b; Kling, Rosenbaum, and Sawyer 2005), context impacts implementation and use (e.g. Kling 2003), and ICT use is situated and context dependent (e.g. Kling, McKim, and King 2003; Sawyer and Rosenbaum 2000). These findings mutually reinforced SI principles and conclusions about the significance of analyzing social variables as they situate and interact with ICTs.

Continued critical analysis also revealed evidence to support new conclusions:

- ICTs and their context are mutually shaping (e.g. Agre 2000a; 2000b; Hara and Kling 2002; Sawyer 2005);
- ICTs are sociotechnical network systems (e.g. Iacono and Kling 2001; Lamb and Kling 2003);
- ICTs have social, technical, and institutional natures (e.g. Lamb and Sawyer 2005; Sawyer 2005);
- ICTs are configurable (Kling, McKim, and King 2003; Kling, Rosenbaum, and Sawyer 2005); and
- Technology affects professional identity (Hara and Kling 2002; Lamb and Davidson 2005).

The introduction of new conclusions and findings augmented the set of explanations available to SI scholars, but perhaps more significant was internal debate surrounding earlier claims. Some SI scholars disagreed over whether ICTs favor or reinforce the status quo (Agre 2002; Ekbia and Kling 2003; Meyer and Kling 2002; Sawyer and Rosenbaum 2000). The subtle tension was important because it indicated a self-critical turn within SI. Expansion and refinement of central tenets and assertions of SI signified its diverse and dynamic status.

Period of Diversification (2006-Present)

Diversification of SI has occurred as 1) researchers have begun to self-identify with other labels for their work (for example, sociotechnical and social aspects of ICTs); and 2) very different approaches have been introduced to address similar problems through new theoretical lenses and different conceptual perspectives (for example, the critical perspective).

Principles

Certain early principles have been now dropped, including overt rejection of determinism, either because SI is no longer tethered to its roots or because discourse has changed over time. The principles guiding SI work include: the sociotechnical (e.g. Davenport 2008; Sawyer and Tyworth 2006; Tapia and Maitland 2009), SI (e.g. Oltmann, Rosenbaum, and Hara 2006; Robbin, et al. 2006; Shachaf and Rosenbaum 2009), social aspects of ICT (e.g. Contractor 2009; Robbin and Day 2006; Shachaf and Hara 2007), critical informatics as an approach (Day 2007; King, Iacono, and Grudin 2007), and the critical perspective (e.g. Day 2007; Robbin and Day 2006).

While this work is labeled in five different ways (sociotechnical, SI, critical informatics, the critical perspective, and social aspects of ICTs), there are two major areas in which all of these types of works are presented and discussed: SI and the sociotechnical. For many researchers, both areas are equally relevant for their work (e.g. Davenport 2008; Sawyer and Tapia 2007), yet for others, these areas differ in relevance and legitimacy (e.g. Contractor 2009). What began as one interdisciplinary set of SI principles is now diverging.

Approaches

Recent SI research has diversified and generated revised theoretical approaches and models for analysis. Interest in network theory (i.e. Contractor 2009; Goggins, Laffey, and Gallagher 2011) and technical action frames (Davenport and Horton 2006; Robbin et al. 2006) continues and older constructs, such as computerization movements, are being revisited (Hara and Rosenbaum 2008). New theories are also being developed, such as IS/IT governance theory (Maldonado, Maitland, and Tapia 2010).

Network constructs enable SI scholars to examine relationships among individuals, institutions, and ICT to identify patterns and sociotechnical interaction (Contractor 2009; Sawyer and Tyworth 2006). Approaches for analysis of networks (Goggins, Laffey, and Gallagher 2011) include the sociotechnical network model (Blincoe, Valetto, and Goggins 2012), social network theory (Contractor 2009), actor-network theory (e.g. Contractor, Monge, and Leonardi 2011; Davenport 2008), and STIN (Meyer 2006; Sawyer and Tyworth 2006; Shachaf and Rosenbaum 2009).

Sociotechnical theory is also developing into a multi-theoretical, integrated framework for sociotechnical studies (Davenport 2008) of interactions (e.g. Sawyer and Tyworth 2006). Specifically, the sociotechnical systems (STS) construct became a popular conceptualization of information systems, which enable and reciprocally impact social processes (Tapia and Maitland 2009).

IS/IT governance theory assesses control and power implications surrounding access and changes to ICTs (Maldonado, Maitland, and Tapia 2010). Political theory and political economics, as for example rational actor theory (Robbin and Day 2006), explain stakeholders' interests and distributions of computerization outcomes (Maldonado, Maitland, and Tapia 2010; Robbin 2007).

Within SI, specifically constructed social theories include, for example group informatics (Goggins 2006) and behavioral complexity theory of media selection (Shachaf and Hara 2007).

Theoretical approaches furthering SI reflect the desire to revise, fortify, and institutionalize SI as a significant and useful approach to the social analysis of computing (Sawyer and Tapia 2007). Many of these approaches apply relevant theories from other domains to define integrated multi-theoretical frameworks. These developments are valuable to frame scholarly work in SI terms, while continuing to be relevant beyond SI.

Concepts

The language and focus of scholarly inquiries in SI continue to focus on the same earlier concepts of control (e.g. Maldonado, Maitland, and Tapia 2010), complexity (e.g. Contractor, Monge, and Leonardi 2011; Tapia and Maitland 2009), and social context (e.g. Hara and Rosenbaum 2008; Robbin and Day 2006).

Researchers have examined organizational (Tapia and Maitland 2009), institutional (Davenport and Horton 2006), sociotechnical (Goggins, Laffey, and Gallagher 2011; King, Iacono, and Grudin 2007), and technical (Orlikowski and Iacono 2008) changes to understand the complexity (e.g. Robbin and Day 2006) and dynamics (e.g. Robbin et al. 2006; Rosenbaum and Shachaf 2010) of sociotechnical interactions and systems (Tapia and Maitland 2009) in context. Specific conceptualizations of sociotechnical interactions complimented the emphasis on sociotechnical theory during this period and formed the core of sociotechnical research as an area somewhat distinct from SI, in terms of researcher self-identification. These sociotechnical concepts, so central to SI, were also of interest to researchers who did not consider themselves to be in SI, such as Bijker (Bijker 2010; Bijker, Hughes, and Pinch 2012).

Organizations and institutions (Contractor 2009; Sawyer and Tapia 2007), as formally bounded social arrangements, are analyzed for their economic and governance implications on local and global societies (Davenport and Horton 2006; Maldonado, Maitland, and Tapia 2010). Communities are studied similarly, though their varied structures and formalization have different implications (e.g. Goggins, Laffey, and Gallagher 2011; Rosenbaum and Shachaf 2010). Analysis of organizational, institutional, and community contexts of ICTs also grounds study of more complex processes and dynamics, including institutionalization (Sawyer and Tapia 2007), values (Robbin and Day 2006; Robbin et al. 2006), identity (Robbin and Day 2006; Rosenbaum and Shachaf 2010), and efficiency (Robbin and Day 2006).

The continued use of a shared vocabulary within SI and sociotechnical research implies that the concepts are still useful in synthesizing findings and shaping common, inclusive discussions about social situated ICTs.

Findings

SI research has verified certain findings such as the socially shaped nature of technology, while directing little attention to a number of earlier findings such as the impact of technology on professional identity. At the same time new conclusions are significant; for example, Orlikowski and Iacono (2008) identified five conceptualizations of ICT as: a tool, an ensemble, a proxy, computational, and nominal.

A major focus continues to be the social analysis of ICTs and change. Research re-emphasizes that ICT users are social actors (e.g. Blincoe, Valetto, and Goggins 2012; Rosenbaum and Shachaf 2010) and ICTs comprise sociotechnical network systems (e.g. Contractor 2009; Orlikowski and Iacono 2008). Social dynamics, including political interests and personal preferences (e.g. Maldonado, Maitland, and Tapia 2010; Shachaf and Hara 2007), describe unequal distributions of social change (e.g. Sawyer and Tapia 2006; Tapia and Maitland 2009) and explain why ICTs benefit the status quo (Robbin et al. 2006), as those in power use their power to protect their interests. Yet, while benefits from new technologies are sometimes predictable, there are certainly paradoxical impacts of ICTs (Oltmann, Rosenbaum, and Hara 2006; Sawyer and Tyworth 2006), in part because: ICTs are not value neutral (e.g. Davenport and Horton 2006; Robbin and Day 2006), there are moral and ethical aspects of ICTs (e.g. Robbin et al. 2006; Sawyer and Tyworth 2006), contexts are complex (e.g. Hara and Rosenbaum 2008; Oltmann, Rosenbaum, and Hara 2006), and contexts impact implementation and use (e.g. King, Iacono, and Grudin 2007; Maldonado, Maitland, and Tapia 2010; Shachaf and Hara 2007).

The constricted focus is consistent with efforts to increase robustness and validity of SI. The collective decrease in variety of claims may have developed from self-critical debate evident in the early 2000s, and is important in consolidating a strong SI core.

Conclusion: Challenges and Opportunities

Considering SI scholarship from past to present, there is a pattern of a central figure, Rob Kling, developing an inclusive space for inquiry and then potential for that space to splinter in his absence.

Early work by Kling and Iacono sought a new social theoretical perspective toward computerization and information systems. SI principles, drawn from early studies, allowed scholars to legitimately account for more diverse variables at a different scale than economists, computer scientists, or sociologists alone at that time. A researcher using the economics of technology approach would likely only consider costs, benefits, and interests and computer scientists would likely only consider technological features and design; SI provided a more holistic, integrated perspective. Furthermore, the sociology of technology would likely consider social statistics and generalize computerization success and failure, while SI explained what happened locally in specific contexts.

Early SI work explained different technological outcomes. However, SI was limited by its relatively nascent stage of scholarship; increased participation and attention were necessary to form a defined approach.

In the 1990s, SI became a more coherent approach, under a common label and with common ideas and terms to explain problems, yet it was not yet recognized as a serious approach to analysis of computing. Scholarly interest was established during this period, providing opportunities for collaboration and consideration of increasingly interdisciplinary and complex situations. Findings and arguments amassed through the 1990s had not yet been internally evaluated or critiqued, despite propensity to question outside arguments and discourse. A challenge as SI further developed would be internal revision and debate over claims, findings, and theories that result from interdisciplinary research on ICTs in society.

The force of Rob Kling as a central, unifying figure was perhaps the most defining feature of the early 2000s. He set an agenda for SI scholarship, collaborated with many of the other primary scholars, and unified SI through a clear definition and opportunities for dialogue through the Center for Social Informatics at Indiana University, Bloomington. His passing posed an enormous challenge to SI to continue and thrive without his critical commentary or contributions. Yet there were also new opportunities to further refine SI, increase scholarship, and extend collaboration in honor of his legacy through the SI institutions and venues he helped to establish.

Recent SI scholarship has begun to redefine and reinvent the approach. New motivations and labels differentiate within SI, and outmoded, contradicted constructs and concepts are abandoned. This refinement in many ways strengthens the value of this work as rigorous, theoretical and empirically grounded, but in other ways challenges researchers who consider the same problems in subtly different ways by dividing them into sociotechnical studies and SI.

From 2006 to the present, there has been a concerted effort to make SI relevant to practitioners and larger scholarly discussions, by considering political and economic themes and networked environments. These efforts imply that SI is becoming an intellectual institution yet it has been challenged by fragmentation, as some scholars identify with labels other than SI to describe their work. There are important opportunities to grow, as SI provides new models for longitudinal, comparative, and larger scale research. SI seems to be progressively more tied to technology and globalization, increasing its cultural relevance and necessitating continued attention.

One cannot avoid raising questions regarding the future of SI, in light of past evolution and its current state. Is SI on the verge of further diversification, which may lead to new concepts and significant findings, or to numbness and extinction, as scholars focus attention on new, more nuanced, challenges and opportunities?

Understanding seminal SI works, and the changes in themes and designs over time, allows researchers to more firmly ground their work, provides a strategy for students to integrate themselves, and maps a trajectory for development in SI approaches.

This chapter seeks to advance the agenda of SI in two ways, by conceptually identifying key concepts and ideas that unify SI, so as to frame future research, and practically identifying the key challenges and opportunities throughout the history of SI, so as provide grounds on which to build and highlight anticipated tensions moving forward. For SI to thrive as an approach and scholarly discussion, identity resolution is important.

References

Agre, Philip E. 2000a. "Infrastructure and Institutional Change in the Networked University." *Information, Communication & Society* 3 (4): 494-507.

—. 2000b. "The Market Logic of Information." *Knowledge, Technology & Policy* 13 (3): 67-77.

—. 2000. "Real-Time Politics: The Internet and the Political Process." *Information Society* 18 (5): 311-331.

Bijker, Wiebe E. 2010. "How is Technology Made? – That is the Question!." *Cambridge Journal Of Economics* 34 (1): 63-76.

Bijker, Wiebe E., Thomas P. Hughes, and Trevor J. Pinch, eds. 2012. *The Social Construction of Technological Systems: New Directions in the Sociology and History of Technology.* Cambridge, Mass.: MIT Press.

Blincoe, Kelly, Giuseppe Valetto, and Sean Goggins. 2012. "Proximity: A Measure to Quantify the Need for Developers' Coordination." *Proceedings of the ACM 2012 Conference on Computer Supported Cooperative Work.* 1351-1360.

Contractor, Noshir. 2009. "The Emergence of Multidimensional Networks." *Journal of Computer-Mediated Communication* 14 (3): 743-747.

Contractor, Noshir. S., Peter R. Monge, and Paul M. Leonardi. 2011. "Multidimensional Networks and the Dynamics of Sociomateriality: Bringing Technology Inside the Network." *International Journal of Communication* 5: 682-720.

Contractor, Noshir S., and David R. Seibold. 1993. "Theoretical Frameworks for the Study of Structuring Processes in Group Decision Support Systems." *Human Communication Research*, 19 (4): 528-563.

Courtright, Christina. 2004. "Which Lessons are Learned? Best Practices and World Bank Rural Telecommunications Policy." *Information Society* 20 (5): 345-356.

—. 2005. "Health Information-seeking Among Latino Newcomers: An Exploratory Study." *Information Research-An International Electronic Journal* 10 (2).

Davenport, Elisabeth. 2001. "Knowledge Management Issues for Online Organisations: 'Communities of Practice' as an Exploratory Framework." *Journal of Documentation* 57 (1): 61-75.

—. 2005. "Social Informatics in Practice: A Guide for the Perplexed." *Bulletin of The American Society For Information Science and Technology* 31 (5): 17-20.

—. 2008. "Social Informatics and Sociotechnical Research – A View from the UK." *Journal of Information Science* 34 (4): 519-530.

Davenport, Elisabeth, and Keith Horton. 2006. "The Production of Services in the Digital City: A Social Informatics Inquiry." In *Social Informatics: An Information Society for All? In Remembrance of Rob Kling*, edited by Jacques Berleur, Markku I. Nurminen, and John Impagliazzo, 233-242. New York: IFIP International Federation for Information Processing.

Day, Ron E. 2007. "Kling and the "Critical": Social Informatics and Critical Informatics." *Journal of the American Society for Information Science and Technology* 58 (4): 575-582.

Ekbia, Hamid R., and Rob Kling. 2003. "Power in Knowledge Management in Late Modern Times." *Academy of Management Proceedings*, D1-D6.

Ekbia, Hamid, and Rob Kling. 2005. "Network Organizations: Symmetric Cooperation or Multivalent Negotiation?." *Information Society* 21 (3): 155-168.

Goggins, Sean P. 2006. "Implications of Group Size on Activity Awareness Tools and Consideration of Information Foraging Theory." Presented at the Conference on Computer Supported Cooperative Work 2006.

Goggins, Sean P., James Laffey, and Michael Gallagher. 2011. "Completely Online Group Formation and Development: Small Groups as Socio-technical Systems." *Information Technology & People* 24 (2): 104-133.

Hara, Noriko, and Rob Kling. 2002. "Communities of Practice With and Without Information Technology." In *Proceedings of the 65th Annual Meeting of the American Society for Information Science and Technology* 39 (1): 338-349.

Hara, Noriko, and Howard Rosenbaum. 2008. "Revising the Conceptualization of Computerization Movements." *The Information Society* 24 (4): 229-245.

Iacono, C. Suzanne. 1996. "The Demise of Meaning-making and Social Agency as Critical Concepts in the Rhetoric of an Information Age." *Information Society* 12 (4): 449-450.

Iacono, Suzanne, John L. King, and Kenneth L. Kraemer. 2003, September. "Rob Kling: A Remembrance." *Communications of AIS* 12: 649-658.

Iacono, Suzanne, and Rob Kling. 2001. "Computerization Movements: The Rise of the Internet and Distant Forms of Work." In *Information Technology and Organizational Transformation: History, Rhetoric, and Practice*, edited by JoAnne Yates and John Van Maanen, 93-137, Organization Science. Thousand Oaks, CA: SAGE Publications.

King, John, Suzanne Iacono, and Jonathan Grudin. 2007. "Going Critical: Perspective and Proportion in the Epistemology of Rob Kling." *Information Society* 23 (4): 251-262.

Kling, Rob. 1994. "Reading "All About" Computerization: How Genre Conventions Shape Non-fiction Social Analysis." *The Information Society* 10 (3): 147-172.

—. 1996. *Computerization and Controversy: Value Conflicts and Social Choices*. San Diego: Academic Press.

—. 1998. "A Brief Introduction to Social Informatics." *Canadian Journal of Information and Library Science – Revue Canadienne des Sciences de l'Information et de Bibliotheconomie* 23 (1-2): 50-85.

—. 1999. "What is Social Informatics and Why Does it Matter?." *D-Lib Magazine* 5 (1).

—. 2000a. "Learning about Information Technologies and Social Change: The Contribution of Social Informatics." *The Information Society* 16 (3): 217-232.

—. 2000b. "Social Informatics: A New Perspective on Social Research about Information and Communication Technologies." *Prometheus: Critical Studies in Innovation* 18 (3): 245-264.

—. 2003. "Critical Professional Education about Information and Communications Technologies and Social Life." *Information Technology & People* 16 (4): 394-418.

Kling, Rob, and Ewa Callahan. 2003. "Electronic Journals, the Internet, and Scholarly Communication." *Annual Review of Information Science & Technology* 37 (1): 127-177.

Kling, Rob, and Christina Courtright. 2003. "Group Behavior and Learning in Electronic Forums: A Sociotechnical Approach." The *Information Society* 19 (3): 221-235.

Kling, Rob, and Noriko Hara. 2004. "Informatics and Distributed Learning." In *Encyclopedia of Distributed Learning*, edited by Anna DiStefano, Kjell Rudestam, and Robert Silverman, 225-227. Thousand Oaks, CA: Sage Publications.

Kling, Rob, and Iacono, Suzanne. 1984a. "Computing as an Occasion for Social Control." *Journal of Social Issues* 40 (3): 77-96.

Kling, Rob, and Iacono, Suzanne. 1984b. "The Control of Information Systems Developments after Implementation." *Communications Of The ACM* 27 (12): 1218-1226.

Kling, Rob, and Suzanne Iacono. 1988. "The mobilization of support for computerization: The role of computerization movements." *Social Problems*, 35, no. 3: 226-243.

Kling, Rob, and Suzanne Iacono. 1989. "The Institutional Character of Computerized Information Systems." *Information Technology & People* 5 (1): 7-28.

Kling, Rob, and Roberta Lamb. 1996. "Bits of Cities: Utopian Visions and Social Power in Placed-Based and Electronic Communities." *Rob Kling Center for Social Informatics Working Papers Series*, WP-96-02. Other versions: Kling, Rob, and Lamb, Roberta. 1998. "Morceaux de Villes. Comment les Visions Utopiques Structurent le Pouvoir Social dans l'Espace Physique et dans le Cyberespace." In *Utopies Urbaines,* edited by Emmanuel Eveno. Toulouse: Presses Universitaires du Mirail.

Kling, Rob, and Roberta Lamb. 1999. "IT and Organizational Change in Digital Economies." *Computers & Society* 29 (3): 17-25.

Kling, Rob, and Geoffrey W. McKim. 2000. "Not Just a Matter of Time: Field Differences and the Shaping of Electronic Media in Supporting Scientific Communication." *Journal of The American Society For Information Science* 51 (14): 1306-1320.

Kling, Rob, Geoffrey W. McKim, and Adam King. 2003. "A Bit More to It: Scholarly Communication Forums as Socio-technical Interaction

Networks." *Journal of The American Society For Information Science and Technology* 54 (1): 47-67.

Kling, Rob, Howard Rosenbaum, and Carol Hert. 1998. "Social Informatics in Information Science: An Introduction." *Journal of the American Society for Information Science* 49 (12): 1047-1052.

Kling, Rob, Howard Rosenbaum, and Steve Sawyer. 2005. *Understanding and Communicating Social Informatics: A Framework for Studying and Teaching the Human Contexts of Information and Communication Technologies.* Medford, N.J.: Information Today.

Kling, Rob, and Leigh Star. 1997. "Human Centered Systems in the Perspective of Organizational and Social Informatics." In *Human Centered Systems*, edited by Thomas Huang and James Flanagan. http://www.ifp.illinois.edu/nsfhcs/final_report/section1.html.

Kling, Rob, and John Tillquist. 1998. "Conceiving IT-enabled Organizational Change." *Rob Kling Center for Social Informatics Working Papers Series*: WP-98-02.

Lamb, Roberta. 1996. "Informational Imperatives and Socially Mediated Relationships." *Information Society* 12 (1): 17-38.

—. 2003. "Memorial: The Social Construction of Rob Kling." *Information Society* 19 (3): 195-196.

Lamb, Roberta, and Elizabeth Davidson. 2005. "Information and Communication Technology Challenges to Scientific Professional Identity." *Information Society* 21 (1): 1-24.

Lamb, Roberta, John King, and Rob Kling. 2003. "Informational Environments: Organizational Contexts of Online Information Use." *Journal Of The American Society For Information Science And Technology* 54 (2): 97-114.

Lamb, Roberta, and Rob Kling. 2003. "Reconceptualizing Users as Social Actors in Information Systems Research." *MIS Quarterly* 27 (2): 197-235.

Lamb, Roberta, and Steve Sawyer. 2005. "On Extending Social Informatics from a Rich Legacy of Networks and Conceptual Resources." *Information Technology & People* 18 (1): 9-20.

Maldonado, Edgar A., Maitland, Carleen F., and Tapia, Andrea H. 2010. "Collaborative Systems Development in Disaster Relief: The Impact of Multi-level Governance." *Information Systems Frontiers* 12 (1): 9-27.

Mansell, Robin. 2005. "Social Informatics and the Political Economy of Communications." *Information Technology & People* 18 (1): 21-25.

Meyer, Eric T. 2006. "Socio-technical Interaction Networks: A Discussion of the Strengths, Weaknesses and Future of Kling's STIN Model." In *IFIP International Federation for Information Processing, Volume*

223, Social Informatics: An Information Society for All? In Remembrance of Rob Kling, edited by Jacques Berleur, Marco I. Numinem and J. Impagliazzo, 37-48. Boston: Springer.

Meyer, Eric T., and Rob Kling. 2002. "Leveling the Playing Field, or Expanding the Bleachers? Socio-technical Interaction Networks and arXiv.org." *Rob Kling Center for Social Informatics Working Papers Series:* WP-02-10.

Oltmann, Shannon M., Howard Rosenbaum, and Noriko Hara. 2006. "Digital Access to Government Information: To What Extent are Agencies in Compliance with EFOIA?." *Proceedings Of The American Society For Information Science And Technology* 43 (1).

Orlikowski, Wanda J., and Suzanne C. Iacono. 2008. "Research Commentary: Desperately Seeking the 'IT' in IT Research: A Call to Theorizing the IT Artifact." In *Information system infrastructure*, edited by Uta Hartung, 280-297. Orriginally published: *Information Systems Research* 12 (2): 121-134.

Robbin, Alice. 2007. "Rob Kling: In Search of One Good Theory." *Information Society* 23 (4): 235-250.

Robbin, Alice, and Ron Day. 2006. "On Rob Kling: The Theoretical, the Methodological, and the Critical." In *Social informatics: An Information Society for All? In Remembrance of Rob Kling*, edited by Jacques Berleur, Markku I. Nurminen, and John Impagliazzo, 25-36. New York: IFIP International Federation for Information Processing.

Robbin, Alice, Roberta Lamb, John L. King, and Jacques Berleur. 2006. "As We May Remember." In *Social Informatics: An Information Society for All? In Remembrance of Rob Kling*, edited by Jacques Berleur, Markku I. Nurminen, and John Impagliazzo, 17-24. New York: IFIP International Federation for Information Processing.

Rosenbaum, Howard, and Pnina Shachaf. 2010. "A Structuration Approach to Online Communities of Practice: The Case of Q&A Communities." *Journal of The American Society For Information Science And Technology* 61 (9): 1933-1944.

Sawyer, Steve. 2005. "Social Informatics: Overview, Principles and Opportunities." *Bulletin Of The American Society For Information Science & Technology* 31 (5): 9-12.

Sawyer, Steve, and Kristin Eschenfelder. 2002. "Social Informatics: Perspectives, Examples, and Trends." *Annual Review Of Information Science and Technology* 36 (1): 427-465.

Sawyer, Steve, and Howard Rosenbaum. 2000. "Social Informatics in the Information Sciences: Current Activities and Emerging Directions." *Informing Science* 3 (2): 89-96.

Sawyer, Steve, and Andrea Tapia. 2005. "The Sociotechnical Nature of Mobile Computing Work: Evidence from a Study of Policing in the United State." *International Journal of Technology And Human Interaction* 1 (3): 1-14.

Sawyer, Steve, and Andrea Tapia. 2006. "Always Articulating: Theorizing on Mobile and Wireless Technologies." *Information Society* 22 (5): 311-323.

Sawyer, Steve, and Andrea Tapia. 2007. "From Findings to Theories: Institutionalizing Social Informatics." *Information Society* 23 (4): 263-275.

Sawyer, Steve, and Michael Tyworth. 2006. "Social Informatics: Principles, Theory, and Practice." In *Social Informatics: An Information Society for All? In Remembrance of Rob Kling*, edited by Jacques Berleur, Markku I. Nurminen, and John Impagliazzo, 49-62. New York: IFIP International Federation for Information Processing.

Shachaf, Pnina, and Noriko Hara. 2007. "Behavioral Complexity Theory of Media Selection: a Proposed Theory for Global Virtual Teams." *Journal of Information Science* 33 (1): 63-75.

Shachaf, Pnina, and Howard Rosenbaum. 2009. "Online Social Reference: A Research Agenda through a STIN Framework." *Proceedings of the 2009 iConference*, Chapel Hill, NC, February 8-11, 2009.

Tapia, Andrea, and Carleen Maitland. 2009. "Wireless Devices for Humanitarian Data Collection." *Information, Communication & Society* 12 (4): 584-604.

Wood-Harper, Trevor, and Bob Wood. 2005. "Multiview as Social Informatics in Action: Past, Present and Future." *Information Technology & People* 18 (1): 26-32.

PART II

PRESENT

CHAPTER THREE

EXAMINING THE HYPHEN: THE VALUE OF SOCIAL INFORMATICS FOR RESEARCH AND TEACHING

ERIC T. MEYER

One and a half decades after the publication of Kling's (1999) article explaining "What is social informatics and why does it matter?", we find ourselves further along the road in terms of understandings of socio-technical configurations, and we must admit as part of any stock-taking that Social Informatics (SI) as an academic pursuit has not achieved the scholarly traction we might have hoped for. While the original article has a fairly healthy number of citations (441 to the 1999 version in *D-Lib Magazine* and another 35 to the version reprinted in the *The Information Society* in 2007, according to Google Scholar), one would be hard-pressed to point to a canon of SI publications that have coalesced into anything resembling a field or discipline or, in fact, anything more than a loosely-knit professional community of like-minded scholars. While Google Scholar reports "about 14,000 results" for the phrase "social informatics", the more narrowly focused Scopus and Web of Science databases indicate much more modest results in the published journal literature (167 articles and 188 articles respectively that include the term "social informatics" in the title, abstract, or keywords as of the beginning of 2013). One of the reasons for the large discrepancy between Google Scholar and the journal databases and for the fact that that SI is much more visible in the gray non-journal literature (such as conference papers, presentations, course materials, and so forth) than in the published academic literature, I will argue, is that the function SI performs for many researchers and students can be thought of as similar to backstage or invisible work (Star and Strauss 1999) that sensitizes researchers to important concepts, but then often recedes into the shadows.

The way I describe SI is as follows. If one considers the hyphenated compound word "socio-technical", SI researchers are interested in the hyphen connecting the social to the technical. While this may seem flippant at first glance, it is actually an important point: inherent in the act of examining the hyphen, as one might think of it, is a balanced view toward the relative importance of the social and the technical aspects of any given socio-technical construct. This is important because many of the alternative frameworks for understanding the socio-technical world rely on *a priori* assumptions, either stated or unstated, that either social considerations or technical considerations are of primary importance.

At one end of the spectrum lie technological determinist accounts of socio-technical systems that view technology as the "cause" of changes in the social order. This can take the form of naïve technological determinism that inhabits so many popular journalistic accounts of technology, such as assertions that internet dating sites cause marriages to fail, or that mobile phones result in the breakdown of parental authority, or any number of other claims one can easily find in the media that link technology directly to positive or negative outcomes without any consideration of contributing and intervening social factors or even human agency. There is also a more sophisticated form of technological determinism that argues that technological changes are a key driving force of history, and that the choices of individuals are inconsequential at this macro scale (Schroeder 2007). It is safe to argue that while there are relatively few technological determinists actively inhabiting the academic social sciences (Schroeder, for instance, happily acknowledges the contrarian nature of his position), nevertheless, unstated determinist assumptions are still remarkably common in, for instance, computing applications and engineering literature.

As one example, while the importance of considering users is frequently mentioned in the context of designing computer applications, all too often, one still hears of the "user" simply as a problem to be overcome with system design, and that lack of adoption can be attributed to the failure of users to adequately understand the technological system. In one meeting observed during research by Meyer and Hjorth (2013) of an arts organization which was working with an outside firm to develop a new web-based platform for artists, the head of the web programming team spent much of the time berating his or her counterparts (who were primarily producers and project managers at that particular meeting) within the arts organization who were unhappy with the platform that had been designed. The platform did not deliver the functions needed to support the organization's objectives, yet the head of the website programming team kept insisting that their platform "worked perfectly" and that it wasn't their fault if nobody was able to use it, or wanted to use it (Meyer and Schroeder, forthcoming). In a key work in the SI literature, Lamb and Kling (2003) specifically addressed this issue when they argued for reconceptualizing "users" as social actors. In their conceptualization, "most people who use ICT applications utilize multiple applications, in various roles, and as part of their efforts to produce goods and services while interacting with a variety of other people, and often in multiple social contexts" (Lamb and Kling 2003, 197). This recasts the person engaging with any given socio-technical configuration as active, rather than in the passive roles suggested by the term "user." For the time being, however, the term "user," and the inherently privileged role of technology in the system that results, remains deeply entrenched in practice and also in theory, particularly in fields such as human-computer interaction (HCI) and user experience design (UXD).

On the opposite end of the spectrum, much of the Science and Technology Studies (STS) literature, as exemplified by work presented at conferences such as 4S (Society for the Social Study of Science) and in journals such as *Science, Technology and Human Values*, implicitly argues that social considerations are the most important to consider and that people shape their technologies. According to this argument (which was a reaction to technological determinist accounts that frequently shaped previous descriptions of technology in society) the characteristics of technologies are shaped and re-shaped almost without regard to any of the inherent aspects of the technologies themselves. This perspective is useful, but risks forgetting the role that technological constructs have in allowing (note: not *causing,* but allowing or enabling) people to reconfigure their relationships (Dutton 2005). In an extended exchange with Woolgar and Grint (Woolgar and Grint 1991; Grint and Woolgar 1992; Kling 1991a; b; 1992a; b) about competing analytical approaches to understanding socio-technical phenomena, Kling argues:

> We agree that the capabilities of technologies are not fixed and depend upon social relationships between users, technologies, and other "close-in" participants. We agree that any relationship between technologies and social effects are socially produced and mediated through complex social networks, institutionalized arrangements, and systems of belief and communication ... But we differ in our beliefs about whether concise characterizations of a technology should be legitimate elements of serious sociological narratives ... Their approach starts with important insights but sacrifices the ability to make strong claims about the consequences of using specific technologies in specific social worlds. It also sacrifices access to important audiences of scholars, policymakers, technologies, and

> others who may be interested in the social consequences of using new technologies. (Kling 1992b, 381-382)

It is worthwhile to touch briefly on at least two theories from the STS literature that have shaped thinking in SI, but also serve to illustrate how SI's open-mindedness towards social shaping versus the power of technological affordances to influence behavior makes it different from the (admittedly larger) STS literature.[1]

The Social Construction of Technology (SCOT) theory is a radical constructivist approach to understanding the development of science and technology (Bijker 2001). Developed starting in the 1980s primarily by Trevor Pinch and Wiebe Bijker, SCOT represents an effort to bring a social constructivist approach, already in common usage in the sociology of scientific knowledge, to the understanding of technology (Bijker, Hughes, and Pinch 1987). A major initial impetus for the development of SCOT was a rejection of technologically deterministic approaches to understanding technological change over time:

> Technological determinism was taken to comprise two elements: (a) technology develops autonomously, and (b) technology determines societal development to an important degree. This view was seen as intellectually poor and politically debilitating. Technological determinism implies a poor research strategy, it was argued, because it entails a teleological, linear, and one-dimensional view of technological development. In addition, it was considered politically debilitating because technological determinism suggests that social and political interventions in the course of technology are impossible, thus making politicization of technology a futile endeavor. (Bijker 2001, 15523)

The term "social construction" in SCOT comes from the sociology of scientific knowledge (SSK) tradition, led by Bloor (1973).[2] In SCOT, social construction is a central concern:

> It is often believed that at the beginning of the process of innovation the problems to be solved are basically technical and that economic, social, political, or indeed cultural considerations come into play only at a later stage … [However,] right from the start, technical, scientific, social, economic, or political considerations have been inextricably bound up into an organic whole. Such heterogeneity and complexity, which everyone

---

[1] The following section is adapted from Meyer (2007a). Copyright the author.

[2] For discussion a complete of the development of SSK, see Collins (1983) and Shapin (1995).

> agrees is present at the end of the process, are not progressively introduced along the way. They are present from the beginning. (Callon 1987, 84)

In other words, the process of the social construction of an artifact is occurring throughout the artifact's development. Using SCOT, analysts both include the social considerations from the beginning of their research and also recognize that social considerations play an important part of the construction of an artifact during its development process. The human actors are part of a social system that is influencing how they will come to understand the artifact.

These understandings are malleable for the SCOT theorists, who argue that the inherent interpretive flexibility in our relationships with our artifacts means that artifacts and experiences can be understood in a variety of ways. "We take words and world to be interpretively flexible and therefore grant that they may be perceived in different ways (that they may have different ontologies for different actors)" (Roth and Duit 2003, 875). Interpretive flexibility allows SCOT researchers to look past the intrinsic technological characteristics of an artifact and deconstruct the artifact into multiple socially interpreted artifacts.[3]

The mutual shaping of people and technology refers to the ongoing interaction between humans and technological artifacts, a process recognized as early as Marshall McLuhan's (1964) discussion of the media, where he observed that "we shape the tools and they in turn shape us." While not overtly emphasized by Bijker and other SCOT founders, mutual shaping has been discussed by other authors as a logical part of SCOT studies (Lievrouw 2002, Boczkowski 2004). Boczkowski in particular is an advocate of this view, stressing the importance of understanding the ongoing and reciprocal nature of shaping while cautioning that:

> This does not mean that the evolution of all new media artifacts is marked by ongoing technological and social transformations, or that these transformations are constant. What a mutual shaping approach implies,

---

[3] See for instance Bijker's (1995) analysis of the social construction of the safety bicycle in late 19th century, in which the high-wheeled Victorian-era 'Ordinary' bicycle, which had a tendency to topple over and was generally risky to ride, was flexibly interpreted. For non-cyclists, their interpretation of this situation was that these features made the bicycle unsafe. However, Bijker points out that for young and generally upper-class men, they exploited these features to "display their athletic skills and daring by showing off in the London parks. To impress the riders' lady friends, the risky nature of the Ordinary was essential. (Bijker 1995, 74-75).

though, is that it is in principle possible that these transformations can occur at multiple points in the shaping and diffusion of the artifact. (Boczkowski 2004, 257)

One key critic of the SCOT approach is Winner who, while acknowledging SCOT's valuable aspects – "its conceptual rigor, its concern for specifics, its attempt to provide empirical models of technological change that better reveal the actual course of events" (1993, 367-368) – believes that SCOT has "an almost total disregard for the social consequences of technical choice" (1993, 368). Winner argues that SCOT takes interpretive flexibility and the relativistic nature of experience too far and as a result "they have no theoretical or practical position on technology and human well-being at all" (1993, 372).

Another prominent STS theory that influences SI, but has important differences from SI, is Actor-Network Theory (ANT), which can be viewed as a subset of SCOT, when SCOT is broadly defined (Bijker 2001). ANT encompasses many elements, but for our purposes here, we can focus on a single key aspect of ANT: the actant. Latour (1987) proposed the term actant as a way to refer to both "people able to talk and things unable to talk" (83). The decision to include non-human artifacts as sources of action within a network is not trivial. Sociological theory, for instance, rarely views technological artifacts as more than a peripheral element that human actors manipulate (Latour 1988; Star 1988); conversely, technological deterministic approaches, which as noted above are strongly criticized by SCOT analysts, that focus on the "impacts" of technology are mechanistic and causal (Griffith and Dougherty 2001). In ANT:

> … elements of any kind may be included: humans, technological artifacts, organizations, institutions, etc. ANT does not distinguish between or define *a priori* any kind of elements…all networks are heterogeneous or socio-technical. There are no networks that consist of only humans or only of technological components. All networks contain elements of both. (Hanseth, Aanestad, and Berg 2004, 118)

Note that Hanseth et al. argue that ANT does not privilege *a priori* between the importance of the social and the technical, but I would argue that in practice, many ANT theorists have an unstated bias in favor of interpreting the social at the cost of disassembling the technical.

Latour argues that the most mundane of artifacts can be actants in socio-technical systems; his analysis of door closing mechanisms as actants is probably the clearest illustration. Latour describes how the simple technological combination of door hinges, which allow walls to temporarily and easily open, with hydraulic spring-operated door closers, which gently restore the wall to an unbroken surface, serve as relatively skilled actants in a socio-technical system allowing human actants to reversibly walk through walls and work in non-entombed but enclosed spaces (Latour 1988).

One of the major sources of criticism of ANT stems from ANT's controversial "claim that there are no differences between non-human and human forms of agency; that animals, machines, or even electrons can be 'actors' in the same sense as human are" (Bruun and Hukkinen 2003, 103). Actor-networks consist "of heterogeneous 'actants' the most durable of which – people, institutions, tools, texts, money, technologies, information, etc. – flow through the network" (Ekbia 2004). However, Bruun and Hukkinen point out that this criticism is based on an overly simplistic reading of ANT. Yes, non-human actants may have agency (the capacity to act) in the sense that agency is about connecting things and intervening in the world, but that does not require that non-living entities have the capacity for intentional behavior, they argue. Instead, it requires that analysts discard purely humanistic notions of action and agency. "Actor-network theory is 'co-constructionist': it seeks to identify how relations and entities come into being together" (Murdoch 2001, 111).

In terms of uptake, ANT is far more prominent than any core SI publications. Latour's book explaining ANT (Latour 2005), for instance has been cited 5,885 times in Google Scholar as of 2013, and his earlier works developing the concept have been cited nearly 8,000 times (Latour and Woolgar 1979) and 14,000 times (Latour 1987), respectively. If so many people have flocked to ANT, and comparatively few to SI, does that mean we should simply acknowledge that we have been less successful at creating our own actor-network, and should simply pack up our bags and go home? Why use the SI perspective at all? Why not just join the crowd and undertake SCOT or ANT research?

The problem is this: both SCOT and ANT have elements that are simply not amenable to SI research without bending or stretching those theories, possibly beyond recognition. As a research domain, SI, as articulated by Kling (1999), tends toward moderation in balancing the ideas of social constructivism with a preference for evidence-based research that takes the technological features of socio-technical systems seriously. As Williams and Edge (1996) point out, the social construction perspective, for its most relativist practitioners, can lead to arguments that artifacts are entirely socially constructed and embody no objective reality whatever. Kling (1992b) was responding to this perspective when he argued that while he agreed "that the capabilities of technologies are not fixed and depend upon social relationships between users, technologies, and other 'close-in' participants" (p. 381), nevertheless one does not need to be a technological determinist to understand that:

> physical objects like guns and roses have some capabilities that are not only arbitrarily derived from the talk about them. It is much harder to kill a platoon of soldiers with a dozen roses than with well-placed high-speed bullets. (Kling 1992a)

One alternative to SCOT and ANT that comes from the SI literature that I have used extensively in research projects is the Socio-Technical Interaction Network (STIN) strategy (Kling, McKim, and King 2003; Meyer 2006). The STIN strategy allows us to draw on the useful insights of SCOT and ANT but does not wholly embrace a relativist perspective and is skeptical of the possibility that non-human actants can exert agency in social situations.

The STIN strategy contains several elements, including a framework for understanding socio-technical systems. These elements include:

1. Identify a relevant population of system interactors
2. Identify core interactor groups
3. Identify incentives
4. Identify excluded actors and undesired interactions
5. Identify existing communication forums
6. Identify resource flows
7. Identify system architectural choice points
8. Map architectural choice points to socio-technical characteristics

(Kling, McKim, and King 2003, 57)

Because I have written about these elements elsewhere (Meyer 2006), I want to focus here only on two which I think make the SI approach embodied in the STIN strategy particularly valuable in contrast to the STS approaches discussed above. The first is part of point number 4: to identify excluded actors. Actor-Network Theory (and other prominent network-based theories such as social network analysis) by their very nature consider those people and technologies and organizations (or actants) *within* the network. They don't generally consider who the network excludes, but in our work on how digital tools for research are resulting in changes across academic disciplines (Meyer and Schroeder, forthcoming) we have found time and again that understanding who is either systematically excluded from a socio-technical construct, or who is excluded during the process of change as systems become computerized, can be key to understanding how technology has entered normal use.

Two quick examples might help understand this point. In the course of a project to understand the impacts digitized library collections are having on various communities and stakeholders (Eccles, Thelwall, and Meyer 2012; Meyer et al. 2009), we discovered that decisions about digitizing a particular library collection had included technical personnel, managers, scholars, community members, and other stakeholders, but had not included the library staff responsible for the original collection. Because we were using the STIN strategy, we probed during interviews to find out who used to be involved before digitization but was no longer part of the process. Once we learned about the excluded staff, we arranged a focus group with them and had an incredibly insightful session in which we learned not only about the history of the collection, but gained considerable insight into the choices that had gone into deciding what to digitize, and how one source of expertise had been excluded from those decisions.

In another study on the uptake of digital photography among marine biologists who study whales, dolphins, and other marine mammals (Meyer 2007a, b), asking questions about excluded actors uncovered a rich vein of information about how volunteers who had previously been a source of both manual labor (keeping paper logs of photographs, organizing slides, or printing black and white prints) and funding (via scientific tourism) were increasingly difficult to involve in the process once organizations had switched from film to digital photography. The volunteer jobs that required minimal training were replaced by jobs requiring more advanced technical skills (including organizing digital collections, designing and updating electronic databases, and maintaining computers, networks and network storage which all required passwords that only employees were allowed access to).

In both cases, sensitivity to the possibility of excluded actors helped to facilitate the discovery of important parts of the analog socio-technical system that had been profoundly affected when various elements of the system became computerized.

Another element of the STIN strategy that makes it more sensitive to the nature of technological developments than other alternatives is point number 7: identifying architectural choice points in the system. What this means is that, as in the Boczkowski quote above, although socio-technical systems evolve, they do not do so continuously. Instead, they follow a type of punctuated equilibrium in which periods of relative stability are punctuated by periods of change. By spending effort during research to focus on these periods of change, the STIN strategy argues, we can learn how decisions have been made that have shaped the resulting sociotechnical configurations, who was involved in (and again, excluded from) making those decisions, and how those decisions later played out when the system entered regular use.

One example of this is the scientific crowdsourcing website *Galaxy Zoo*, which was established in 2007 to solve a very practical problem: a group of researchers at Oxford University needed to classify a million galaxies from the Sloan Digital Sky Survey, and found that they did not have sufficient time or manpower to do the job themselves (Meyer et al. 2012; Raddick et al. 2010). In a meeting in an Oxford pub (Lintott, personal communication), the founders of Galaxy Zoo found themselves at an architectural choice point: their existing systems of technology and people clearly needed re-thinking, and several options were open to them. The choice they made, to build an online platform that would let anyone make a series of simple choices to help classify the galaxies, to open it up to the world via the internet, and to make additional information available for enthusiasts to go beyond the limits of the normal interface, has shaped the careers of the Galaxy Zoo scientists ever since. The platform has been extraordinarily successful, not only serving the original purpose of classifying large numbers of galaxies, but also enabling unexpected new discoveries to emerge (Cardamone et al. 2009; Lintott et al. 2009).

While the discovery of excluded actors or the examination of important decision points could of course happen regardless of one's discipline or theoretical perspective, I would argue that STIN in particular, and SI's openness to both technological and social drivers more generally, make discoveries such as these more likely. Horton and Davenport (2005) have argued that the STIN strategy "is a useful foil for examining over-exuberant claims about [communities of practice]" (61) and argue that the tight coupling between the social and the technical in the STIN strategy makes it more able to predict the likelihood of certain types of relationships compared to the generally post hoc approach usually taken by actor network approaches.

I have argued elsewhere that the STIN strategy is not a theory per se, which is one of the reasons, I would argue, that it has seen less uptake than it might otherwise have done in the published literature.

> It is fairly clear that STIN does not reach the level of theory, nor is it a proper methodology. What I would like to suggest is that STIN is really an analytic strategy. No particular methods are tied to STIN research; in fact, STIN research, like most of SI, is wide-ranging in the selection of specific methods that can be used to gather the data necessary to construct STIN explanations at the analytic level. I suggest the term STIN strategy is appropriate in the sense that a strategy is a goal-oriented plan of action.

> The goal in this case is to find more complete explanations and thorough understandings of the relationship between the social and the technical in socio-technical systems. (Meyer 2006, 44)

The inability to claim that STIN is sufficiently robust to be either a theory or a method is consistent with Robbin's (2007) argument that Kling's publication record in general did not "create, (re)construct, or extend theory, or create new methodologies for understanding the empirical world of computers in organizations" (244). Instead, Robbin argues, Kling took a practical approach to appropriating theory and method as necessary to explain computerization in organizations and to build a corpus of empirically-based research that "made the unobvious, the taken-for-granted, and the ignored explicit, problematic, and visible" (245).

One could think of the STIN strategy and other SI ideas such as the social actor concept (Lamb and Kling 2003) and computerization movements (Kling and Iacono 1988; Elliott and Kraemer 2008) as lenses into understanding socio-technical systems from an SI viewpoint. In a key volume on SI (Kling, Rosenbaum, and Sawyer 2005), there are extensive discussions of SI concepts and how to teach and communicate those concepts, but there is relatively little discussion of how one actually goes about researching and uncovering these concepts. This makes SI research questions particularly difficult to frame adequately; lacking appropriate robust theories and methods, most SI researchers must draw on other disciplines for their approaches that they hope will yield results of interest to an SI audience. SI researchers come from, and work in departments representing, a variety of disciplines, and bring their theories and methods with them. The problem is translating these disparate approaches into something coherent enough to contribute scholarship meaningful to other researchers in SI, such as in this book. This problem is particularly acute for new researchers wanting to enter this field who may be daunted by the wide variety of disciplinary approaches that are brought to bear by SI researchers and the large literature that must be mastered to make sense of these approaches.

For students wishing to understand how technology interacts with society and social constructs, however, I would argue that an SI lens has proven extremely useful. And the evidence shows that I am not alone in this: searching for the phrase ["social informatics" syllabus] in Google shows about 5,000 results, including entire courses or course modules at many universities around the world. While journal publications explicitly using the phrase social informatics may have lagged, the addition of SI to core curricula in information science, computer science, informatics, and business departments is a sign of the power of the concepts communicated by SI to engage students.

The SI viewpoint is an extraordinarily useful sensitizing concept when trying to teach students to think critically about what technology is, what technology does, and how technology plays a role in society and organizations. For instance, when I teach methods to post-graduate students, I frequently use the STIN strategy discussed above to show students how one can use a framework to know which questions to ask of research participants, but also how one can identify which people and which socio-technical configurations should be engaged as research participants. I have had many students use this approach in their papers and projects, and I find that gives them a solid footing when approaching a new research topic.

Likewise, the concept of computerization movements (Kling and Iacono 1988; Elliott and Kraemer 2008) plays an important role in how I teach parts of a course on networks of collaboration, and the Lamb and Kling (2003) concept of social actors is useful for sensitizing students to the problems with uncritically accepting the term "user" and its inherent passivity, as discussed earlier.

The disappearance of SI into the academic shadows after it has done its work sensitizing researchers to these concepts is at least slightly ironic, in that backstage work is one of the topics that SI researchers have sought to understand. Invisible work (Nardi and Engeström 1999) is often done behind the scenes, preparing the ground for the visible work that organizations do. The invisible work that SI is doing, I would argue, is to prepare students and researchers to be aware of and, hopefully, to engage both sides of the socio-technical in their jobs and research.

The greater dominance of SI in curricula and in gray literature than in the official published journal literature is both encouraging and troubling. Encouraging, for it demonstrates the usefulness of SI in communicating how socio-technical systems function in the real world and sensitizing students to the importance of understanding the hyphen that connects the social to the technical. Troubling, for unless new research continues to be generated and the community of SI researchers continues to grow, the insights offered by Kling and his students and colleagues risk growing out-of-date and fading into irrelevance for researchers and students alike.

References

Bijker, Wiebe E. 1995. *Of Bicycles, Bakelites, and Bulbs: Toward a Theory of Sociotechnical Change*. Cambridge, MA: The MIT Press.

—. 2001. "Social Construction of Technology." In *International Encyclopedia of the Social & Behavioral Sciences*, edited by N.J. Smelser and P.B. Baltes, 15522-15527. Oxford: Elsevier Science Ltd.

Bijker, Wiebe E., Thomas P. Hughes, and Trevor Pinch. 1987. *The Social Construction of Technological Systems: New Directions in the Sociology and History of Technology*. Cambridge, MA: The MIT Press.

Bloor, David. 1973. "Wittgenstein and Mannheim on the Sociology of Mathematics." *Studies in the History and Philosophy of Science Part A* 4 (2):173-191.

Boczkowski, Pablo J. 2004. "The Mutual Shaping of Technology and Society in Videotex Newspapers: Beyond the Diffusion and Social Shaping Perspectives." *The Information Society* 20 (4):255-267.

Bruun, Henrik, and Janne Hukkinen. 2003. "Crossing Boundaries: An Integrative Framework for Studying Technological Change." *Social Studies of Science* 33 (1):95-116.

Callon, Michel. 1987. "Society in the Making: The Study of Technology as a Tool for Social Analysis." In *The Social Construction of Technological Systems*, edited by Wiebe E. Bijker, Thomas P. Hughes and Trevor Pinch, 83-103. Cambridge, MA: The MIT Press.

Cardamone, Carolin, Kevin Schawinski, Marc Sarzi, Steven P Bamford, Nicola Bennert, CM Urry, Chris Lintott, William C Keel, John Parejko, and Robert C Nichol, Daniel Thomas, Dan Andreescu, Phil Murray, M. Jordan Raddick, Anze Slosar, Alex Szalay, and Jan VandenBerg. 2009. "Galaxy Zoo Green Peas: Discovery of a Class of Compact Extremely Star-forming Galaxies." *Monthly Notices of the Royal Astronomical Society* 399 (3):1191-1205.

Collins, H. M. 1983. "The Sociology of Scientific Knowledge: Studies of Contemporary Science." *Annual Review of Sociology* 9:265-285.

Dutton, William H. 2005. "The Internet and Social Transformation: Reconfiguring Access." In *Transforming Enterprise: The Economic and Social Implications of Information Technology*, edited by William H. Dutton, Brian Kahin, Ramon O'Callaghan and Andrew W. Wyckoff, 375-397. Cambridge, MA: MIT Press.

Eccles, Kathryn E., Mike Thelwall, and Eric T. Meyer. 2012. "Measuring the Web Impact of Digitised Scholarly Resources." *Journal of Documentation* 68 (4):512-526.

Ekbia, Hamid. 2004. "How IT Mediates Organizations: Enron and the California Energy Crisis." *Journal of Digital Information* 5 (4).

Elliott, Margaret S., and Kenneth L. Kraemer. 2008. *Computerization Movements and Technology Diffusion: from Mainframes to Ubiquitous Computing*. Medford, N.J.: Information Today.

Griffith, Terri L., and Deborah J. Dougherty. 2001. "Beyond Socio-technical Systems: Introduction to the Special Issue." *Journal of Engineering and Technology Management* 18 (3-4):207-218.

Grint, Keith, and Steve Woolgar. 1992. "Computers, Guns, and Roses: What's Social about Being Shot?" *Science, Technology, & Human Values* 17 (3):366-380.

Hanseth, Ole, Margunn Aanestad, and Marc Berg. 2004. "Actor-network Theory and Information Systems. What's So Special?" *Information Technology & People* 17 (2):116-123.

Horton, Keith, Elisabeth Davenport, and Trevor Wood-Harper. 2005. "Exploring Sociotechnical Interaction with Rob Kling: Five "Big" Ideas." *Information Technology & People* 18 (1):50-67.

Kling, Rob. 1991a. "Computerization and Social Transformations." *Science, Technology, & Human Values* 16 (3):342-367.

—. 1991b. "Reply to Woolgar and Grint: A Preview." *Science, Technology, & Human Values* 16 (3):379-381.

—. 1992a. "Audiences, Narratives, and Human Values in Social Studies of Technology." *Science, Technology, & Human Values* 17 (3):349-365.

—. 1992b. "When Gunfire Shatters Bone: Reducing Sociotechnical Systems to Social Relationships." *Science, Technology, & Human Values* 17 (3):381-385.

—. 1999. "What is Social Informatics and Why Does it Matter?" *D-Lib Magazine* 5 (1).

Kling, Rob, and Suzanne Iacono. 1988. "The Mobilization of Support for Computerization: The Role of Computerization Movements." *Social Problems* 35 (3):226-243.

Kling, Rob, Geoffrey McKim, and Adam King. 2003. "A Bit More to It: Scholarly Communication Forums as Socio-Technical Interaction Networks." *Journal of the American Society for Information Science and Technology* 54 (1):46-67.

Kling, Rob, Howard Rosenbaum, and Steve Sawyer. 2005. *Understanding and Communicating Social Informatics: A Framework for Studying and Teaching the Human Contexts of Information and Communication Technologies*. Medford, NJ: Information Today, Inc.

Lamb, Roberta, and Rob Kling. 2003. "Reconceptualizing Users and Social Actors in Information Systems Research." *MIS Quarterly* 27 (2):197-235.

Latour, Bruno. 1987. *Science in Action: How to Follow Scientists and Engineers Through Society*. Cambridge, MA: Harvard University Press.

—. 1988. "Mixing Humans and Nonhumans Together: The Sociology of a Door-Closer." *Social Problems* 35 (3):298-310.

—. 2005. *Reassembling the Social: An Introduction to Actor-Network-Theory*. Oxford: Oxford University Press.

Latour, Bruno, and Steve Woolgar. 1979. *Laboratory Life: The Social Construction of Scientific Facts*. Beverly Hills: Sage.

Lievrouw, Leah A. 2002. "Determination and Contingency in New Media Development: Diffusion of Innovations and Social Shaping of Technology Perspectives." In *Handbook of New Media: Social Shaping and Consequences of ICTs*, edited by Leah A. Lievrouw and Sonia Livingstone, 183-199. London: SAGE Publications.

Lintott, Chris J., K. Schawinski, W. Keel, H. Van Arkel, N. Bennert, E. Edmondson, D. Thomas, D.J.B. Smith, P.D. Herbert, and M.J. Jarvis. 2009. "Galaxy Zoo:'Hanny's Voorwerp', a Quasar Light Echo?" *Monthly Notices of the Royal Astronomical Society* no. 399 (1):129-140.

McLuhan, Marshall. 1964. *Understanding Media: The Extensions of Man*. Cambridge, MA: MIT Press.

Meyer, Eric T. 2006. "Socio-technical Interaction Networks: A Discussion of the Strengths, Weaknesses and Future of Kling's STIN model." In *IFIP International Federation for Information Processing, Volume 223, Social Informatics: An Information Society for All? In Remembrance of Rob Kling*, edited by Jacques Berleur, Marco I. Numinem and J. Impagliazzo, 37-48. Boston: Springer.

Meyer, Eric T. 2007a. *Socio-technical Perspectives on Digital Photography: Scientific Digital Photography Use by Marine Mammal Researchers*. PhD diss., Indiana University, Bloomington.

—. 2007b. "Technological Change and the Form of Science Research Teams: Dealing with the Digitals." *Prometheus* 25 (4):345-361.

Meyer, Eric T., Monica Bulger, Avgousta Kyriakidou-Zacharoudiou, Lucy Power, Peter Williams, Will Venters, Melissa Terras, and Sally Wyatt. 2012. "Collaborative yet Independent: Information Practices in the Physical Sciences." *A Research Information Network Report*. London: Research Information Network.

Meyer, Eric T., Kathryn Eccles, Michael Thelwall, and Christine Madsen. 2009. Final Report to JISC on the Usage and Impact Study of JISC-funded Phase 1 Digitisation Projects & the Toolkit for the Impact of Digitised Scholarly Resources (TIDSR). http://microsites.oii.ox.ac.uk/tidsr/system/files/TIDSR_FinalReport_20July2009.pdf.

Meyer, Eric T., and Isis Hjorth. 2013. *Digitally Scratching New Theatre: London's Battersea Arts Centre engaging via the web.* London: Nesta.

Meyer, Eric T., and Ralph Schroeder. Forthcoming. *Knowledge Machines: Digital Transformations in the Sciences and Humanities*. Cambridge, MA: The MIT Press.

Murdoch, Jonathan. 2001. "Ecologising Sociology: Actor-Network Theory, Co-Construction and the Problem of Human Exemptionalism." *Sociology-The Journal of The British Sociological Association* 35 (1):111-133.

Nardi, Bonnie A, and Yrjö Engeström. 1999. "A Web on the Wind: The Structure of Invisible Work." *Computer Supported Cooperative Work (CSCW)* 8 (1-2):1-8.

Raddick, M. Jordan, Georgia Bracey, Pamela L. Gay, Chris J. Lintott, Phil Murray, Kevin Schawinski, Alexander S. Szalay, and Jan Vandenberg. 2010. "Galaxy Zoo: Exploring the Motivations of Citizen Science Volunteers." *Astronomy Education Review* 9.

Robbin, Alice. 2007. "Rob Kling In Search of One Good Theory." *The Information Society* 23 (4):235-250.

Roth, Wolff-Michael, and Reinders Duit. 2003. "Emergence, Flexibility, and Stabilization of Language in a Physics Classroom." *Journal of Research in Science Teaching* 40 (9):869-897.

Schroeder, Ralph. 2007. *Rethinking Science, Technology, and Social Change*. Stanford: Stanford University Press.

Shapin, Steven. 1995. "Here and Everywhere: Sociology of Scientific Knowledge." *Annual Review of Sociology* 21:289-321.

Star, Susan Leigh. 1988. "Introduction: The Sociology of Science and Technology." *Social Problems* 35 (3):197-205.

Star, Susan Leigh, and Anselm Strauss. 1999. "Layers of Silence, Arenas of Voice: The Ecology of Visible and Invisible Work." *Computer Supported Cooperative Work* 8:9-30.

Williams, Robin, and David Edge. 1996. "The Social Shaping of Technology." *Research Policy* 25:865-899.

Winner, Langdon. 1993. "Upon Opening the Black Box and Finding It Empty: Social Constructivism and the Philosophy of Technology." *Science, Technology, & Human Values* 18 (3):362-378.

Woolgar, Steve, and Keith Grint. 1991. "Computers and the Transformation of Social Analysis." *Science, Technology, & Human Values* 16 (3): 368-378.

CHAPTER FOUR

SOCIAL INFORMATICS, HUMAN VALUES, AND ICT DESIGN

KENNETH R. FLEISCHMANN

Human values provide useful insights into human thought and behavior, and, as such, they can serve as an important lens for Social Informatics (SI) research (Kling 1978; 1983; 1996). Human values can be defined as "guiding principles of what people consider important in life" (Cheng and Fleischmann 2010, 2). Values drive decision-making in all facets of life (Schwartz 2007). Since values vary from one person to the next, any activity involving multiple individuals inevitably involves value conflicts. Technology can exacerbate these value conflicts, since human values become embedded in technology by their designers (Fleischmann 2007a; Johnson 1997; Nissenbaum 2001; Sclove 1995). This chapter explores the emerging literature on values and design as part of the present of SI.

This chapter begins with a brief trip to the past, to explore pioneering work in the history of SI research that helped to inspire research on values and design. It then spends the majority of its time in the present, considering the multi-faceted literature on values and design as an example of contemporary SI. Finally, it looks briefly into the future, with some speculation about the future of values and design and how it is transforming and will continue to transform how we think of SI.

The Past: Pioneering Social Informatics Research on Values and Design

Participants in an NSF-funded workshop in 1997 defined SI as "the interdisciplinary study of the design, uses, and consequences of ICTs [information and communication technologies] that takes into account their interaction with institutional and cultural contexts" (Kling, Rosenbaum, and Sawyer 2005, 6). Certainly, one important institutional and cultural context is human values. Values intermediate between the group level and the individual level (Hitlin and Piliavin 2004), as values are contained within individuals, but values are also transmitted through various forms of communication (including technology design) from one individual to another within a group, organization, or society (McConatha, Tahmaseb, and Schnell 1995).

Rob Kling did some of the pioneering research on the role of human values in the design and use of information technologies. In a 1978 article, he explores the role of human values in the design of electronic funds transfer systems. Kling explores how values such as reliability, security, and privacy are inherent within various models for the design of these systems. Kling calls for public debate surrounding the design of these systems, demonstrating an emphasis on inclusiveness and participatory design that strongly foreshadows more contemporary research on values and design.

In a 1983 article, Kling adds a second case, instructional computing in primary and secondary schools. He also considers future IT developments and the role that values may play within them. Next, he expands the scope from national to international, with explicit consideration of differences between developed and developing countries, with a comparison between the United States and Brazil. Kling writes, "the value conflicts catalyzed by new computing developments are sometimes subtle, and their political dimensions are often more important in the long run than in the short run" (Kling 1983, 34). Thus, Kling advocates adopting a long-term view of the role of values in the design of information technologies. Kling further states, "socially sensitive proposals for computerization should take explicit account of the values sacrificed or compromised as well as those fostered by new forms of computerization" (Kling 1983, 34). Kling is arguing for and advocating the type of value sensitive design that is now taking place within the values and design space.

In 1991, Kling published an edited book, which went into second edition in 1996, on the role of value conflicts in computerization. The book included a wide range of prominent scholars from fields such as science and technology studies, information studies, management information systems, and human-computer interaction. One particularly striking passage within the early chapters written by Kling is, "unfortunately, it is hard to find balanced accounts that carefully examine the social character of different packages of social and technological alternatives and the values which they each support" (Kling 1991, 24).

Importantly, this has since become a major motivating point for values and design research, demonstrating the importance and impact of his work in pioneering research in values and design.

Finally, in a 2003 article, Kling addresses the small but growing literature on values and design. He notes, "of course, there has been a small North American literature about IT applications, human values (and conflicts about them)" and goes on to cite his own edited book as well as a similar edited volume by Batya Friedman (1997a), the founder of the field of value sensitive design. Thus, from Kling's perspective, value sensitive design and other values and design literatures clearly fit into the big tent of SI (Fleischmann 2007b; 2009).

The Present: The Emerging Literature on Values and Design

As noted above, Kling's interest in the relationship between values and design has been explored in great detail in the literature, from a variety of perspectives. First, there is basic research to understand the values of users. Next, there is applied research that involves design interventions that directly connect design to the values of users. There is also basic research to understand the values of designers. Finally, there is applied research to develop educational interventions to educate designers about users' values. This chapter explores each of these facets of the ongoing values and design field.

Studying the Values of Users

What do users value? Users are, first and foremost, people, so the literature on understanding human values and cultural differences in values is extremely relevant here. For example, Schwartz (2006) analyzed data from 73 countries and identified seven transnational cultural groupings: English-speaking, West European, East European, Latin American, Confucian influenced, South Asian, and African/Middle Eastern. It is reasonable to assume that many of these individuals are already users of information technology in some form, and certainly all are potential users. Thus, understanding cultural differences in values can help us to better understand the values of particular groups, which, in turn, can help us to design for those values.

Batya Friedman's value sensitive design begins with studying the values of users, although it certainly does not end there, as we will discuss in the next section. For example, she has studied online trust (Friedman,

Kahn, and Howe 2000), users' understanding of Web security (Friedman et al. 2002a), and users' conceptions of online harms and risks (Friedman et al. 2002b). Her students have carried this research into even more domains, such as urban planning (Davis 2006), interaction by children with personified agents (Freier 2008), and ecovillages for sustainability (Nathan 2009).

Recently, there has been a particular focus on the values of vulnerable populations, including, notably, individuals who are homeless. This more recent value sensitive design research builds on earlier work such as Schmitz et al. (1995). In this paper, the authors explore the role of the Public Electronic Network in Santa Monica during the late 1980s and early 1990s. They found that ICTs can help to bridge communication gaps between groups, such as the homeless and the homed. They also found that value choices in the design of such systems significantly influence the outcome of their use.

Among the recent value sensitive design studies of values related to homelessness and ICTs, Le Dantec and Edwards (2008) conduct a photo-elicitation interview to study how homeless individuals interact with and envision ICTs. They identify the importance of staying connected, identity management, information access, health information, and navigation, among other themes. Similarly, Woelfer et al. (2011) ask homeless young people, service providers, police officers, and community members to complete a value sketch that includes indicating on a map which places are safe and unsafe for homeless young people. This study provides insights into the relationship between physical space, safety, ICTs, and homelessness. Finally, Koepfler and Fleischmann (2012) perform a content analysis of tweets by individuals who self-identify as homeless or formerly homeless along with a comparison group. They identify nine values that are expressed more frequently in tweets by homeless individuals than in tweets by non-homeless individuals, including broad-mindedness, equality, freedom, helpfulness, identity, justice, responsibility, spirituality, and wealth. These studies as well as other studies of the values of users set the stage for design interventions to connect design to the values of users.

The study by Koepfler and Fleischmann (2012) is also an example of studying values in communication, using content analysis. Similar studies include exploration of the role of human values in the Net neutrality debate, using both manual (Cheng 2012; Cheng et al. 2010; 2012) and automatic (Fleischmann et al. 2009; Ishita et al. 2010) content analysis of prepared testimonies from Federal Communications Commission (FCC) and Congressional hearings. Another project involved employing crowdsourcing to detect human values by comparing value survey responses and agreement with paragraphs on controversial topics such as the Net neutrality debate, and once again successfully automating the process (Fleischmann, Templeton, and Boyd-Graber 2011; Templeton and Fleischmann 2011; Templeton, Fleischmann, and Boyd-Graber 2011a; 2011b). The findings of these studies can then be applied to design, potentially including design of systems to support computer-mediated communication, understanding political debates, or searching for articles that span a variety of value perspectives.

Design Interventions to Connect Design to the Values of Users

Most value sensitive design projects culminate in a design intervention to design a new technology that is more sensitive to the values of users. Indeed, Friedman and Kahn's (2003) primary criticism of (most) SI research is that it does not focus sufficiently on design. Friedman, Kahn, and Borning (2006) define value sensitive design as a tripartite methodology including conceptual, empirical, and technical investigations. One of the examples of technical investigations that they provide is to design a new technology, and this is a major focus of value sensitive design research.

One of Friedman's most influential and widely used design interventions was to create a web browser plugin to improve cookie management to ensure privacy and informed consent online. Friedman (1997b) identified privacy as an important consideration in adolescents' online behavior, which has the potential to undermine trust in online interactions (Friedman, Kahn, and Howe 2000). These insights led to design recommendations (Millett, Friedman, and Felten 2001), which Friedman and her team then applied to the Mozilla browser (Friedman, Howe, and Felten 2002). They employed an iterative design process that involved prototyping and developing the browser plugin and then evaluating its use. As they note, "our work also demonstrates the viability of the Value-Sensitive Design methodology in the context of a real-world large-scale software system" (Friedman, Howe, and Felten, 255). Their research not only led to usable software but also contributed to a significant degree of increased awareness of cookies and their risks, and increased user control of cookie management.

Another important and wide-reaching project originating in the Value Sensitive Design Lab was the value sensitive design of an urban simulation. UrbanSim (Borning, Friedman, and Kahn 2004) incorporates a wide range of stakeholder values, including both direct and indirect stakeholders (thus expanding beyond just considering end users). Values considered within UrbanSim include democratic engagement, freedom from bias, and political legitimacy (Davis et al. 2006). They also conducted a mixed-method quantitative and qualitative evaluation of UrbanSim (Friedman et al. 2008). Through projects such as UrbanSim, there is the potential to impact the lives of many individuals beyond just those who directly interact with technologies.

The values and design literature has also produced projects that focus on incorporating values into the design of new technologies. For example, the Values at Play project (Flanagan, Howe, and Nissenbaum 2005) involves values discovery, identifying values-based conflicts, implementation and prototyping, and values verification. One of the important elements of this project is ensuring gender equity as part of a larger focus on social inclusion (Flanagan and Nissenbaum 2007). Further, there is significant emphasis within the values and design literature on studying and influencing the values of designers, which is explored in more detail below.

Studying the Values of Designers

What do designers value? Geert Hofstede (2001) conducted one of the first studies of the values of designers, based on an analysis of data from IBM employees from 1967-1973. In his original analysis, he identified four value dimensions: power distance, uncertainty avoidance, individualism and collectivism, and masculinity and femininity. It is important to note that Hofstede takes a macro-type approach similar to Schwartz's (2006) comparison of the values of different national cultures, while most values and design research takes a much more micro perspective. Interestingly, there is a connection back to Kling, as Kumar and Bjorn-Andersen (1990) published a similar comparison of information system designers across national culture contexts published by *Communications of the ACM* within the area of Social Aspects of Computing, which was edited by Rob Kling.

Fleischmann (2003; 2004) employed multi-sited ethnographic methods to qualitatively study the values of dissection simulation designers. The main finding of the paper was the discovery of a convergence of the values of these designers and of one of the major stakeholders in dissection simulation: animal advocates. While these two groups maintained distinct core values, they latched onto each other's peripheral values, as demonstrated by their statements as well as the marketing and even the design of the simulations themselves. For example, Digital Frog was marketed as "frog-friendly software" (Fleischmann 2003; 2004) and Prodisector, which was led by a medical illustrator who also had experience as a simulation designer (Fleischmann 2004; 2006), redefined the anatomy experience by allowing students to make the layers of the frog transparent, rather than relying on the physical metaphor of dissection (Fleischmann 2004; 2007c).

Fleischmann and Wallace (2006; 2009; 2010; *3rd Hawai'i International Conference on System Sciences* 2010; 2011a; 2011b) conducted a multi-sited ethnographic study of computational modelers. Three field sites were used; an academic lab, a corporate lab, and a government lab. Data collection included surveys with 76 modelers, including the Schwartz (1994) Value Survey and questions about the role of values and value conflicts in the design of computational models, as well as interviews with 40 of the modelers to explore their survey answers in more detail. A number of specific values were identified as important in computational modeling, including perhaps most notably transparency, since revealing the processes underlying the model is indicative of the reality and values used to design the model (Fleischmann and Wallace 2009). Value conflicts affected both the process and products of modeling (Fleischmann and Wallace 2010), and the survey results revealed that certain values held by modelers, most notably equality, were correlated with decreases in reports of value conflicts with other stakeholders (Fleischmann, Wallace, and Grimes 2011b).

Shilton (In Press) conducted an ethnographic study of a research laboratory developing new mobile sensing technologies and identified several practices employed within this lab that tend to highlight values issues. For example, participating in internal prototype testing involves asking designers to take on the role of users, which helps to connect them to users' values as well as their own. Also, working on interdisciplinary teams was another activity that promoted values discussion and consideration, based on the inherent value differences between different fields. Shilton labels these as "value levers," and suggests the possibility of encouraging or facilitating similar activities in other design contexts.

Educational Interventions to Inform Designers about Users' Values

As noted above, the literature on studying designers' values has revealed that designers' values matter a lot during the design process and interventions may be required to ensure that designers are conscious about and aware of users' values. The goal is not to turn "bad" designers into "good" ones, in a moral or ethical sense, but rather to increase awareness of the value-laden-ness of design decisions so that designers do not fall prey to what Langdon Winner (1986) terms "technological somnambulism," or sleepwalking through design (without considering the ethical implications of design). Designers can then seek to learn more about users' values as well as their own, to ensure that the systems that they design are sensitive to and compatible with the values of users and other stakeholders.

One recent educational intervention within the value-sensitive design space is the Envisioning Cards (Friedman et al. 2011; Friedman and Hendry 2012). As Friedman and Hendry explain, "through their form and structure the cards position researchers and designers to consider values, time, pervasiveness, and stakeholders; that is, to attend to what is important in people's lives" (Friedman and Hendry 2012,1148). They further explain that they "seek systematic ways to place them within design processes and educational settings, to make HCI an even more human-centered practice" (Friedman and Hendry 2012,1148). Thus, the Envisioning Cards represent a highly creative approach to helping designers to think about the values of users and others.

The Values at Play project has developed a game that focused on values embedded in video games, Grow-A-Game (Belman et al. 2011). Players brainstorm ideas for new games, working in groups, with an emphasis on prioritizing human values. As they explain, "the cards require designers to identify and/or articulate the values that are relevant to their project, and to translate them into mechanics" (Belman et al. 2011,13). The Values at Play project has also developed and made freely and publicly available an entire curriculum for graduate and undergraduate students studying game design entitled "values conscious design."

Finally, Fleischmann, Robbins, and Wallace (2009; 2011a; 2011b; Fleischmann et al. 2011) have developed two tools used teach information ethics, focusing on salient values in design. The first tool is a case-based educational simulation that involves open-ended and closed-ended resolution of a realistic information ethics dilemma. These mini-cases differ from traditional case-based learning in that, instead of focusing on a single perspective from which to engage with the case, the cases all involve multiple, interconnected perspectives, such that the decisions made by one stakeholder directly affect the ethical dilemmas that are confronted by others (Fleischmann, Robbins, and Wallace 2009). The second tool is a graphical user interface for developing cases that can be played within the simulation. As a result, anyone can create cases for others to play, without requiring any programming skills. This combination provides an innovative and sustainable approach (in that others are enabled and encouraged to create cases for others to play) that has shown preliminary promise in achieving successful outcomes in ethics education.

The Future: Reconnecting the Values and Design and Social Informatics Literatures

Recent research in values and design has built upon and greatly expanded research within SI. The great emphasis on stakeholders in design, including but not limited to the end user, is reminiscent of SI and provides a point of differentiation between, for example, value sensitive design and other human-computer interaction approaches, such as participatory design and co-design. The values and design literature has also continued to update and expand the scope of relevant research, not only involving early work-related computerization such as that studied by Kling, but also game design in the case of Values at Play.

One fundamental difference thus far is that SI, while it is based in part on field research, tends to take a fairly macro-scale view on the world, while the values and design literature has tended to focus more on the micro-scale in terms of specific individuals' interactions with particular technologies. There is great value in both micro-scale and macro-scale research. One interesting point is whether there might be ways to further unify these two perspectives. One approach that has the potential to do this is a computational social science approach that can work to scale up the thick, rich, and deep findings from methods such as ethnography and content analysis (Cheng et al. 2008; Fleischmann et al. 2009; 2012; 2013).

Another fundamental difference, as noted above, is the lesser emphasis on design in SI (Friedman and Kahn 2003). Values and design is not only critical, but also constructive, in developing new approaches to design as well as new designs that better incorporate values. SI can make a clearer and stronger case for its usefulness and importance by ensuring that the insights gained through SI are applied back to design, to actively work to make the world a better place.

The values and design and SI literatures are clearly far more powerful, effective, and influential together than they are separately. Broadening the scope of SI to fully incorporate the offshoots that it has helped to produce, such as values and design, can help to ensure that SI is not only a thing of the past, or even the present, but carries on into the future in new and exciting ways. Certainly, there is much that the values and design and SI literatures have learned and still can learn from each other.

References

Belman, Jonathan, Helen Nissenbaum, Mary Flanagan, and Jim Diamond. 2011. "Grow-A-Game: A Tool for Values Conscious Design and Analysis of Digital Games." *Proceedings of DiGRA 2011 Conference*, Utrecht, The Netherlands.

Borning, Alan, Batya Friedman, and Peter H. Kahn, Jr. 2004. "Designing for Human Values in an Urban Simulation System: Value Sensitive Design and Participatory Design." *Proceedings of the Eighth Biennial Participatory Design Conference*, 67-71, Toronto, Canada.

Cheng, An-Shou. 2012. "Values in the Net Neutrality Debate: Applying Content Analysis to Testimonies from Public Hearings" PhD diss., University of Maryland.

Cheng, An-Shou and Kenneth R. Fleischmann. 2010. "Developing a Meta-Inventory of Human Values." *Proceedings of the 73rd Annual Meeting of the American Society for Information Science and Technology*, Pittsburgh, PA.

Cheng, An-Shou, Kenneth R. Fleischmann, Ping Wang, Emi Ishita, and Douglas W. Oard. 2010. "Values of Stakeholders in the Net Neutrality Debate: Applying Content Analysis to Telecommunications Policy." *Proceedings of the 43rd Hawai'i International Conference on System Sciences*, Kauai, HI.

Cheng, An-Shou, Kenneth R. Fleischmann, Ping Wang, Emi Ishita, and Douglas W. Oard. 2012. "The Role of Innovation and Wealth in the Net Neutrality Debate: A Content Analysis of Human Values in Congressional and FCC Hearings." *Journal of the American Society for Information Science and Technology* 63 (7):1360-1373. doi: 10.1002/asi.22646.

Cheng, An-Shou, Kenneth R. Fleischmann, Ping Wang, and Douglas W. Oard. 2008. "Advancing Social Science Research by Applying Computational Linguistics." *Proceedings of the 71st Annual Meeting of the American Society for Information Science and Technology*, Columbus, OH.

Davis, Janet. 2006. "Value Sensitive Design of Interactions with UrbanSim Indicators." PhD diss., University of Washington.

Davis, Janet, Peyina Lin, Alan Borning, Batya Friedman, Peter H. Kahn, and Paul A. Waddell. 2006. "Simulations for Urban Planning: Designing for Human Values." *Computer* 39 (9):66-72.

Flanagan, Mary, Daniel C. Howe, and Helen Nissenbaum. 2005. "New Design Methods for Activist Gaming." In *Worlds in Play: International Perspectives on Digital Games Research*, edited by Suzanne de Castell and Jennifer Jenson. New York: Peter Lang.

Flanagan, Mary and Helen Nissenbaum. 2007. "A Game Design Methodology to Incorporate Social Activist Themes." *Proceedings of CHI 2007*, San Jose, CA.

Fleischmann, Kenneth R. 2003. "Frog and Cyberfrog are Friends: Dissection Simulation and Animal Advocacy." *Society and Animals* 11: 123-143.

—. 2004. "Exploring the Design-Use Interface: The Agency of Boundary Objects in Educational Technology." PhD diss., Rensselaer Polytechnic Institute.

—. 2006. "Do-It-Yourself Information Technology: Role Hybridization and the Design-Use Interface." *Journal of the American Society for Information Science and Technology* 57 (1):87-95.

—. 2007a. "Digital Libraries and Human Values: Human-Computer Interaction Meets Social Informatics." *Proceedings of the 70th Annual Meeting of the American Society for Information Science and Technology*, Milwaukee, WI.

—. 2007b. "Digital Libraries with Embedded Values: Combining Insights from LIS and Science and Technology Studies." *Library Quarterly* 77 (4):409-427.

—. 2007c. "The Evolution of Agency: Spectra of Bioagency and Cyberagency." *The Information Society.* 23 (5):361-371.

—. 2009. "Sociotechnical Interaction and Cyborg-Cyborg Interaction: Transforming the Scale and Convergence of HCI." *The Information Society* 25 (4):227-235.

Fleischmann, Kenneth R., An-Shou Cheng, Thomas Clay Templeton, Jes A. Koepfler, Douglas W. Oard, Jordan Boyd-Graber, Emi Ishita, and William A. Wallace. 2012. "Content Analysis for Values Elicitation." *Proceedings of CHI 2012*, Austin, TX.

Fleischmann, Kenneth R., Sean P. Goggins, James Howison, Matthew Lease, and Douglas W. Oard. 2013. "Calling All Computer Scientists and Social Scientists: Establishing a Research Agenda for Computational Social Science." *Proceedings of the 8th Annual iConference*.

Fleischmann, Kenneth R., Jes A. Koepfler, Russell W. Robbins, and William A. Wallace. 2011. "CaseBuilder: A GUI Web App for Building Interactive Teaching Cases." *Proceedings of the American Society for Information Science and Technology* 48 (1):1-4.

Fleischmann, Kenneth R., Douglas W. Oard, An-Shou Cheng, Ping Wang, and Emi Ishita. 2009. "Automatic Classification of Human Values: Applying Computational Thinking to Information Ethics." *Proceedings of the 72nd Annual Meeting of the American Society for Information Science and Technology*, Vancouver, BC, Canada.

Fleischmann, Kenneth R., Russell W. Robbins, and William A. Wallace. 2009. "Designing Educational Cases for Intercultural Information Ethics: The Importance of Diversity, Perspectives, Values, and Pluralism." *Journal of Education for Library and Information Science* 50 (1):4-14.

Fleischmann, Kenneth R., Russell W. Robbins, and William A. Wallace. 2011a. "Information Ethics Education in a Multicultural World." *Journal of Information Systems Education* 22 (3):191-202.

Fleischmann, Kenneth R., Russell W. Robbins, and William A. Wallace. 2011b. "Collaborative Learning of Ethical Decision-Making via Simulated Cases." *Proceedings of the 6th Annual iConference*, Seattle, WA.

Fleischmann, Kenneth R., Thomas Clay Templeton, and Jordan Boyd-Graber. 2011. "Modeling Diverse Standpoints in Text Classification: Learning to Be Human by Modeling Human Values." *Proceedings of the 6th Annual iConference*, Seattle, WA.

Fleischmann, Kenneth R. and William A. Wallace. 2006. "Ethical Implications of Values Embedded in Computational Models: An Exploratory Study." *Proceedings of the 69th Annual Meeting of the American Society for Information Science and Technology*, Austin, TX.

Fleischmann, Kenneth R. and William A. Wallace. 2009. "Ensuring Transparency in Computational Modeling." *Communications of the ACM* 52 (3):131-134.

Fleischmann, Kenneth R. and William A. Wallace. 2010. "Value Conflicts in Computational Modeling." *Computer* 43 (7):57-63.

Fleischmann, Kenneth R., William A. Wallace, and Justin M. Grimes. 2010. "The Values of Computational Modelers and Professional Codes of Ethics: Results from a Field Study." *Proceedings of the 43rd Hawai'i International Conference on System Sciences*, Kauai, HI.

Fleischmann, Kenneth R., William A. Wallace, and Justin M. Grimes. 2011a. "Computational Modeling and Human Values: A Comparative Study of Corporate, Academic, and Government Research Labs." *Proceedings of the 44th Hawai'i International Conference on System Sciences*, Kauai, HI.

Fleischmann, Kenneth R., William A. Wallace, and Justin M. Grimes. 2011b. "How Values Can Reduce Conflicts in the Design Process: Results from a Multi-Site Mixed-Method Field Study." *Proceedings of the 74th Annual Meeting of the American Society for Information Science and Technology*, New Orleans, LA.

Freier, Nathan G. 2008. "Children Attribute Moral Standing to a Personified Agent." *Proceedings of CHI 2008*, Florence, Italy.

Friedman, Batya, ed. 1997a. *Human Values and the Design of Computer Technology*. New York: Cambridge University Press.

Friedman, Batya. 1997b. "Social Judgments and Technological Innovation: Adolescents' Understanding of Property, Privacy, and Electronic Information." *Computers in Human Behavior* 13 (3):327-351.

Friedman, Batya, Alan Borning, Janet L. Davis, Brian T. Gill, Peter H. Kahn, Jr., Travis Kriplean, and Peyina Lin. 2008. "Laying the Foundations for Public Participation and Value Advocacy: Interaction Design for a Large Scale Urban Simulation." *Proceedings of the 9th Annual International Digital Government Research Conference*, Montreal, Canada.

Friedman, Batya and David G. Hendry. 2012. "The Envisioning Cards: A Toolkit for Catalyzing Humanistic and Technical Imagination." *Proceedings of CHI 2012*, Austin, TX.

Friedman, Batya, Daniel C. Howe, and Edward Felten. 2002. "Informed Consent in the Mozilla Browser: Implementing Value-Sensitive Design." *Proceedings of the 35th Hawai'i International Conference on Systems Sciences*, Big Island, HI.

Friedman, Batya, David Hurley, Daniel C. Howe, Edward Felten, and Helen Nissenbaum. 2002a. "Users' Conceptions of Web Security: A Comparative Study." *Extended Abstracts of CHI 2002*, Minneapolis, MN.

Friedman, Batya and Peter H. Kahn, Jr. 2003. "Human Values, Ethics, and Design." In *The Human-Computer Interaction Handbook*, edited by Julie A. Jacko and Andrew Sears. Mahwah, NJ: Lawrence Erlbaum Associates.

Friedman, Batya, Peter H. Kahn, and Daniel C. Howe. 2000. "Trust Online." *Communications of the ACM* 43 (12):34-40.

Friedman, Batya, Lisa Nathan, Shaun Kane, and John Lin. 2011. *Envisioning Cards*. Seattle, WA: University of Washington.

Friedman, Batya, Helen Nissenbaum, David Hurley, Daniel C. Howe, and Edward Felten. 2002b. "Users' Conceptions of Risks and Harms on the

Web: A Comparative Study." *Extended Abstracts of CHI 2002*, Minneapolis, MN.

Hitlin, Steven and Jane Allyn Piliavin. 2004. "Values: Reviving a Dormant Concept." *Annual Review of Sociology* 30: 359-393.

Hofstede, Geert. 2001. *Culture's Consequences: Comparing Values, Behaviors, Institutions, and Organizations Across Nations, Second Edition*. Thousand Oaks, CA: Sage Publications.

Ishita, Emi, Douglas W. Oard, Kenneth R. Fleischmann, An-Shou Cheng, and Thomas Clay Templeton. 2010. "Investigating Multi-Label Classification for Human Values." *Proceedings of the 73rd Annual Meeting of the American Society for Information Science and Technology*, Pittsburgh, PA.

Johnson, Deborah. 1997. "Is the Global Information Infrastructure a Democratic Technology?" *Computers and Society* 27 (3):20-26.

Kling, Rob. 1978. "Value Conflicts and Social Choice in Electronic Funds Transfer Systems Developments." *Communications of the ACM* 21 (8): 642-657.

—. 1983. "Value Conflicts in the Deployment of Computing Applications: Cases in Developed and Developing Countries." *Telecommunications Policy* 7 (1):12-34.

—. ed. 1996. *Computerization and Controversy: Value Conflicts and Social Choices, Second Edition*. San Francisco, CA: Academic Press.

Kling, Rob. 2003. "Critical Professional Education about Information and Communication Technologies and Social Life." *Information Technology and People* 16 (4):394-418.

Kling, Rob, Howard Rosenbaum, and Steve Sawyer. 2005. *Understanding and Communicating Social Informatics: A Framework for Studying and Teaching the Human Contexts of Information and Communication Technologies*. Medford, NJ: Information Today.

Koepfler, Jes A. and Kenneth R. Fleischmann. 2012. "Studying the Values of Hard-to-Reach Populations: Content Analysis of Tweets by the 21st Century Homeless." *Proceedings of the 7th Annual iConference*, Toronto, Canada.

Kumar, Kuldeep and Niels Bjorn-Andersen. 1990. "A Cross-Cultural Comparison of IS Designers' Values." *Communications of the ACM* 33 (5):528-538.

Le Dantec, Christopher A. and W. Keith Edwards. 2008. "Designs on Dignity: Perceptions of Technology Among the Homeless." *Proceedings of CHI 2008*, Florence, Italy.

McConatha, Jasmin Tahmaseb and Frauke Schnell. 1995. "The Confluence of Values: Implications for Educational Research and Policy." *Educational Practice and Theory* 17 (2):79-83.

Millett, Lynette I., Batya Friedman, and Edward Felten. 2001. "Cookies and Web Browser Design: Toward Realizing Informed Consent Online." *Proceedings of CHI 2001*, Seattle, WA.

Nathan, Lisa. 2009. "Ecovillages, Sustainability, and Information Tools: An Ethnography of Values, Adaptation, and Tension." PhD diss., University of Washington.

Nissenbaum, Helen. 2001. "How Computer Systems Embody Values." *IEEE Computer* 120 (3):118-119.

Schwartz, Shalom H. 1994. "Are There Universal Aspects in the Structure and Contents of Human Values?" *Journal of Social Issues* 50 (4):19-45.

—. (2006). Value orientations: Measurement, antecedents and consequences across nations. In *Measuring attitudes cross-nationally – lessons from the European Social Survey*, edited by Roger Jowell, Caroline Roberts, Rory Fitzgerald, and Gillian Eva. London: Sage. 169-200.

—. 2007. "Value Orientations: Measurement, Antecedents, and Consequences Across Nations." In *Measuring Attitudes Cross-Nationally: Lessons from the European Social Survey*, edited by Roger Jowell, Caroline Roberts, Rory Fitzgerald, and Gillian Eva. London: Sage Publications.

Sclove, Richard E. 1995. *Democracy and Technology*. New York: Guilford Press.

Schmitz, Joseph, Everett M. Rogers, Ken Phillips, and Donald Paschal. 1995. "The Public Electronic Network (PEN) and the Homeless in Santa Monica." *Journal of Applied Communication Research* 23 (1): 26-43.

Shilton, Katie. In Press. "Value Levers: Building Ethics into Design." *Science, Technology, and Human Values*.

Templeton, Thomas Clay and Kenneth R. Fleischmann. 2011. "The Relationship Between Human Values and Attitudes Toward the Park51 and Nuclear Power Controversies." *Proceedings of the 74th Annual Meeting of the American Society for Information Science and Technology*, New Orleans, LA.

Templeton, Thomas Clay, Kenneth R. Fleischmann, and Jordan Boyd-Graber. 2011a. "Comparing Values and Sentiment Using Mechanical Turk." *Proceedings of the 6th Annual iConference*, Seattle, WA.

Templeton, Thomas Clay, Kenneth R. Fleischmann, and Jordan Boyd-Graber. 2011b. "Simulating Audiences: Automating Analysis of Values, Attitudes, and Sentiment." *Proceedings of the Third IEEE International Conference on Social Computing*. Boston, MA.

Winner, Langdon. 1986. *The Whale and the Reactor: A Search for Limits in an Age of High Technology*. Chicago: University of Chicago Press.

Woelfer, Jill Palzkill, Amy Iverson, David G. Hendry, Batya Friedman, and Brian T. Gill. 2011. "Improving the Safety of Homeless Young People with Mobile Phones: Values, Form, and Function." *Proceedings of CHI 2011*, Vancouver, Canada.

CHAPTER FIVE

FRAMEWORKS FOR UNDERSTANDING KNOWLEDGE SHARING IN ONLINE COMMUNITIES: BOUNDARIES AND BOUNDARY CROSSING

NORIKO HARA AND PNINA FICHMAN

Introduction

Earlier studies of Social Informatics aimed to understand Information and Communication Technologies (ICTs) in organizational context (Dutton 2005). In the 1970s and 1980s, ICTs were primarily developed for and used in organizations such as universities, corporations, and governments. As the price of computer devices decreased, more computers were found in private homes, and studies of personal computers were added to the corpus of SI studies (e.g., Hara and Kling 2000). Then, in the 1990s, as more and more people gained access to the Internet, SI researchers started focusing on Internet use in various settings (e.g., Kling 1996; Kling, Rosenbaum, and Sawyer 2005). In the early 21st century, there has been a surge in social media use, which has led to a wave of studies seeking insight into user relationships with social media and the consequences of these activities (e.g, Turkle 2011). In line with this trend this chapter calls for studies of knowledge sharing in the social media setting from an SI perspective.

Knowledge sharing in online communities

Knowledge sharing activities online have been flourishing with the advent of social media. Web 2.0 platforms, such as Facebook, Twitter, and Wikipedia, facilitate knowledge sharing in open online communities, which are not constrained by existing organizational boundaries (Qualman

2011).[1] As organizations invest more in crowdsourcing (Doan, Ramakrishnan, and Halevy 2011), sharing knowledge and collaborating online become easier and more frequent. As such, it is imperative to better understand how knowledge sharing occurs on Web 2.0 platforms and in these open online communities (Allen 2010; Hara, Shachaf, and Stoerger 2009; Lee and Cole 2003; Vakkayil 2012). While much attention has been given to knowledge sharing over the years, the focus of prior research has generally been limited to its practice within organizations. Wang and Noe (2010), for example, provide an excellent overview of research conducted in the area of knowledge sharing, primarily within organizations. They report that the focus of these studies ranges from motivational factors (e.g., Hew and Hara 2007; Wasko and Faraj 2005) to organizational context (e.g., Brown and Duguid 2001).

Further, Wang and Noe (2010) claim that more investigations of knowledge sharing that apply various theoretical perspectives are needed. They found that the main theories employed include the theory of reasoned action, social exchange theory, and social capital and network theories. This chapter aims to explore the usefulness of employing frameworks of boundaries and boundary crossing in the examination of knowledge sharing in open online communities, in line with Vakkayil (2012), who found the concept of boundaries to be informative for understanding knowledge sharing and creation.

Boundary Crossing

The literature on boundary crossing includes conceptual frameworks that are relevant to understanding knowledge sharing. Efforts to investigate the concepts and properties of boundaries have been published in disciplines such as Science and Technology Studies (STS), sociology, and organization science (e.g., Lamont and Molnár 2002; Star and Griesemer 1989; Watkins 2006). For example, scholars have previously investigated how to communicate across disciplines and professions by crossing boundaries, primarily via "boundary objects" (Star and Griesemer 1989) and through "brokers" (Wenger 1998).

Boundary objects, or shared objects that facilitate bridging across different groups and assist the intersecting of different communities of practice (Star and Ruhleder 2001), are used when crossing boundaries to

[1] Open online communities are those that function outside the boundaries of one organization and that involve participants from many groups, organizations, countries and so on.

communicate with people who belong to different groups and have various backgrounds (Star and Griesemer 1989). Wenger (1998), inspired by Star, elaborates on the idea of boundary crossing in the context of communities of practice. He argues that an established practice not only creates separation from others, i.e., boundaries, but also develops opportunities to interact with people in other practices. He explains that boundary objects help bridge different communities of practice, and that they can be digital documents or spaces, standardized methods or concepts.

The concept of boundary objects has been widely used in studies examining the use of ICTs (e.g., Barrett and Oborn 2010; Fox 2011). In particular, previous research has investigated how boundary objects support collaboration in various settings and between various groups, including an interdisciplinary team of designers in a museum (Lee 2007), simulation designers and users (Fleischmann 2006), and air traffic managers (Landry et al. 2010). This concept has also been used to understand the knowledge transfer processes among consultants (Miller 2005) and engineers (Carlile 2004; Hsiao, Tsai, and Lee 2012). In addition, boundary objects are frequently used to understand ICT use in communities of practice; they facilitate collaboration across these groups and allow experts to easily extract meaning from a large quantity of information (Landry et al. 2010).

Lee (2007) advances the conceptualization of boundary objects and argues that artifacts can be used to "push boundaries rather than merely sailing across them" (308). She identifies five types of boundary negotiation artifacts: 1) Self-explanation Artifacts privately used for "learning, recording, organizing, remembering, and reflecting" (319), e.g., notes, sketches, and journals; 2) Inclusion Artifacts used for developing "alliances with sympathetic communities of practice" (321); 3) Compilation Artifacts applied to cultivating shared meaning; 4) Structuring Artifacts employed to "coordinate media and understand" (330), but are frequently used when conflicts are found between two communities of practice; and 5) Borrowed Artifacts that are appropriated from one community to the other.

Based on two empirical case studies, Levina and Vaast (2005) have found that boundary objects-in-use have a common identity in practice and have articulated three conditions for their emergence. 1) For artifacts to acquire a local usefulness, agents must use and make sense of them in the context of each field of practice (drawn from Bourdieu and Wacquant 1992); 2) To acquire a common identity, they have to stem from a shared symbolic capital coming from a joint field within which agents jointly recognize and value the artifact; 3) To establish the local usefulness of boundary objects-in-use and to establish their common identity, organizations rely on boundary spanners-in-practice. Similarly, Hsiao et al. (2012) emphasizes the importance of understanding boundary crossing in light of learning in situ and examines how engineers interact with boundary objects to engage in problem solving.

Although digital objects as boundary objects tend to support knowledge sharing and collaboration across diverse groups, digital objects are also problematic and can hinder knowledge sharing in this context. For example, Joyce, Butler, and Pike (2011) examine biographies of living persons in Wikipedia and argue that some shared digital objects can introduce conflicts, which they call contentious objects. Dougherty and Dune (2012) also discuss how digitalization may hinder knowledge sharing, and consequently innovation. They identify knowledge boundaries between two types of scientists, therapy and digital scientists, during drug discovery processes. Therapy scientists are traditional laboratory scientists and "work in multi-science teams centered on therapeutic or disease areas" whereas digital scientists "work on computers and other digital technologies" (Dougherty and Dune, 2102; 1469) to manipulate data and conduct experiments. Although digital scientists assist in drug discovery in innovative ways, the emergence of these scientists has also created knowledge boundaries between the two types of scientists. Dougherty and Dune (2012) propose ways to overcome these boundaries to allow for new drug innovations. For example, they suggest that it is critical to develop new common ground between the two types of scientists, who should also possess competencies for boundary-spanning and concrete boundary objects.

Similarly, Kimble, Grenier, and Goglio-Primard (2010) discuss how boundary objects and brokers are interconnected. They present two case studies, one with a software company and the other with a healthcare company, in which brokers strategically selected boundary objects to bridge two communities. They contend that these case studies reveal how "the broker acts as *tertius gaudens* ("the third who benefits") rather than *tertius iungens* ("the third who joins") (Kimble, Grenier, and Goglio-Primard 2010, 443, italics original).

Wenger further elaborates on the boundary-crossing concept by referring to a broker in addition to boundary objects. According to Wenger (1998), brokers can move from one group to another in order to bridge two communities. For example, a doctoral student who works with professors in different disciplines becomes a broker by serving as a liaison between the two disciplines (Hara, Solomon, Kim, and Sonnenwald 2003). At times brokers are also called boundary spanners (e.g., Levina and Vaast 2005;

Shachaf and Hara 2005; Hsiao, Tsai, and Lee 2012). Levina and Vaast (2005) identify three compulsory conditions for a broker to become a boundary spanner-in-practice by grounding their ideas in two field studies. First, the boundary spanner becomes a legitimate, but possibly peripheral participant in the practices of both fields. Second, the boundary spanner has legitimacy as a negotiator on behalf of the field whose interest they represent. Third, the boundary spanner considers spanning boundaries an advantage.

These conceptualizations of boundary objects and brokers/boundary spanners are used widely in the frameworks of identifying types and properties of boundaries.

Types and Properties of Boundaries

Lamont and Molnár (2002) conduct an extensive literature review of a multitude of studies on boundaries in general and conclude that further work to investigate the types and properties of boundaries would be fruitful. Akkerman and Bakker (2011) concur with this need following their study of learning mechanisms that occur when crossing boundaries. During the last decade, a few frameworks to analyze knowledge sharing and transmission have been developed (e.g., Carlile 2004; Hernes 2004; Sturdy et al. 2009; Werr, Blomberg, and Löwstedt 2009; Wright 2009); these frameworks are described next and summarized in Table 1. Interestingly, the development of these frameworks has been primarily grounded in the literature of organization theories. While the authors use various terminologies, all of the boundaries fall within one of the following categories: physical, cognitive, social, and political. Physical boundaries are those that are concrete, such as boundaries created by buildings, technologies, and locations. Cognitive boundaries are those that are mentally created, such as personal beliefs, worldviews, and understanding. Social boundaries are created by cultures, social interactions, and tradition. Political boundaries are formed by contentious situations, such as negotiations, conflicts, and control. While this can be considered a sub category of social boundaries, researchers tend to define a distinct category for political boundaries.

Carlile (2004) has developed one of the frameworks to classify boundaries in a context of knowledge transfer that inspires innovation. He discusses three approaches to categorizing boundaries found in the literature: 1) a syntactic or information processing boundary; 2) a semantic or interpretive boundary; and 3) a pragmatic or political boundary. The first approach, the syntactic boundary approach, deals with the situation in which knowledge transfer occurs between two actors in a syntactic form (0s and 1s). This perspective is rooted in the information-processing approach whose focus is "on the storage and retrieval of knowledge" (Carlile 2004, 558). As such, this category can be considered as physical boundaries. Second, the semantic or interpretive boundary can be found when knowledge exchange happens between two actors whose backgrounds are different. This situation requires some kind of common ground, such as "shared meanings" (558) to overcome differences. Hence, this category can be interpreted as social boundaries. Third, the pragmatic or political boundary refers to when actors involved in knowledge sharing have a conflict of interest. Boundary objects are one of the useful tools for handling the political boundary.

Hernes (2004) develops another framework for analyzing boundaries. Unlike other frameworks that tend to be one-dimensional, this framework is composed of two dimensions: the first addresses the "types of process that a boundary represents" (Hernes 2004, 13) and the second addresses "the effects that boundaries have on the organization" (Hernes 2004, 15). The first dimension includes three types of boundaries – physical, social and mental boundaries. Physical boundaries are explicit boundaries, such as physical structures including buildings or formal rules, whereas social boundaries consist of identity and norms that would divide one group from another. Mental boundaries refer to beliefs and core ideas that are central to organizations. The second dimension includes three effects of boundaries on organizations: boundaries as ordering agents, distinctions, or thresholds. According to Hernes (2004), boundaries can be used as forces to affect certain behaviors, play a role in distinguishing one group from another, and determine how easy it is to cross boundaries by setting standards for thresholds. When the threshold for a certain boundary is low, the boundaries become more permeable. The concept of thresholds is highly relevant to the idea of "permeable" boundaries that was articulated by March and Simon in 1958.

Sturdy et al. (2009) provide another framework for analyzing boundaries. They argue that sociological approaches to boundaries tend to focus on the multiplicity of boundaries (i.e., individuals move from one boundary to another) and that previous organizational research has identified physical, cultural, and political boundaries. They argue that physical boundaries refer to "physical and technological arrangements" created by "architecture, and various boundary objects including human agents" (Sturdy et al. 2009; 633). Cultural boundaries consist of cognitive and emotional dimensions. Cognitive boundaries are similar to the "semantic boundaries" proposed by Carlile (2004) above, and crossing cognitive boundaries involves socio-cultural learning (Vygotsky 1978). Emotional boundaries refer to the idea that people have emotional attachments to knowledge, which may make the flow of knowledge difficult. Finally, there are political boundaries, which are created by power relations through structural differences within organizations. In addition, Sturdy et al. affirm the dynamic nature of these boundary dimensions by studying the organizational boundaries of knowledge flow among management consultancies.

Werr et al.'s (2009) framework includes five dimensions of boundaries for knowledge exchange: interests, interpretive frameworks, trust, private/organizational, and priority: 1) Individuals' interests construct and constrain boundaries; 2) Interpretive frameworks develop mental boundaries based on the understanding of the world; 3) Trust helps or hinders relationships, which in turn builds boundaries; 4) The boundaries to distinguish the private/personal and the organizational/public are determined by relationships between "the self" and "the other;" 5) The priority dimension influences the way boundaries are constructed to determine the knowledge/resource flow and personal relationships. If one perceives a lack of time, knowledge exchange may be reduced, which then creates a boundary for relationships that constrain knowledge sharing.

The final framework for analyzing boundaries is proposed by Wright (2009) who claims that individuals construct their organizational membership around four key boundary dimensions: their role and position in the organizational hierarchy (structural boundaries), their expertise and functional activities (knowledge boundaries), their organizational legitimacy and power (political boundaries) and their personal relationships with clients and other stakeholders (interpersonal boundaries).

These frameworks are useful for understanding knowledge sharing; yet, they are somewhat limited in that they were developed based on and for the use in organizational contexts. As knowledge production outside of organizations in open online communities is increasing (Allen 2010; Hara et al. 2009; Rau, Neyer, and Möslein 2012), it is imperative to examine whether any of these frameworks are useful when traditional organizational structures are challenged.

Table 1: Summary of types of boundaries described in the literature

Authors	Terminology of Boundary Types			
	Physical	*Cognitive*	*Social*	*Political*
Carlile (2004)	Syntactic		Semantic	Pragmatic
Hernes (2004)	Physical	Mental	Social	
Wright (2009)	Structural	Knowledge	Interpersonal	Political
Sturdy et al. (2009)	Physical	Cultural (emotional)	Cultural (cognitive)	Political
Werr et al. (2009)		Mental (interest, interpretive framework, priority)	Social (trust, private-organizational)	

Conclusion

As we move forward in the 21st century, the foci of SI studies are expanding from analyzing computing use in organizations to studies that include social media that are external to organizations. Along the same line, the frameworks for analyzing boundary types and properties, as well as the process of boundary spanning, have been predominantly developed in an organizational context, but much knowledge sharing today happens outside of these organizational boundaries. It is possible that the utility of these theories is inadequate in the context of knowledge sharing in mass open collaborative projects and the social web. As such, boundary crossing processes and frameworks for analyzing boundary types and properties may need to be modified and extended to explain knowledge-sharing processes in this complex environment. Rau et al. (2012) indicated that previous research has not paid enough attention to crossing semantic and pragmatic boundaries in Web 2.0 environments. Table 1 in the previous section is a synthesis of the previous literature. Our own future research aims to investigate further development of boundary types in online communities.

References

Akkerman, Sanne F., and Arthur Bakker. 2011. "Boundary Crossing and Boundary Objects." *Review of Educational Research* 81 (2): 132-169.

Allen, Jonathan P. 2010. "Knowledge-Sharing Successes in Web 2.0 Communities." *IEEE Technology and Society Magazine* 29 (1): 58-64.

Barrett, Michael, and Eivor Oborn, 2010. "Boundary Object Use in Cross-Cultural Software Development Teams." *Human Relations* 63 (8): 1199-1221.

Bourdieu, Pierre, and Loic J. D. Wacquant. 1992. *An Invitation to Reflexive Sociology*. Chicago: University of Chicago Press.

Brown, John Seely, and Paul Duguid, P. 2001. "Knowledge and Organization: A Social-Practice Perspective." *Organization Science* 12 (2): 198-213.

Carlile, Paul R. 2004. "Transferring, Translating, and Transforming: An Integrative Framework for Managing Knowledge Across Boundaries." *Organization Science* 15 (5): 555-568.

Doan, Anhai, Raghu Ramakrishnan, and Alon Y. Halevy. 2011. "Crowdsourcing Systems on the World-Wide Web." *Communications of the ACM* 54 (4): 86-96.

Dougherty, Deborah, and Danielle D. Dune. 2012. "Digital Science and Knowledge Boundaries in Complex Innovation." *Organization Science* 23 (5): 1467-1484.

Dutton, William H. 2005. Foreword to *Understanding and Communicating Social Informatics: A Framework for Studying and Teaching the Human Contexts of Information and Communication Technologies* by Rob Kling, Howard Rosenbaum, and Steve Sawyer. Medford, NJ: Information Today.

Fleischmann, Kenneth R. 2006. "Boundary Objects with Agency: A Method for Studying the Design-Use Interface." *The Information Society* 22 (2): 77-87.

Fox, Nick J. 2011. "Boundary Objects, Social Meanings and the Success of New Technologies." *Sociology* 45 (1): 70-85.

Hara, Noriko, and Rob Kling. 2000. "Students' Distress with a Web-Based Distance Education Course." *Information, Communication and Society* 3 (4): 557-579.

Hara, Noriko, Pnina Shachaf, and Sharon Stoerger. 2009. "Online Communities of Practice Typology Revisited." *Journal of Information Science* 35 (6): 740-757.

Hara, Noriko, Paul Solomon, Seung-Lye Kim, and Diane H. Sonnenwald. 2003. "An Emerging View of Scientific Collaboration: Scientists' Perspectives on Collaboration and Factors that Impact Collaboration." *Journal of the American Society for Information Science & Technology* 54 (10): 952-965.

Hernes, Tor. 2004. "Studying Composite Boundaries: A Framework of Analysis." *Human Relations* 57 (1): 9-29.

Hew, Khe Foon, and Noriko Hara. 2007. "Knowledge Sharing Among Professionals in Three Online Environments: A Qualitative Case Study." *Journal of the American Society for Information Science & Technology* 58 (14): 2310-2324.

Hsiao, Ruey-Lin, Dun-Hou Tsai, and Ching-Fang Lee. 2012. "Collaborative Knowing: The Adaptive Nature of Cross-Boundary Spanning." *Journal of Management Studies* 49 (3): 463-491.

Joyce, Elisabeth, Brian Butler, and Jacqueline Pike. 2011. "Handling Flammable Materials: Wikipedia Biographies of Living Persons as Contentious Objects." In Proceedings of iConference 2011, Seattle, Washington, February 8-11, 2011.

Kimble, Chris, Corinne Grenier, and Karine Goglio-Primard. 2010. "Innovation and Knowledge Sharing Across Professional Boundaries: Political Interplay Between Boundary Objects and Brokers." *International Journal of Information Management* 30: (5): 437-444.

Kling, Rob, ed. 1996. *Computerization and Controversy: Value Conflicts and Social Choices* (2nd ed.). San Diego: Academic Press.

Kling, Rob, Howard Rosenbaum, and Steve Sawyer. 2005. *Understanding and Communicating Social Informatics: A Framework for Studying and Teaching the Human Contexts of Information and Communication Technologies*. Medford, NJ: Information Today.

Lamont, Michèle, and Virág Molnár. 2002. "The Study of Boundaries in the Social Sciences." *Annual Review of Sociology* 28: 167-195.

Landry, Steven, Kerry Levin, Dennis Rowe, and Monicarol Nickelson. 2010. "Enabling Collaborative Work Across Different Communities of Practice Through Boundary Objects: Field Studies in Air Traffic Management." *International Journal of Human-Computer Interaction* 26 (1): 75-93.

Lee, Charlotte P. 2007. "Boundary Negotiating Artifacts: Unbinding the Routine of Boundary Objects and Embracing Chaos in Collaborative Work." *Computer Supported Cooperative Work* 16 (3): 307-339.

Lee, Gwendolyn K., and Robert E. Cole. 2003. "From a Firm-Based to a Community-Based Model of Knowledge Creation. The Case of the Linux Kernel Development." *Organization Science* 14 (6): 633-649.

Levina, Natalia, and Emmanuelle Vaast. 2005. "The Emergence of Boundary Spanning Competence in Practice: Implications for Implementation and Use of Information Systems." *MIS Quarterly* 29 (2): 335-363.

March, James G., and Herbert A. Simon. 1958. *Organizations*. New York: Wiley.

Miller, Richard. 2005. "Creating Boundary Objects to Aid Knowledge Transfer." *Knowledge Management Review* 8 (2): 12-15.

Qualman, Erik. 2011. *Socialnomics: How Social Media Transforms the Way we Live and Do Business*. Hoboken, NJ: Wiley.

Rau, Christiane, Anne-Katrin Neyer, and Kathrin M. Möslein. 2012. "Innovation Practices and Their Boundary-Crossing Mechanisms: A Review and Proposals for the Future." *Technology Analysis & Strategic Management* 24 (2): 181-217.

Shachaf, Pnina, and Noriko Hara. 2005. "Team Effectiveness in Virtual Environments: An Ecological Approach." In *Teaching and Learning with Virtual Teams*, edited by Sharmila Pixy Ferris and Susan Godar, 81-106. Hershey, PA: Idea Group Publishing.

Star, Susan Leigh, and James R. Griesemer. 1989. "Institutional Ecology, 'Translations' and Boundary Objects: Amateurs and Professionals in Berkeley's Museum of Vertebrate Zoology." *Social Studies of Science* 19 (3): 387-420.

Star, Susan Leigh, and Karen Ruhleder. 2001. "Steps Toward an Ecology of Infrastructure: Design and Access for Large Information Spaces." In *Information Technology and Organizational Transformation: History, Rhetoric, and Practice*, edited by JoAnne Yates and John Van Maanen, 305-345, Organization Science. Thousand Oaks, CA: SAGE Publications.

Sturdy, Andrew, Timothy Clark, Robin Fincham, and Karen Handley. 2009. "Between Innovation and Legitimation – Boundaries and Knowledge Flow in Management Consultancy." *Organization* 16 (5): 627-653.

Turkle, Sherry. 2011. *Alone Together: Why we Expect More from Technology and Less From Each Other*. New York: Basic Books.

Vakkayil, Jacob D. 2012. "Boundaries and Organizations: A Few Considerations for Research." *International Journal of Organizational Analysis* 20 (2): 203-220.

Vygotsky, Lev S. 1978. *Mind in Society: The Development of Higher Psychological Processes*. Cambridge: Harvard University Press.

Wang, Sheng, and Raymond A. Noe. 2010. "Knowledge Sharing: A Review and Directions for Future Research." *Human Resource Management Review* 20 (2): 115-131.

Wasko, Molly McLure, and Samer Faraj. 2005. "Why Should I Share? Examining Social Capital and Knowledge Contribution in Electronic Networks of Practice." *MIS Quarterly* 29 (1): 35-57.

Watkins, Ceri. 2006. "Boundaries, Boundary Work and the Art of Management and Organisation Conferences: New Lines of Knowing." *Culture & Organization* 12 (1): 3-10.

Wenger, Etienne. 1998. *Communities of Practice: Learning, Meaning, and Identity*. Cambridge, UK: Cambridge University Press.

Werr, Andreas, Jesper Blomberg, and Jan Löwstedt. 2009. "Gaining External Knowledge – Boundaries in Managers' Knowledge Relations." *Journal of Knowledge Management* 13 (6): 448-463.

Wright, Christopher. 2009. "Inside Out? Organizational Membership, Ambiguity and the Ambivalent Identity of the Internal Consultant." *British Journal of Management* 20 (3): 309-322.

CHAPTER SIX

USE REGIMES: A THEORETICAL FRAMEWORK FOR SOCIAL INFORMATICS RESEARCH ON INTELLECTUAL AND CULTURAL PROPERTY

KRISTIN ESCHENFELDER

Introduction to the Use Regimes Framework

This chapter describes a theoretical framework called use regimes first presented in Eschenfelder, Desai and Downey (2011). This chapter further develops the framework, comparing and contrasting it to related theories and explaining its relationship to the broader field of Social Informatics (SI). Use regimes focuses on a particular area of inquiry – the practices through which people arrange and carry out the transfer of intellectual and cultural works. Eschenfelder (2011) defines use regimes as *temporary stabilizations of networks of associations related to the practices of transferring or distributing creative and intellectual works*. The use regimes framework represents the present of SI because the framework reflects many of the tensions currently felt in SI. On one hand, it embodies the core principles of SI (e.g., information and communication technologies (ICTs) are interpreted and used in different ways by different people; ICTs enable and constrain social actions and relationships, etc. (Kling, Rosenbaum, and Sawyer 2005)). But the framework expands what is commonly understood to be "Social Informatics" research in several ways.

Use regimes expand SI by departing from the problem-oriented, systems-improvement focus of research that many have equated with SI (Sawyer and Eschenfelder 2002). But as others have argued, understandings of SI research should expand to include scholarship that does not necessarily immediately help us to build better information systems, but rather challenges what we are doing and encourages us to challenge what others tell us ought to be the case (Day 2007). Use regimes also expand our conception of SI in that they point scholars' attention to larger problems associated with digital information and cultural works, rather than just those immediately tied to ICTs. While ICTs play an important role in a use regimes analysis of digital works, this analysis should follow the works well beyond any implicated ICT. ICT tools may be important, but they are not necessarily the primary focus. Finally, use regimes' longitudinal nature highlights how, while any given ICT changes over time, the larger problems related to the distribution of the intellectual and cultural works remain. By moving the focus of inquiry off ICTs, use regimes help blur the distinctions between any given ICT and its social context, a dichotomous trope that remains in place in much SI research, toward the trope of ICTs as one part of constantly shifting ensembles or networks of associations (e.g., Latour 2005).

Studying Use Rights for Digital Intellectual and Cultural Works

As we come to rely more on digital platforms and media to make use of educational materials, business information, and entertainment sources, understanding the origins and the history of the use rights we enjoy related to those materials becomes more important because of the greater ability of digital systems and media to control primary and downstream uses of works. Investigating the long term stability or instability and contingent nature of any given use right broadens our perspective on contemporary conflicts about what uses of digital works are acceptable. Moreover, examination of past use rights debates allows us to see patterns of change in claims about uses that might not be apparent in a shorter time frame.

The use regimes framework is a sociotechnical analytic tool that provides a guide to study changes in use practices over time or across geography. My goal in developing it was to assist other researchers in studying complex intellectual and cultural property issues by providing a sociotechnical framework specifically focused on intellectual and cultural property use disputes. It draws on my own experiences in studying use disputes surrounding a range of cultural materials (e.g., Eschenfelder et al. 2010; Eschenfelder and Caswell 2011; Eschenfelder and Johnson in press). The framework draws out associations between different understandings of "use," claims about what uses are acceptable, and broader sociotechnical developments. The framework should be useful in analyzing controversies about uses of a variety of intellectual and cultural works from digital music to e-books.

The purpose of the use regimes framework is to encourage and guide investigation. The framework does not represent a set of generalizable findings, and other scholars should seek to elaborate the framework to fit a range of intellectual and cultural property use disputes. While it suggests a certain focus and inclusion of general areas of inquiry, the particulars will vary in different use cases (e.g., disputes over cartographic data use rights, questions about public domain image use rights in art museums, etc.). But as a framework, use regimes should provide a starting point for investigation and development of findings about use disputes related to a range of digital media forms and practices because the dimensions of the use regime framework (described below) are common across a range of types of intellectual and cultural property issues.

The use regimes framework facilitates a combination of contemporary and historical data collection and analysis. For example in past work, we took a contemporary largely taken-for-granted use right associated with citation downloading, and traced its history to show how it was previously hotly debated, and then how it came to be taken-for-granted (Eschenfelder, Desai, and Downey 2011). This approach borrows from infrastructure studies' strategy of beginning with taken-for-granted infrastructures and working backwards to uncover forgotten conflicts (Bowker 2006; Bowker and Star 1999; Edwards 2010; Star 1999). One could also begin with a contemporary controversy and work backwards to uncover origins and progenitor controversies.

The use regimes framework consists of two parts. At its core is the close critical examination of the uses of cultural and intellectual works. Surrounding this is an examination of the legal, market, cultural, and technical dimensions of use. Use regimes draw on three existing bodies of theory: sociotechnical, institutional and regime theory.

Intellectual Foundations of Use Regimes

Sociotechnical Ensemble

Any particular use regime should be understood as a sociotechnical ensemble. The term "sociotechnical" is from science and technology studies (STS) and refers to the idea that technology, rather than standing apart from society, is inextricably bound up with social practices like distribution, product packaging, cultural expectations and legal or contractual rules. STS theorists argue that you cannot neatly separate the social from the technological in analysis, and even technology is inherently sociotechnical. The term "ensemble" refers to the notion that development, use, and changes in technological systems can only be explained with reference to a messy, contingent network of associations of both human and nonhuman elements. The development, deployment, adoption, and use of technologies are always shaped by a variety of ingrained social processes, values, and conceptualizations. New technologies conversely influence a variety of social processes, values and conceptualizations (Bijker, Hughes, and Pinch 1999; Bijker and Law 1992; Bijker 1995; Kline and Pinch 1999; Winner 1986).

The arrangement of elements in an ensemble is contingent and unstable; one should expect change over time. For example, technology changes what uses are possible and what stakeholders expect to be able to do with works. Markets shift as competitors develop new relationships or competing works emerge. International treaties may force change of national level laws, and widespread best practices may become recognized in case law. Because of the contingency of ensembles, actors who benefit from a particular arrangement must actively work to maintain important associations in the ensemble; otherwise, other stakeholders may undermine the current ensemble (Bijker and Law 1992; Bijker, Hughes, and Pinch 1999). Latour (2005) tells of how stakeholders must constantly re-align and re-assemble social and technological phenomena to maintain arrangements which benefit them.

The use regimes approach examines digital intellectual and cultural works, and the practices of transferring or distributing, them as sociotechnical phenomena composed of contingent ensembles of social and technical elements.

Institutional Theory

Use regimes also draw from institutional theory, which seeks to explain the creation, reproduction or deterioration of institutions, or social structures with a high degree of resilience that provides meaning and stability to social life (Scott 2008; 2004). The use regimes approach focuses on very particular institutions – *the networks of associations related to the practices of transferring or distributing creative and intellectual work.* Most would agree that stable practices for transferring or distributing creative and intellectual works have existed for periods of time. For example, journal publishers have sold subscriptions to libraries for hundreds of years. But numerous details of these long standing institutions are shifting: book publishers still sell books to bookstores, but they also sell e-books through Amazon.

Institutional theory suggests that institutions are composed of cultural-cognitive, normative, and regulative elements in relation to "associated activities and resources" (Scott 2008). The regulative pillar of institutions is composed of indicators like rules, laws and sanctions. The normative pillar is composed of phenomena like certifications, accreditations, or commonly held norms and values. The cultural-cognitive pillar includes common beliefs, shared logics of action, shared categories and definitions, and how isomorphism occurs (Scott 2008).

The four use regimes dimensions (outlined later in the chapter) are inspired by institutional theories three pillars of institutional theory, and a use regimes approach would strive to explain use practices in light of each. But, as explained in a later section of this chapter, each pillar might appear in more than one dimension of use regimes.

Regimes

Within studies of scholarly communications, scholars adopted the term *regime* to explore institutionalized patterns of relationships, practices, discourses and beliefs, and how they enable or constrain information flows (Hilgartner 1995; 2012; Kling, Spector, and Fortuna 2004). The concept of regime is very common in International Relations (IR), where scholars developed "regime theory" to study informal cooperative relationships between nation states. An example of a regime in IR would be regimes of money and trade, for example balance of payments financing system (Cohen 1982). Regimes are "sets of implicit or explicit principles, norms, rules and decision making procedures around which actors' expectations converge" (Krasner 1982). IR regimes focus on deep structures of principles, norms, rules and procedures. The argument is that the deep structures facilitate overlying agreements, arrangements or relationships (Krasner 1982). Ruggie (1982) describes regimes as a "generative grammar" or "language" for action in a field that defines "underlying principles of order and meaning" including: what knowledge has fact status, beliefs about causation in the field, and expectations about rights and obligations.

It is unclear how deep one must go to uncover the bones of a regime and what counts as regime change. In IR, scholars distinguish between foundational norms underlying a regime (e.g., capitalism as a system for distributing goods) and norms specific to an area of action (e.g., contemporary copyright law or contract terms). Krasner suggests thinking in terms of hierarchies, with deeper structures influencing more specific norms in domains of interest. In this view, true regime change requires change at foundational levels. Scholarship using the regime concept in scholarly communications is similar in many ways, but seems less concerned with distinguishing levels of regimes or what constitutes a regime change. Instead of focusing on hierarchies, Hilgartner suggests a relationship of "entanglement" between the multiple regimes that might operate in a given environment (2012).

There are many similarities and differences between the above three theoretical areas and each provides input for the use regimes approach.

Parts of the Use Regimes Framework

The use regimes framework consists of two parts. At its core is the close critical examination of the uses of cultural and intellectual works. Surrounding this is an examination of the legal, market, cultural, and technical dimensions of use.

Uses

First, use regimes foreground the concept of "use," or what people can do, or believe they should (or should not) be able to do, with intellectual and cultural works. The framework emphasizes the socially constructed nature of claims about acceptable uses, and it encourages consideration of the motivations behind any beliefs or claims about acceptable or unacceptable uses.

Use regimes emphasize the socially constructed nature of claims about the acceptable and unacceptable uses of digital works. It encourages examination of motivations for claims or beliefs about legitimacy or illegitimacy of use, and counter arguments to those claims. In this approach, acceptable use is a social construct that changes over time (given a long enough scale). As Johns (2010) pointed out in his history of copyright, what counts as an acceptable use today may be piracy tomorrow, or vice versa. Given this, our current legal, social, or contractual understandings of acceptable uses are neither pre-ordained nor static – they emerge from past conflicts and historically contingent decisions (Bowker 2006; Burkhart and McCourt 2006; Downey 2008; Fisher 2004; Gillespie 2007; Wirten 2008).

Borrowing from the tradition of the social shaping of technology, the use regimes framework encourages examination of how stakeholders can develop their beliefs about acceptable or unacceptable uses and what motivates their beliefs and claims about uses. Actors may seek to define certain uses as unacceptable for a variety of reasons including: legal risks related to intellectual property or privacy, a desire to obtain social or monetary credit, and stewardship responsibility to avoid irresponsible or socially damaging uses (Eschenfelder and Caswell 2010). Stakeholder groups continually create, promote or seek to change dominant understandings of what is acceptable or unacceptable (Bijker and Law 1992; Hackett et al. 2007; Johns 2010; Pinch and Bijker 1984).

Rules, Market, Cultural and Technological Dimensions

Second, to undertake a rich examination of use, the use regimes framework suggests examination of four different dimensions of use: market, legal, cultural expectations, and technological. Analysis of each dimension draws on institutional theory's three pillars, the idea of sociotechnical ensembles, and other core concepts from SI. Consideration of each dimension leads to a slightly different perspective on the concept of "use." Importantly, the dimensions are interlinked and overlapping. Beginning a trace in one dimension should inevitably lead into consideration of the other dimensions. Given space constraints, I mention only some possible areas of analysis within each dimension.

Market analysis: From a market perspective, "use" may refer to product attributes or features developed by an organization that makes one version of a work more attractive to customers than others. Marketing often emphasizes that the product allows or facilitates certain uses. For example, in our study of citation downloading, in the 1990s, when downloading rights were disputed, some database vendors advertised downloading as a product feature. Later in the 2000s after the creation of citation software, vendors were again advertising the ability to download to software like EndNote as a product feature (Eschenfelder, Desai, and Downey 2011). In a study of data repositories, the ability to control downstream use of data was sometimes an advertised feature that would encourage scientists to deposit their data (Eschenfelder and Johnson, in press).

In terms of the range of associations to investigate, market analysis includes consideration of the economic, symbolic, or practical value of works and their packaging and pricing models. With intellectual and cultural works this often includes the information economics concept of "versioning," or variation of characteristics of works (e.g., update rates, coverage) to create different versions of the work at different price points that appeal to different sets of customers (Shapiro and Varian 1999; Kahin and Varian 2000). Market analysis therefore includes a robust investigation of how the work has been packaged and priced over time or across borders with an eye to understanding changes in pricing and packaging in relation to changes in technologies, competing works or different regulatory structures (e.g., Farjoun 2002; Eschenfelder et al. 2005).

Market analysis should also involve examination of the relationships between entities that facilitate the transfer or distribution of works and the transaction costs inherent in those arrangements. This would include tracing chains of distribution and investigating how and why those relationships may change over time – for example how change in technology or legal rules may facilitate or impede certain types of relationships. It is also important to include unofficial or unsanctioned relationships.

Market analysis would include questions like the following: What uses of this work are economically valuable and why? How has this work been packaged and priced over time? How have competing works been packaged and priced? What relationships are involved in the creation and distribution of this work? How have these relationships changed over time and why? What relationships support distribution of competing works?

Rules analysis: From a rules perspective, "use" typically refers to clauses describing sanctioned or prohibited practices associated with a work in copyright law, contract stipulations, terms of use, or other formal texts. Use can also refer to the varying claims based on differing interpretations of the above clauses if ambiguity allows for different interpretations.

Analysis of rules associations includes, but should not be limited to, examination of the formal clauses describing claims about acceptable and unacceptable uses, including those provided by statute (e.g., the Copyright Act), judicial case law or regulation, or those specified in a contract or license. In many cases, rules specified in contracts or terms of use may be as, or more, important than those specified in law because contracts and terms of use allow for much more specific acceptable use claims. Further, lack of formal claims about use may be important because ambiguity creates space in which different interpretations of use rights can exist as competing claims about what uses are acceptable.

Further, it is important to understand that rules may have little or no influence on actual use. Researchers therefore should not end their analysis with rules. If users pay little or no attention to rules, it may be that cultural norms play a more important role as described in the next dimension, cultural expectations.

Rules analysis would include questions such as the following: What uses are legally or contractually allowable and what uses are not? How did a particular use come to be formally ordained as acceptable while another was labeled not acceptable? In what areas does ambiguity or silence about rules exist and why? How have rules about acceptable use related to a particular type of work changed across geography or over time? How and why do rules about acceptable use vary across groups?

Cultural expectation analysis: From a cultural expectations perspective, "use" refers to social norms about acceptable or unacceptable uses that stakeholders in a given field believe should be true, regardless of formal rules such as laws or contracts. Norms about use within groups may be explicit or implicit, and one should expect that competing social norms exist in a field of interest.

A cultural analysis would include investigation of the expectations, beliefs, or social norms that a particular set of users might have with regard to a given work and the relationship of those beliefs to their larger lives. Norms scholars point to how norms develop from within day-to-day work or recreation and therefore are typically developed and shared within an industry, workgroup or culture (Ellickson 1991; Hechter and Opp 2001). They may be reinforced by professional or social affiliations, expectations, and work or recreation patterns and value structures (Eschenfelder and Caswell 2010; Fine 2001; Lamb, King, and Kling 2003; Lamb and Kling 2003a).

Social norms about use may be explicit or implicit. For example, within the domain of intellectual and cultural property, explicit norms in the form of "best practices" and "model licenses" have recently become important. These statements argue for particular interpretations of acceptable uses. Examples include the *Documentary Filmmakers' Statement of Best Practices in Fair Use,* which presents explicit claims about use norms within the documentary film community (Association of Independent Video and Filmmakers et al. 2005), and the LIBLICENSE model license for electronic journal subscriptions, which makes claims about what use terms e-journal licenses ought to include (Council on Library and Information Resources et al. 2008).

A cultural expectations analysis would include questions such as: Do any explicit statements of norms exist? What uses (or restrictions) are seen as sensible or normal within stakeholder groups? How did these norms develop and change across space or over time? What differences in use (or restrictions) norms exist between groups? How do groups enforce particular use norms implicitly or explicitly?

Technologies analysis: From a technological perspective, "use" typically refers to what a given technological system allows a user to do with content – perhaps the system encourages some uses by making them obvious and easy to enact, but discourages others by making them more less obvious to find or more difficult to enact.

A technological associations analysis examines the various technologies related to the distribution and sharing of the intellectual and cultural works over time. Its main focus is on how technology facilitates or prohibits uses, and the associations between technology enabled/disabled uses and the other three dimensions of use: market, rules, and cultural expectations.

In terms of direct impact on use, a distribution system may include a technological protection measure that makes some uses difficult or just very onerous (Eschenfelder 2008; 2011; Gillespie 2007). One important consideration in examining impact on use is the fuzzy relationship between technological protection and rule-based protection measures (e.g., contractual) such as terms of use. Often the two are mixed; for example, systems may require a user to click a radio button indicating agreement with terms of use statement before proceeding to a work. Because of this, it may be conceptually helpful to blur the distinction between technological protection measure and rule based protection measure to look at how use is managed through any means. Technological analysis should also consider the importance of any blocked or discouraged uses within the context of the social and professional norms, expectations, and relationships of users. Finally, a use regimes analysis should expect users to actively reconfigure and resist protection measures of any type that impede desirable uses (Akrich 1992; Oudshoorn and Pinch 2005).

A second important aspect of technology to consider is how technological change facilitates new uses over time. Certain uses of digital works just were not possible in the past because the technology did not exist, or was not widely available, to facilitate that use. A use regimes technology analysis should therefore track changes in technology and how those changes may have led to completely new uses of works. For example, in our past study of bibliographic citations, the use of "downloading" was not possible prior to the widespread adoption of personal computers with local storage devices. One cannot download without a target storage device (Eschenfelder, Desai, and Downey 2011). Importantly, this means the range of possible uses of a work changes over time as technology changes.

Moreover, changes in other non-directly related technologies may be important if they change users' expectations about what they ought to be able to do with the work or how they should be able to gain access to the work. Further, technology also facilitates new distribution chains and packaging and pricing models which may lead to the creation of new competing works or generate new audiences for a digital work that change the range of possible uses of a work.

The technological analysis would include questions such as: How do distribution systems facilitate or impede certain uses? How have changes in technology over time changed the uses of the work that are possible? How have changes in technology affected how the work is packaged and priced over time, or how the work has been distributed? Do users' experiences with similar technologies lead to changes in users' expectations about use?

In summary, the use regimes framework employs a sociotechnical ensemble approach in order to investigate uses of digital, intellectual, and cultural works from four different perspectives: market, laws, cultural expectations, and technologies. This section described how the meaning of the term "use" shifts depending on whether one focuses on markets, rules, cultural expectations, or technologies. Second, it outlined how to trace the associations within and among the market, rules, cultural expectations, and technological aspects of use when studying use disputes related to digital intellectual and cultural works.

The Use Regimes Framework's Contribution to Social Informatics

The agenda of SI is promotion of the interdisciplinary study of the design, uses, and consequences of ICTs that takes into account their interaction with institutional and social contexts (Kling, Rosenbaum, Sawyer 2005). Use regimes advance the agenda of SI both theoretically and empirically. Theoretically, it advances the agenda of SI by expanding the focus of SI from just ICT to the larger problem associated with digital intellectual or cultural works that are often delivered via complex ICT systems. In doing so, it provides a means to investigate questions about digital works that include, but are not limited to the various ICT associated with that problem. This facilitates investigations of big, complex problems that span multiple ICT or where the ICT is part of a much larger socio-cultural issue.

Use regimes also advance the agenda of SI theoretically through its field or industry level of analysis. Research using individual and group levels of analysis are very common in SI research, and this work should be complemented by research at the field or industry level of analysis that can ask and answer complementary sets of questions. Use regimes point to bodies of theory that can help scholars manage the complexities of field and industry level of analysis.

The use regimes advance the analytic agenda of SI by providing an example of historically informed research. SI definitional works have pointed to the temporal dimensions of ICT, "ICT-based systems evolution is as much social history as technical progress." (Kling et al. 2005, 94) But, a historical focus is still unusual in SI research. I hope that the use regimes framework will provide a useful example that might encourage other scholars to include historical perspectives on contemporary SI questions. It encourages consideration of changes in acceptable uses over time and space.

Like Hilgartner's and Kling's use of the regimes concept, the use regimes framework maps the interconnections in the sociotechnical ensemble and seeks to track and explain change in a sociotechnical ensemble over time and across geography. It takes as a starting point that widespread acceptance of any particular use as legitimate or illegitimate is always contingent on the regimes associated with that use. As underlying elements shift, perceptions of the acceptability or unacceptability of use may also shift. This is particularly important to scholarship making arguments about "fair use" or "fair dealing" rights. The concept of fair use, like acceptable use, is a sociotechnical construct intertwined with changing business models, social mores, and technologies (Bracha 2005). One must consider claims about fair use or fair dealing in relationship to the other four dimensions. The complex linkages between the regime elements, combined with change over time in each, make any comparison between digital and pre-digital use rights challenging. Studies of use rights, especially those that make claims about impacts on fair use, ideally would address fair use and fair dealing as socially constructed claims about what uses are acceptable within the context of the markets, expectations, and technologies.

Use regimes also advance the analytic agenda of SI through the complex consideration of what "use" of a digital work means – it requires investigators to consider use in relationship to other dimensions: markets, rules, expectations/norms, and technologies. It encourages tracing of how changes in one dimension of the framework influence phenomena in the other dimensions. It provides a tool for organizing the investigation and analysis of complex, messy situations. No framework can include everything, and scholars must be sensitive to the unique attributes of their particular cases; however, the framework provides a useful jumping off point and a reminder of the breadth of things to consider.

In summary, use regimes are *temporary stabilizations of networks of associations related to the practices of transferring or distributing creative and intellectual works*. The use regimes framework offers a guide to aid scholars in the investigation of complex digital intellectual and cultural property issues. The concept of a use regime draws on concepts from science and technology studies, institutional theory and regime theory. But it offers unique contributions in that it focuses particularly on use disputes related to intellectual and cultural property and highlights those sociotechnical elements most likely to come into play with intellectual and cultural property disputes. It is also unique in that it places use rights as the center of analysis. A use regime analysis can be similar in spirit to full-fledged historical studies of changes in cultural and intellectual property and information systems (e.g., Bourne and Bellardo-Hahn 2003; Bowker 2006; Burkart and McCourt 2006; Downey 2008; Edwards 2010; Johns 2010); however, the use regimes framework offers more structure. Some may see this as a feature guiding and encouraging research, and others as a bug, overly determining what is included in an investigation.

The use regimes framework foregrounds the insight that the closure of research is always arbitrary and conclusions are always contingent on the current arrangement of the sociotechnical ensemble. Hilgartner (1995) reminds us that, while regimes stabilize for periods of time, they are always subject to competition from new alternative regimes. Thus, regime element changes that seem to resolve disputes are likely to be only temporary.

References

Akrich, Madeline. 1992. "The De-scription of Technical Objects." In *Shaping Technology/Building Society: Studies in Sociotechnical Change*, edited by Wiebe Bijker and John Law, 205-224. Cambridge, MA: MIT Press.

Association of Independent Video and Filmmakers; Independent Feature Project; International Documentary Association; National Alliance for Media Arts and Culture; Women in Film and Video, Washington, D.C., Chapter. 2005. "Documentary Film Makers' Statement on Best Practices in Fair Use." Washington DC: American University Washington College of Law. http://www.centerforsocialmedia.org/sites/default/files/fair_use_final.pdf.

Bijker, Wiebe E., and John Law. 1992. *Shaping Technology/Building Society: Studies in Sociotechnical Change*. Cambridge, MA: MIT Press.

Bijker, Wiebe E., Thomas P. Hughes, and Trevor Pinch., eds. 1999. *The Social Construction of Technological Systems: New Directions in the Sociology and History of Technology*. Cambridge, MA: MIT Press.

Bijker, Wiebe E. 1995. *Of Bicycles, Bakelites and Bulbs: Toward a Theory of Sociotechnical Change*. Cambridge, MA: MIT Press.

Bowker, Geoffrey C. 2006. *Memory Practices in the Sciences*. Cambridge, MA: MIT Press.

Bowker, Geoffrey C., and Susan L. Star. 1999. *Sorting Things Out: Classification and Its Consequences*. Cambridge, MA: MIT Press.

Bourne, Charles P., and Trudi Bellardo-Hahn. 2003. *A History of Online Information Services, 1963-1976*. Cambridge, MA: MIT Press.

Bracha, Oren. "Owning Ideas: A History of Anglo-American Intellectual Property." SJD diss., Harvard Law School, 2005. http://www.obracha.net/oi/oi.htm.

Burkart, Patrick, and Tom McCourt. 2006. *Digital Music Wars: Ownership and Control of the Celestial Jukebox*. Lanham, MD: Rowman & Littlefield Publishers Inc.

Cohen, Benjamin J. 1982. Balance-of-payments financing: evolution of a Regime. International Organizations 36(2):457-478.

Council on Library and Information Resources, the Digital Library Federation, and Yale University Library. 2008. *Liblicense Model License*. Chicago: Center for Research Libraries. http://liblicense.crl.edu/licensing-information/model-license/.

Day, Ronald E. 2007. "Kling and the Critical: Social Informatics and Critical Informatics." *Journal of the American Society for Information Science and Technology* 58(4):575-682.

Downey, Gregory J. 2008. *Closed Captioning: Subtitling, Stenography, and the Digital Convergence of Text with Television*. Baltimore, MD: Johns Hopkins University Press.

Edwards, Paul N. 2010. *A Vast Machine: Computer Models, Climate Data, and the Politics of Global Warming*. Cambridge MA: MIT Press.

Eschenfelder, Kristin R., Tien-I Tsai, Xiaohua Zhu and Brenton Stewart. 2013. "How Institutionalized are Model License Use Terms: An Analysis of E-Journal License Use Rights Clauses from 2000–2009." *College and Research Libraries.* 74(4).

Eschenfelder, Kristin R., Anuj C. Desai, and Gregory J. Downey. 2011. "The 1980's Downloading Controversy: The Evolution of Use Rights for Licensed Electronic Resources." *The Information Society* 27(2).

Eschenfelder, Kristin R., and Michelle Caswell. 2010. "Digital Cultural Collections in an Age of Reuse and Remixes." *First Monday* 11(1).

Eschenfelder, Kristin R. 2008. "Every Library's Nightmare: Digital Rights Management and Licensed Scholarly Digital Resources." *College and Research Libraries* 69(3).

Eschenfelder, K.R.; Desai, A.C.; Alderman, I.; Sin, J.; Shen Yi. 2005 "The Limits of DeCSS Posting: A Comparison of Internet Posting of DVD Circumvention Devices in the European Union The People's Republic of China, Hong Kong and Macau." Journ*al of Information Science* 31 (4), pg. 317-331.

Ellickson, Robert C. 1991. *Order Without Law: How Neighbors Settle Disputes*. Cambridge, MA: Harvard University Press.

Farjoun, Moshe. 2002. "The Dialectics of Institutional Development in Emerging and Turbulent Fields: The History of Pricing Conventions in the On-line Database Industry." *Academy of Management Journal* 45(5):848–74.

Fine, Gary A. 2001. "Enacting Norms: Mushrooming and the Culture of Expectations and Explanations." In *Social Norms,* edited by Michael Hechter, and Kar-Dieter Opp, 139-164. New York: Russel Sage Foundation.

Fisher, William W. 2004. *Promises to Keep: Technology, Law and the Future of Entertainment*. Stanford CA: Stanford Law and Politics.

Gillespie, Tarleton. 2007. *Wired Shut: Copyright and the Shape of Digital Culture*. Cambridge, MA: MIT Press.

Hackett, Edward J., Olga Amsterdamska, Michael E. Lynch, and Judy Wajcman, eds. 2007. *The Handbook of Science and Technology Studies*. Cambridge MA: MIT Press.

Hechter, Michael, and Karl-Dieter Opp, eds. 2001. *Social Norms*. New York: Russell Sage Foundation.

Hilgartner, Stephen. 1995. "Biomolecular Databases: New Communication Regimes for Biology?" *Science Communication,* 17(2):240-263.

—. 2012. "Selective Flows of Knowledge in Technoscientific Interaction: Information Control in Genome Research. *The British Journal for the History of Science,* 45(2), 267-280.

Johns, Adrian. 2010. *Piracy: The Intellectual Property Wars from Gutenberg to Gates.* Chicago: University of Chicago Press.

Kahin, Brian, and Hal R. Varian, eds. 2000. *Internet Publishing and Beyond: The Economics of Digital Information and Intellectual Property*. Cambridge, MA: MIT Press.

Kline, Ronald, and Trevor Pinch. 1999. "The Social Construction of Technology." In *The Social Shaping of Technology*, edited by Donald MacKenzie, and Judy Wajcman, 113-115. Buckingham: Open University Press.

Kling, Rob, Howard Rosenbaum, and Steve Sawyer. 2005. *Understanding and Communicating Social Informatics: A Framework for Studying and Teaching the Human Contexts of Information and Communications Technology.* Medford NJ: Information Today.

Kling, Rob, Lisa B. Spector, and Joanna Fortuna. 2004. "The Real Stakes of Virtual Publishing: The Transformation of E-biomed into PubMed Central." *Journal of the American Society for Information Science and Technology*, 55(2):127-148.

Krasner, Stephen D. (1982). Structural causes and regime consequences: regimes as intervening variables. International Organization, 36, pp 185-205.

Lamb, Roberta, John L. King, and Rob Kling. 2003. "Informational Environments: Organizational Contexts of Online Information Use." *Journal of the American Society for Information Science and Technology*, 54(2):97-114.

Lamb, Roberta, and Rob Kling. 2003a. "Reconceptualizing Users as Social Actors in Information Systems Research." *MIS Quarterly*, 27(2):197-235.

Latour, Bruno. 2005. *Reassembling the Social: An Introduction to Actor-Network-Theory.* Oxford: Oxford University Press.

Oudshoorn, Nelly, and Trevor Pinch, eds. 2005. *How Users Matter: The Co-Construction of Users and Technology*. Cambridge, MA: MIT Press.

Ruggie, John G. 1982. International regimes, transactions, and change: embedded liberalism in the postwar economic order. *International Organizations* 36(2):379-415.

Pinch, Trevor, and Wiebe Bijker. 1984. "The Social Construction of Facts and Artefacts: Or How the Sociology of Science and the Sociology of Technology Might Benefit Each Other." *Social Studies of Science,* 14:399-441.

Sawyer, Steve and Eschenfelder, Kristin R. 2002. "Social Informatics: Perspectives, Examples, Trends" in Cronin B. (Ed.) *Annual Review of Information Science and Technology*, 36. Information Today: Medford, NJ, 427-465.

Scott, W. Richard 2004. "Institutional theory" in *Encyclopedia of Social Theory*, George Ritzer, ed. Thousand Oaks, CA: Sage, p 408-14.

—. (2008). *Institutions and Organizations, Third Edition*. Thousand Oaks, CA, Sage.

Shapiro, Carl, and Hal R. Varian. 1999. *Information Rules: A Strategic Guide to the Network Economy*. Boston, MA: Harvard Business School Press.

Star, Susan L. 1999. "The Ethnography of Infrastructure." *American Behavioral Scientist*, 43(3):377-391.

Winner, Langdon. 1986. The *Whale and the Reactor: A Search for Limits in an Age of High Technology*. Chicago: University of Chicago Press.

Wirten, Eva H. 2008. *Terms of Use: Negotiating the Jungle of the Intellectual Commons*. Toronto: University of Toronto Press.

CHAPTER SEVEN

DON'T TAP ON THE GLASS, YOU'LL ANGER THE FISH! THE INFORMATION WORLDS OF DISTRIBUTED SCIENTIFIC TEAMS

GARY BURNETT, KATHLEEN BURNETT, MICHELLE M. KAZMER, PAUL F. MARTY, ADAM WORRALL, BRIAN KNOP, CHARLES C. HINNANT, BESIKI STVILIA AND SHUHENG WU

Introduction

Historically, scientific inquiry was conducted individually; in recent years specialized research teams have worked collaboratively to solve increasingly complex problems (Hinnant et al. 2012; Stvilia, et al. 2011; Borgman, Wallis, and Enyedy 2007; Sonnenwald 2007; Cummings and Kiesler 2005). This trend is apparent in the increased frequency of citation of multi-authored compared to single-authored publications (Wuchty, Jones, and Uzzi 2007). Today, many teams are geographically distributed (Hinds and Bailey 2003) and include members with multiple disciplinary and institutional affiliations. Team members communicate, coordinate, and collaborate through information and communication technologies (ICTs) (Lamb and Davidson 2005; Walsh and Bayma 1996; Walsh et al. 2000). Often, these teams operate in a hybrid modality, where predominantly virtual teams have short but intense periods of physical interaction (Griffith and Neale 2001). Given the importance of teams in the discovery and dissemination of scientific knowledge, many researchers are studying contextual factors – disciplinary, technical, organizational, informational, and social – that play a role in collaborative work, especially work that is distributed, virtual, or hybrid (Finholt 2005; Kraut, Egido, and Galegher 1988).

Analysis of the social and behavioral characteristics of scientists working in these environments can provide important information that may be used to improve the performance and longevity of scientific teams. As teams form and work together to employ specialized scientific instruments, technologies, and professional and support staff located within the labs, the relationships between team characteristics and knowledge production become important phenomena of inquiry (Lee and Bozeman 2005; Thorsteinsdóttir 2000). In this chapter, we report on a Social Informatics (SI) study of scientists working at the National High Magnetic Field Laboratory in Tallahassee, Florida.

National High Magnetic Field Laboratory

The National High Magnetic Field Laboratory (Lab) near Florida State University in Tallahassee represents a large national investment in advanced infrastructure for e-science funded by the National Science Foundation to facilitate the wider sharing of expensive science instruments and curated datasets, and to enable more effective and efficient scientific collaborations, learning, and professional development (Atkins et al. 2003). The Lab is the largest and highest-powered magnet laboratory in the world, and includes sites at the Los Alamos National Laboratory in New Mexico and the University of Florida in Gainesville. Teams of scientists from all over the world travel to the Lab to conduct physics, materials science, chemistry, biochemistry, biology, and biomedicine experiments requiring the use of unique magnets designed and built onsite. In addition to the magnets themselves, scientists rely on various ICTs to gather, analyze, and share data. To facilitate sharing of expertise across disciplinary, institutional, and national boundaries, the composition of such teams may be multidisciplinary, multi-institutional, and multinational.

The ability to share information across time and space is essential to advancement of scientific knowledge everywhere. Even more crucial to the research carried out at the Lab is the ability to share information across disciplinary, institutional, political, and national boundaries. Disciplinary values, institutional norms, social structures, and cultural factors may either constrain or encourage the adoption and use of technology or data in a given research endeavor. Similarly, ICTs and other technologies may influence social structures and enable or constrain social interaction, data sharing, and collaboration (Birnholtz and Bietz 2003; Orlikowski 1992; Kling 2000; Stvilia et al. 2008).

Theory of Information Worlds

The theory of information worlds (IWs) (Jaeger and Burnett 2010; Burnett and Jaeger 2008; Burnett, Besant, and Chatman 2001) guided our investigation of how social and organizational factors support or constrain the transition of short-term experiment-focused multidisciplinary virtual scientific collaborations to long-term productive and innovative programs of scientific research. This SI theory seeks to describe the intertwined processes of information exchange and social interaction in a wide variety of social and professional settings. The theory draws upon LIS scholar and theorist Elfreda Chatman's conceptualization of "small worlds," (which she defined as localized and, socioeconomically constrained social groupings of people tied together through a shared set of normative behaviors, beliefs, and views) (Burnett, Besant, and Chatman 2001; Chatman 1991; 1992; 1999); and Jurgen Habermas' "lifeworld," which envisions a shared culture-wide social world replete with a vast body of information and resources (Habermas 1992).

Positioned between these two extremes, IWs can be understood as definable social groups that share views about the kinds of behaviors that are acceptable and the information that is worth attention. IWs do not exist in isolation, but rather in relationship with one another. Worlds may be contiguous with one another – e.g., fire and police departments exist next to each other within the same community, share certain contextual characteristics, but their activities, interests, information needs and values clearly diverge. An IW may, like a neighborhood within a city or a city within a state, be embedded within another (e.g., a university's information technology support staff operates as a definable social entity within the larger IW of the university as a whole).

Similarly, individuals may be members of multiple IWs; the same person may be both a university professor (and, thus, a member of the IW of her campus' faculty) and a guitar player, sharing a very different IW with other musicians. However, that individual's behaviors and concerns will likely be quite different as she moves back and forth between the two worlds; she will, that is, tend to function according to the norms and values of the world in which she is present at any given time.

The IW of the scientific teams visiting the Lab manifest a set of common characteristics that make them of special interest. These teams are intrinsically transient. They come together at the Lab to work for specific periods of time and to focus on specific projects. Even when teams persist beyond the period of time spent at the Lab (for ongoing work related to their current project or for other projects) their work at the Lab itself is structured by a very precise lifecycle with distinct beginning and ending points, as well as clearly demarcated activities, information needs, technical and other support from Lab staff, etc.

Although the teams visiting the Lab share many characteristics and needs, the IW of teams can also be seen as being quite distinct from one another, since each team focuses on its own particular area of scientific concern, and comes with its own social types, social norms, information values, and information behaviors.

The remainder of the chapter uses a set of concepts from the theory of information worlds (social types, boundaries, information value, social norms, and information behavior) to describe the IWs that we observed and interviewed at the Lab.

The Information Worlds of the Lab

Although each of the individual IWs of the teams working at the Lab brings its own blend of social norms and types, information behaviors, and information values into play, the fact that teams are embedded within the larger IW of the Lab itself while they conduct experiments there means that certain characteristics are held in common across teams, both because they are, as noted above, subject to the pre-established lifecycles for their visits and because they must fit into the norms and behaviors expected of all users of the lab. In what follows, we do not dig deeply into the distinctive features of any specific team, but rather explore some of the broad outlines of how the work in which teams engage is structured while at the Lab. These comments grow out of numerous observations and interviews conducted as part of an NSF-funded project intended to investigate both the social aspects of scientific work taking place at the Lab and the life-cycles of teams engaged in scientific research.

Boundaries and Social Types

Two of the theory's concepts – boundaries and social types – can help to explain the ways in which each team is a distinct IW while simultaneously embedded within the larger world of the Lab, and co-existing and interacting with other worlds present in the Lab.

The concept of boundaries acknowledges the fact that IWs do not exist in isolation, but are connected to other worlds in a variety of ways. Each world shares boundaries, is embedded within, or is contiguous with a number of other worlds. At the Lab, each scientific team undertakes its work separately. Each team conducts its own experiments using a magnet within the literal boundary of the physical walls that separates it from all of the other rooms. Each visiting team therefore inhabits its own physical world, using its own magnet according to its own schedule, without drawing upon the resources brought to the site by other teams or using the skills of individuals from other visiting teams. At the same time, all visiting teams share common resources and staff support provided by the Lab as a whole. Each team maintains autonomy from other teams – and may even be competing with other teams, if they are conducting similar experiments – while coexisting with those other teams within the larger world of the Lab.

Similarly, the Lab as a whole is also a definable world that exists quite literally within a larger IW: it is part of the larger world of the national Lab, part of the FSU world at large, and even part of the larger political and economic world of Tallahassee, the state of Florida, and the extensive national – and international – world of scientific research. Not surprisingly, the fact that the Lab is embedded in so many different ways within other worlds manifests itself in a clear understanding of the boundaries involved, and a keen awareness of the various challenges involved as those boundaries are negotiated daily.

Two types of boundaries are particularly worth noting. The first is internal and is built into the actual structure of the discipline of physics: theoretical and experimental physics, by and large, are separate (if related) IWs – their values, norms, practices, and information behaviors are clearly distinct from one another. And yet, by bringing these two worlds together – that is, by crossing the boundaries between them – the Lab is able to improve the quality of the work in which both are engaged. As one scientist put it:

> People are clever enough to understand that they are different. And adjust themselves. Usual example, maybe it's multidisciplinary, it's when you have theorists and experimentalists. Very different way of thinking, but it's … very beneficial.

The second type of boundary is the inescapable relationship between the Lab (and, by extension, the university with which it is affiliated) and the broader non-scientific world in which it is embedded. In our observations and interviews, this theme emerged repeatedly, with an emphasis on the importance of crossing this boundary in order to advocate for the Lab to local, state, and national politicians and funding sources, as well as to the region's general population. The Lab employs a number of staff (or social types) whose jobs are explicitly defined as providing an interface between these worlds. One staff member, for instance, focuses on reaching out to K-12 schools in the region and beyond to bring science education into those schools and to attempt to recruit scientists of the future. In a more general sense, many who work at the lab are very concerned with their image in the broader social world, above and beyond either the goals of the science itself or the Lab's educational mission. One scientist bemoaned the fact that some high profile scientists (not affiliated with the Lab) openly espouse atheism. Because the world in which the Lab is embedded is the largely rural and very religious deep south – this scientist commented that this is "a bad idea, because it can make the public hostile to science," which can only serve to make its work more difficult and, in a worst-case scenario, lead to overt conflict between the lab and the outside world in the public space of local (and state) political discourse and the pages of local newspapers. To put it in terms of the theory of information worlds, the ways in which those outside the Lab understand the IW within – their social norms, practices, information behaviors, and values – can be just as important as how insiders understand their own activities.

The concept of social types refers to the ways that participants are perceived within their IW, as well as the ways in which members of different worlds perceive each other. The latter may play out simply as a political reality, resulting in the necessity for someone to fulfill the social type of mediator between inside and outside. As one staff member described, mediators play the role of "an interface between the sterile world and technology," teaching newcomers how to work with the technology – ICTs and other tools – and working to explain what the Lab does and why it is important to outsiders who may see it as nothing more than a waste of taxpayer money. Such work is necessary to situate the Lab effectively in the broader community; it is important that the Lab is perceived by the broader community to be a socially useful entity providing value for investment, a good citizen rather than a drain on resources or a haven for eccentrics and eggheads (or, as a recurring theme in letters to the local newspaper would have it, a disrupter of regular weather patterns). At the same time, because it is its own world that undertakes sharply focused work, perceptions of social types may sometimes be reduced to the simple binary insiders and outsiders. As one interviewee put it, "Maybe you don't understand because you're not a physicist."

Within the Lab itself, many people fall into definable categories based on criteria that are integral to the setting. For instance, many can be categorized as specific social types by virtue of where they fall in the hierarchies of their profession or the roles they play in the day-to-day activities (visiting scientists, staff scientists, technicians, principal investigators of specific projects), stages of their careers (doctoral students, post-docs, junior and senior faculty), nationalities, scientific domains, etc. Such distinct types can also be found within a specific domain: for instance, many users are physicists, but this category includes experimental physicists, theoretical physicists, and "sample growers" who provide the materials for experiments. Within teams, the activities of individuals are often at least in part a function of these types; for instance, principal investigators of particular projects often participate in experiments only from a distance, while doctoral students and post-docs often spend very long hours at the Lab handling the day-to-day work related to the experiment. In terms of SI, this last phenomenon – with certain types actively engaged in the hands-on aspects of the experiments while other types are not physically present on site – necessitates the ongoing use of ICTs (discussed more fully below) to support ongoing communication and information exchange throughout the course of the Lab visit.

Information Value

The concept of information value suggests that, within an IW, members tend to share a belief about what kinds of things – activities, issues, and other sorts of phenomena – are of value and, thus, worth the time and energy required for obtaining, collecting, and exchanging information about; it should be noted that this concept denotes a shared belief or perception that may or may not be explicitly stated, but that may manifest itself in observable activities (to be discussed below, in relation to social norms and information behavior). The core information value of the Lab is defined in the first part of its mission (as of July 2, 2013): "promote magnet-related research to serve an interdisciplinary scientific user community spanning materials science, condensed matter physics, magnet technology, chemistry, and biology." Any information related to this mission is, by definition, perceived as being of value.

Our observations and interviews confirm this. During team visits, it is common that one member remains onsite at all times so that the experiments can continue around the clock, since the quality and value of the information emerging from the experiment depends on such intensive effort. Similarly, it is clear that a closely related value is a belief that more can be achieved through collaboration than through work in isolation, in part because multiple collaborators bring with them multiple areas of expertise, knowledge of related work, and subject-specific information necessary to complete the experiment. As one interviewee (a staff scientist) put it when asked whether he continued to work with particular teams out of choice or out of obligation,

> By choice, of course. I have continued to work with them by choice, yes. This is from the beginning the almost ideal collaboration. Those ... [collaborations are] the ideal fulfillment of the Magnet Lab's mission. So there is a group, far away from here, an excellent group. And we can offer excellent service. It's service but it's collaboration. Here, complementary, in our know-how, in our knowledge and background in Physics. And that produces good results.

At the same time, information values are never uniform, and differences in values within and across worlds may lead to overt conflict or, more subtly, unresolved tensions or, even more subtly, interesting patterns of behavior and activity that do not seem to match a world's core values but still add complexity and texture to a world's behaviors, beliefs, and interactions. The ongoing letters to the editor of the local newspaper mentioned earlier can be seen in this light: some of the general public perceive the weather, because it is more directly experienced, to be of higher value than the science taking place in the Lab. Within the Lab itself, there are also varying perceptions of information value; that is, while the Lab's mission explicitly defines the core value at work there, many other types of information are also perceived as being worth a certain amount of effort and commitment. During our observations, we witnessed a number of such mismatches in perceptions of information value, ranging from the innocuous (e.g., shared interests in fantasy football or other pastimes occasionally trumping a sustained focus on science), to the more challenging (e.g., the political dimension of conducting science in a publicly funded lab; the difficulties of doing scientific research while maintaining a personal life; and the barriers to gender equity in the sciences).

At the Lab, these mismatches appear most often to be taken for granted, and to function as part of the overall fabric of a fairly stable IW rather than perceived as threats to the future of that world. Although pursuing such interests is not directly relevant to the immediate value of furthering scientific knowledge, they, and the information surrounding them, are perceived of as having value.

Several interviewees commented that the difficulty of maintaining a personal life while conducting successful scientific work is a challenge faced more often by women than men, and a clear factor in the under-representation of women in the sciences. This is largely perceived as a simple fact of life, over which the values of scientific work have precedence:

> So, at some point you have to find a balanced life. And that's what's difficult with this job. We have the demands of NSF as a user facility, but at this lab we'll be recognized by the quality of the people we have inside. And the quality of people is not just a service. It is intellectual quality, technical quality, and the skills of people here. This is an art. To do experimental physics and be published in the best places is an art. It's the art of choosing the right problem, it's the art of asking the right question, it's the art of getting the right answers using the–developing the right technique for the right answers and being able to present them the right way when you go to conferences and to write papers.

Participants in the Lab's IW appear to hold as a fundamental value the belief that one of the primary ways to overcome or mediate these challenges and mismatches is to take special care in communication to ensure the accuracy of information exchange within and across teams, while acknowledging that the process of communication is often fraught with the potential for misunderstanding:

> I think that communication is key and, you know, in communication you've got to have a sender and a receiver and you've got to make sure that what you say the person hears. And what you hear is what the person says. Human beings are very good at filling in gaps, and a lot of time we are filling gaps where there are no gaps.

They are acutely aware that a primary challenge is to "fill in the gaps" or, to find ways to effectively negotiate boundaries between different IWs; visiting teams' use of ICTs is integral to this effort; the next section of this chapter investigates the role of ICTs in more detail.

Social Norms and Information Behavior

The theory's concept of social norms refers to a shared understanding of the rightness and wrongness of overt and observable *behaviors* within or across IWs. At the Lab, this often manifests itself as a sense of the purely routine nature of daily activities. Social norms play such a strong role in daily activities that they can become almost invisible. During our observations, we were regularly told that we would find everything we witnessed to be "boring" because there was nothing at all remarkable about any of the activities under way except the science itself, which we would not understand.

Obviously, much activity at the Lab is not only routine, but expressly work related, at least for the visiting scientists and lab staff. Teams follow standard protocols and procedures for conducting experiments over the course of their stay, and the lifecycle of a visit typically follows predictable patterns, with clear stages for planning the work (most often prior to the visit), setting up and testing the equipment, powering up and shutting down the magnets, gathering the data and conducting preliminary analysis, and finalizing the work.

The concept of social norms can also account for the degree to which members of an IW tolerate–or encourage–activities and behaviors that do not necessarily appear to be "normative," whether because they are not purely routine or because they are not always work related. Such activities observed at the Lab ranged widely, from the expected (use of ICTs for information gathering activities unrelated to work – e.g., to look up the results of the day's basketball games) to the seemingly eccentric (the fact that one project depended almost exclusively on the availability and ongoing functionality of a unique bit of individually-programmed software and the very outdated computer required to run it). In most cases, such seemingly extraneous activities served to make what is an intrinsically very high-pressure and busy IW a more human – or even "real life" rather than "work only" – environment. While it is clear that the Lab's predominant social norms emphasize the centrality of work, the Lab is both a work environment and a social setting. It was not at all uncommon to encounter clearly important and socially meaningful bits of levity or irreverence, such as the sign taped to the window of one of the magnet control rooms: "Don't tap on the glass, you'll anger the fish."

The concern of the theory of information worlds is with the place of, and activities related to, information in a variety of social contexts. The concept of information behavior, following Chatman's work (Chatman 1991; 1992; 1999), has to do with how a world's participants engage with information – how they seek, acquire, share, and distribute it, avoid it, etc.; it also focuses on the kinds of tools and technologies used to enact these behaviors.

Because the Lab supports distributed science of teams from all around the world, not all of whom may be present in Tallahassee during experiments, ICTs play a crucial role in ensuring that routine activities continue satisfactorily and successfully, through facilitation and support for information sharing and documentation. One staff scientist emphasized the importance of these ICTs for exchanging information and otherwise supporting the work of teams:

> Skype is very good for keeping people in regular contact. And the video is nice because, well, you can see people and I believe that face-to-face contact–face time is very important. So it's hard to engage in distance science but science is an international discipline. I think in the old days people tended to work with other members of their own department, or across departments in their own university. And now we have choices. We can work with people all over the world. So, the people who do it better will succeed more.

Appropriate utilization of ICTs is essential not only for the work itself – the planning and scheduling of the experiments, interacting with remote research partners during experiments, searching for, retrieving, and reviewing literature relevant to the experiment at hand etc. – but also for other routine aspects of activity, including logistics and social concerns. The interviewee continued:

> And then probably about two months [before the visit to the Lab] we started exchanging emails about kind of what are the experiments very precisely. So it was kind of relatively intriguing emails until about two weeks before, where then also the administrative talk and organizational talk: the student stayed in one of our apartments in alumni village. Does she drive? This sort of thing. She didn't drive, so 'do you have a bicycle?' Kind of organizational things.

Communication activities using ICTs, thus, are inextricably interwoven with information and information behaviors necessary to complete the work of the teams. Throughout our observations, it was clear that ICTs were not simply used for communication, but that almost all communication activities were focused on information exchange; thus, ICTs can be seen as one of many tools (along with logbooks, pen and paper, posters, and scribbles on post-it notes) used to collect, analyze, record, and share experiment data and other important information. In our observations and interviews, scientists and staff emphasized the importance of ICTs such as Skype, email, online databases and file sharing sites, and other technologies they used for day-to-day communication and planning and for the storage and exchange of both small work files and huge datasets; they said that these tools allowed them to make progress in a wide variety of work-related activities at a distance when they were not gathered together to actually conduct experiments.

One scientist noted an important advantage offered by ICTs over face-to-face interaction: ICTs not only support communication, but can also automatically document that communication for future reference; in other words, the "I" of ICTs (information) is just as important in their use as the "C" (communication):

> And I prefer, as many people also prefer email for all this load, all these collaborators, it is good to have something written. It's like a trace. We keep trace of what's going on. We can discuss some details on the phone quickly, but you really exchange emails just to have a record.

Similarly, the storage and distribution capabilities of ICTs support the storage and distribution of data in a way not limited by either time or space:

> We had to try and figure out data, places where we could try and dump some of this data, because the files that we were getting were, like, huge amounts of data for these things. So I think we actually ended up doing a combination of emailing attached files, and then dropping them somewhere … we had access to a server.

Still, ICTs do not solve all problems that scientists working in teams across large geographic distances encounter, especially because not all work that must be done can be done asynchronously. As one scientist noted, both asynchronous tools such as email and synchronous tools like Skype can support certain types of communication, but cannot overcome limitations imposed by distance such as collaborating across multiple time zones, nor can they overcome the limitations of the different habits, normative communication and information practices, and other day-to-day activities of the very human members of the IW.

> Sometimes, especially with international users, it's just a difference in time. [With] European collaborators, you really have to be here early in the morning. And we have some users in Sydney nowadays. So that is very strange. I myself am not always the quickest to answer emails. Whereas other people, you send them an email and in five minutes they write you back. But some people answer very easily and some people, they answer the email, but not really what you're asking them. Which is annoying sometimes.

Further, every ICT comes with its own particular set of capabilities and characteristics. Teams working at a distance must choose tools from the variety available and use them for their specific needs at a given time and taking into account the makeup (and location) of their team:

> If you're talking in a group, you can't really use Skype. We had one project with one in London, one in Utah, one in Sydney, and one here in Tallahassee. So then you teleconference and Skype.

This brief overview of information behavior and the role of ICTs, does not really do justice to the pervasiveness of activities and practices related to information at the Lab. Simply put, ICTs are integral to nearly everything; they are used almost constantly and for a very wide range of activities from the essential (e.g., troubleshooting at a distance when an experiment is not going well) to the trivial. And, because of the centrality of information in all of these activities, ICTs are key components that support the various IWs found within the Lab.

Conclusions

Scientific inquiry has moved from individualized inquiry to distributed team science, to engage scientists from multiple disciplines, institutions, and nations in the solution of complex problems. National science laboratories are designed to support sharing of costly scientific instruments and expertise. In this chapter, we applied the concepts of the theory of information worlds to the analysis of information behaviors, social norms, social types, information values, and boundaries of intrinsically transient distributed scientific teams during that portion of their life-cycles while they were embedded in the IW of the Lab.

SI examines the roles and uses of information technology in social and organizational contexts (Kling, Rosenbaum and Sawyer 2005). We found that ICT use is a pervasive and integral information behavior across the visiting teams, facilitating connectivity between onsite and offsite members, and providing essential documentation of the decisions made, but that the social norms related to this use may vary from team to team. We learned that a wide variety of social types are engaged in the work, and that these create both synergy and friction between the visiting scientists and the Lab staff, and within the teams themselves. The individual teams have intrinsic social norms that are shared between onsite and offsite members. Sometimes these norms are in conflict with those of the Lab, and while embedded there, must be modified. Mismatches in the social types and social norms within and across IWs demonstrate the permeability of boundaries between the embedded worlds. While the visiting teams and staff scientists alike share the information value that is articulated through the Lab's mission, this value is not necessarily shared by the non-scientific community and political context in which the Lab is embedded. In order for the work of the Lab to be successful, both the intrinsically transient visiting teams and the resident staff scientists must be respectful of these boundaries and tend them with care.

Acknowledgments

The authors would like to express their gratitude to Larry Dennis, Dean of the College of Communication and Information, for suggesting the Lab as a research site and facilitating access to the scientists and staff. Thanks also to Dr. Gregory Boebinger, director of the Lab, and Pat Dixon and Kathy Hedick for their support of this project. Wilhelmina Randtke and Jessica Roberts helped with the data collection and coding. This research was supported in part by the National Science Foundation under Grant OCI T0942855. The article reflects the findings and conclusions of the authors, and does not necessarily reflect the views of the National Science Foundation or the National High Magnetic Field Laboratory.

References

Atkins, Daniel, Kelvin K. Droegemeier, Stuart I. Feldman, Hector Garcia-Molina, Michael L. Klein, David G. Messerschmitt, Paul Messina, Jeremiah P. Ostriker, and Margaret H. Wright. 2003. Revolutionizing Science and Engineering Through Cyberinfrastructure: Report of the National Science Foundation Blue-ribbon Advisory Panel on Cyberinfrastructure. http://arizona.openrepository.com/arizona/handle/10150/106224.

Birnholtz, Jeremy, and Matthew Bietz. 2003. "Data at Work: Supporting Sharing in Science and Engineering." In *Proceedings of the 2003 International ACM SIGGROUP Conference on Supporting Group Work* 339-348.

Borgman, Christine L., Jillian C. Wallis, and Noel Enyedy. 2007. "Little Science Confronts the Data Deluge: Habitat Ecology, Embedded Sensor Networks, and Digital Libraries." *International Journal on Digital Libraries*. 7: 17-30. doi:10.1007/s00799-007-0022-9.

Burnett, Gary, and Paul T. Jaeger. 2008. "Small Worlds, Lifeworlds, and Information: The Ramifications of the Information Behaviors of Social Groups in Public Policy and the Public Sphere." *Information Research* 13 (2). http://InformationR.net/ir/13-2/paper346.html.

Burnett, Gary, Michele Besant, and Elfreda A. Chatman. 2001. Small Worlds: Normative Behavior in Virtual Communities and Feminist Bookselling. *Journal of the American Society for Information Science and Technology* 52 (7): 517-535.

Chatman, Elfreda. A. 1991. Life in a Small World: Applicability of Gratification Theory to Information-seeking Behavior. *Journal of the American Society for Information Science* 42: 438-449.

—. A. 1992. *The Information World of Retired Women.* Westport, CT: Greenwood.

—. 1999. A Theory of Life in the Round. *Journal of the American Society for Information Science,* 50: 207-217.

Cummings, Jonathon N., and Sara Kiesler. 2005. "Collaborative Research Across Disciplinary and Organizational Boundaries." *Social Studies of Science* 35 (5): 703-722.

Finholt, Thomas A. 2005. "Collaboratories." *Annual Review of Information Science and Technology* 36: 73-107. doi: 10.1002/aris.1440360103.

Griffith, Terri L., and Margaret A Neale. 2001. "Information Processing in Traditional, Hybrid, and Virtual Teams: From Nascent Knowledge to Transactive Memory." *Research in Organizational Behavior* 23: 379-421. doi: 10.1016/S019-308(01)23009-3.

Habermas, Jurgen. 1992. Further Reflections on the Public Sphere. In J. Calhoun (Ed.), *Critical Social Theory: Culture, Theory and the Challenge of Difference* (pp. 421-462). Oxford: Blackwell.

Hinds, Pamela J., and Diane E. Bailey. 2003. "Out of Sight, Out of Sync: Understanding Conflict in Distributed Teams." *Organization Science* 14 (6): 615-632.

Hinnant, Charles. C., Besiki Stvilia, Shuheng Wu, Adam Worrall, Gary Burnett, Kathleen Burnett, Michelle M. Kazmer, and Paul F. Marty. 2012. "Author Team Diversity and the Impact of Scientific Publications: Evidence from Physics Research at a National Science Lab." *Library and Information Science Research* 34 (4): 249-257. doi:10.1016/j.lisr.2012.03.001.

Jaeger, Paul T. and Gary Burnett. 2010. *Information Worlds: Behavior, Technology, and Social Context in the Age of the Internet*. New York: Routledge.

Kling, Rob. 2000. "Learning about Information Technologies and Social Change: The Contribution of Social Informatics." *The Information Society* 16 (3): 217-232.

Kling, Rob, Howard Rosenbaum, and Steve Sawyer. 2005. *Understanding and Communicating Social Informatics: A Framework for Studying and Teaching the Human Contexts of Information and Communications Technologies*. Medford, New Jersey: Information Today, Inc.

Kraut, R., Carmen Egido, and Jolene Galegher. 1988. "Patterns of Contact and Communication in Scientific Research Collaboration. In

Proceedings of the 1988 ACM Conference on Computer Supported Cooperative Work, edited by Irene Greif, 1-12. New York: ACM.

Lamb, Roberta, and Elizabeth Davidson. 2005. "Information and Communication Technology Challenges to Scientific Professional Identity." *The Information Society* 21 (1): 1-24. doi: 10.1080/01972240 590895883.

Lee, Sooho., and Barry Bozeman. 2005. "The Impact of Research Collaboration on Scientific Productivity." *Social Studies of Science* 35 (5): 673-702.

Orlikowski, Wanda. 1992. "Learning from Notes: Organizational Issues in Groupware Implementation." In *Proceedings of the Conference on Computer-Supported Cooperative Work* 362-369.

Stvilia, Besiki, Michael B. Twidale, Linda C. Smith, and Les Gasser. 2008. "Information Quality Work Organization in Wikipedia." *Journal of the American Society for Information Science and Technology* 59 (6): 983–1001.

Stvilia, Besiki, Charles C. Hinnant, Katy Schindler, Adam Worrall, Gary Burnett, Kathleen Burnett, Michelle M. Kazmer, and Paul F. Marty. 2011. "Composition of Scientific Teams and Publication Productivity at a National Science Lab." *Journal of the American Society for Information Science and Technology* 62 (2): 270-283. doi: 10.1002/asi.21464.

Thorsteinsdóttir, O. Halla. 2000. "External Research Collaboration in Two Small Science Systems." *Scientometrics* 49 (1):145-160.

Walsh, John P., and Todd Bayma. 1996. "The Virtual College: Computer-mediated Communication and Scientific Work." *Information Society* 12 (4): 343-363.

Walsh, John P., Stephanie Kucker, Nancy G. Maloney, and Shaul Gabbay. 2000. "Connecting Minds: Computer-mediated Communication and Scientific Work." *Journal of the American Society for Information Science* 51 (14): 1295-1305.

Wuchty, Stephan, Benjamin F. Jones, and Brian Uzzi. 2007. "The Increasing Dominance of Teams in Production of Knowledge." *Science* 316 (5827): 1036-1039. doi:10.1126/science.1136099.

PART III

FUTURE

CHAPTER EIGHT

REFRAMING THE SOCIO-TECHNICAL PROBLEM: A WAY FORWARD FOR SOCIAL INFORMATICS

LYSANNE LESSARD

Introduction

The research area of Social Informatics (SI) has greatly contributed to a socio-technical understanding of the design, management, and use of information and communication technologies (ICTs) (Sawyer and Rosenbaum 2000). SI research typically provides in-depth investigations of the contexts of ICTs' design and use, moving beyond simplistic understandings of ICTs as tools that have deterministic impacts (Kling 2000). However, current approaches have been criticized for using oversimplified models of ICTs and their mutual relationship with social actors (Sawyer and Rosenbaum 2000; Sawyer and Tyworth 2006). Thus, while SI is fundamentally concerned with ICTs in context, theoretical models that underlie studies in this area, such as Social Construction of Technology (SCOT) (Bijker 2001; 1995), may provide a better analytical grip on the contextual dimension than on the ICT dimension of this relationship. This issue can make it difficult to translate the implications of SI research into accurate design guidelines for ICTs. Indeed, the material properties of technological artifacts need to be addressed in order to account for the apparently paradoxical effects of their use (Volkoff, Strong, and Elmes 2007; Jones and Orlikowski 2009).

In order to move forward and have a greater impact on the way in which ICTs are understood and designed, SI theorizing efforts need to better account for the nature and roles of ICTs (Sawyer and Tyworth 2006). This could imply developing more sophisticated models of ICTs to be integrated into current SI theories. Doing so, however, could violate the basic socio-technical principles that guide these theories; these principles, such as that of the seamless web, emphasize that technology cannot meaningfully be isolated from its social context of design and use (Sawyer and Tyworth 2006). Instead, this chapter argues for the need to reframe the socio-technical problem as one that concerns the understanding and representation of structure, action, and their relationship. This alternative perspective could support theorizing efforts within SI in a way that is aligned with its basic socio-technical principles; it could also help to extend nascent SI theories such as Socio-Technical Interaction Networks (STIN) (Kling, McKim, and King 2003) and the Social Actor approach (Lamb and Kling 2003).

This paper thus proposes to use Critical Realism as a means to further develop socio-technical theorizing within SI. Critical Realism is a philosophical perspective whose basic insight is that the patterns of events that we observe in the world are ontologically distinct from the structures, powers and generative mechanisms that cause them (Bhaskar and Lawson 1998). Through empirical investigation, researchers produce explanations of these patterns that are tentatively accepted if, and as long as, these explanations better account for a given phenomenon than competing accounts. Critical Realism thus recognizes that knowledge is incomplete, fallible and value-laden, and that alternative accounts of a phenomenon can be valid, embracing a relativist epistemology and a realist ontology (Maxwell 2012)

In Critical Realism, structures and interactions are two objects of study that mutually shape and imply each other in any socio-technical phenomenon, but that nonetheless can be analytically separated in time (Archer 1995). This position is in line with Bijker's (1993) proposition to consider socio-technical ensembles as the main unit of analysis, but assumes an ontological distinction between the structures and (inter)actions that co-constitute these ensembles; in other words, structure and agency are taken to be "real" objects that possess different properties. In particular, Critical Realism differs from the constructivist groundings of SI by positing that structure always precedes agency, conditioning though not determining action (Archer 1995).

While Critical Realism is not inherently a "socio-technical" philosophy, it has been found to be a useful basis for developing midrange theories of information technology in organizations (Strong and Volkoff 2010; Volkoff, Strong, and Elmes 2007). The concept of structural conditioning developed in the morphogenetic approach, a Critical Realist theory of organizational change (Archer 1995), is particularly relevant to account for the materiality of information technology while enabling the understanding of its evolution through time (Volkoff, Strong, and Elmes 2007). The morphogenetic approach is a social theory that understands social structures as pre-existing current action, which can then transform (morphogenesis) or reinforce (morphostatis) these structures (Archer 1995); from this perspective, organizational actors are conditioned – both enabled and constrained – by the emerging properties of existing ICTs part of organizational structures. These properties give them reasons (which they may or may not act upon) to act in certain ways (Archer 1995). Using Critical Realism as a research perspective could thus provide a solid foundation for extending current SI theories guiding the understanding and design of ICTs in context.

The remainder of the chapter focuses on information and knowledge infrastructures as a means to illustrate the implications of adopting such a perspective. The following section first introduces the notion of knowledge infrastructures as a type of information infrastructure focusing on the creation and use of knowledge. Indeed, the concept of knowledge infrastructures is particularly relevant for distributed and fluid forms of knowledge exchange and recombination that have been facilitated by information infrastructures such as the World Wide Web (Ciborra and Andreu 2001). Since knowledge infrastructures have not been investigated from a socio-technical perspective, related work on information infrastructures is then presented and re-interpreted through a Critical Realist perspective; doing so conveys how Critical Realism can help to guide the understanding and design of knowledge infrastructures. The chapter then revisits the socio-technical foundations of SI, and discusses how Critical Realism can provide a stronger analytical grip on ICT development in a manner that is aligned with these foundations.

Knowledge Infrastructures

Knowledge infrastructures have been defined as ICT platforms that support collaboration, knowledge sharing, and learning within knowledge processes (Maier, Hädrich, and Peinl 2009). However, this definition reflects a dichotomy between technologies and the social world that SI has been striving to depart from (Kling 2000). Taking a socio-technical perspective, a knowledge infrastructure is composed of ICT platforms, knowledge processes, and knowledge-related activities undertaken by actors – as well as the actors themselves.

Knowledge infrastructures can be found within large organizations (Maier, Hädrich, and Peinl 2009). They also emerge in the context of inter-organizational networks such as those formed through consortiums or research and development efforts. Indeed, actors in these networks typically collaborate over long periods of time on projects related to a domain of interest such as municipal service delivery (Lessard and Yu

2013), videogame development (Lessard and Yu 2012), health care staff training, etc. Knowledge from actors' expertise and from past projects acts as a resource for the creation of new knowledge through each new project. While not necessarily explicit, knowledge creation in this type of phenomena is supported by a knowledge infrastructure in the form of technical artifacts, people, policies, practices, and more.

Knowledge infrastructures have not been studied from a socio-technical perspective to the author's knowledge. It is thus perhaps more fruitful to understand knowledge infrastructures as a special kind of information infrastructures, a concept which has been explored through a socio-technical lens. The following section presents a brief overview of two propositions for understanding and designing information infrastructures (Hanseth and Lyytinen 2010; Star and Ruhleder 1996). The subsequent section will then suggest that their apparent contradiction results from a different understanding of the socio-technical object (Bygstad 2008). This understanding is then applied to the design of knowledge infrastructures.

Related Work on the Design of Information Infrastructures

The first proposition comes from Star and Ruhleder's (1996) well-known work on information infrastructures. They propose that infrastructures are not "things", but relations that are enacted in the context of organizational practices. This move does away with the "what" of an infrastructure, with its "thinginess", in order to focus on "when" it becomes recognizable as an infrastructure by given actors:

> An infrastructure occurs when the tension between local and global is resolved. That is, an infrastructure occurs when local practices are afforded by a larger-scale technology, which can then be used in a natural, ready-to-hand fashion. (Star and Ruhleder 1996, 114).

The authors studied the development of the Worm Community System (WCS), an infrastructure aimed at supporting the research work of molecular biologists in the United States. They concluded that the ultimate failure of the WCS to become widely used could be mainly attributed to discontinuities, or gaps, between varied contexts of use. The authors propose addressing these gaps by having multi-disciplinary development teams; providing technical education to users; and developing the computing infrastructure (hardware, software, and technical services part of the information infrastructure) in a way that is open to change. These recommendations are intended to guide the development of practices surrounding information infrastructures in a way that "minds" the technical side, but falls short of providing clear guidance for its design and development (e.g., how does one go about designing a flexible computing infrastructure?).

A contrasting proposition is that of Hanseth and Lyytinen (2010). They propose socio-technical design principles for promoting the evolution and growth of information infrastructures. While agreeing with Star and Ruhleder about the importance of local shaping of information infrastructures by different communities, their definition focuses on the installed base:

> We will define an II as a shared, open (and unbounded), heterogeneous and evolving socio-technical system (which we call installed base) consisting of a set of IT capabilities and their user, operations and design communities. (Hanseth and Lyytinen 2010, 4).

In this view, the structure of an information infrastructure is a recursive organization of information technology (IT) capability, while its "social" side concerns the recursive organization of its rules by users who both follow and shape them. Drawing from complex adaptive systems theory, they develop design principles able to address the growth (bootstrap problem) and adaptation (adaptability problem) of infrastructures. These principles are further decomposed into design rules that focus on means to develop IT capabilities and artifacts in a way that meets these principles. In contrast with Star and Ruhleder, Hanseth and Lyytinen thus propose design guidelines that are mindful of social dynamics, but that mainly focus on the information technologies that influence and are shaped by them (e.g., using rules as a proxy for use).

Interestingly, both sets of authors' detailed discussions of information infrastructures as phenomena show a good amount of overlap; importantly for the present discussion, they are also explicitly based on a socio-technical perspective. Yet, their definitions of information infrastructures and the design guidelines provided for their development differ significantly. A cursory understanding of their propositions might lead to a categorization of Star and Ruhleder's work as "social", and of Hanseth and Lyytinen's work as "technical". Indeed, while the former use the term "computer infrastructure" and the later refer to "users" and "design communities", the way to tackle these dimensions from a design standpoint is not clearly explicated in either text. But such a proposition would not do justice to the work of either set of authors, who both show a true concern for and a sophisticated understanding of the way in which social and technical issues are intertwined.

A Critical Realist Understanding of Information Infrastructures

A different explanation of these apparently contradictory propositions for information infrastructures comes from the use of a Critical Realist philosophical perspective (Archer et al. 1998). Critical Realism views the world as composed of objects possessing generative mechanisms – causal powers and liabilities – by virtue of their intrinsic structures (Bhaskar and Lawson 1998; Sayer 2010). In this view, underlying structures and generative mechanisms are real and produce the events and behaviors that can be observed in the empirical world; moreover, structures and social interactions can be analytically separated in order to understand how they shape each other in turn (Archer 1995). This does not entail that events can be predicted since the world, in particular the social world, is taken to be an open system where mechanisms can interact with or counteract each other (Collier 1994).

Critical Realism is increasingly being proposed as a basis from which to conduct studies in organization science, management, information systems and information science (Budd 2012; Dobson, Myles, and Jackson 2007; Mingers 2004; Strong and Volkoff 2010; van Aken 2004; Volkoff, Strong, and Elmes 2007). It has also been used as a perspective from which to explore the ontological nature of information infrastructures (Bygstad 2008). From this view, socio-technical networks such as information infrastructures are composed of two socio-technical objects: one concerning structure, and one concerning action. While intimately related, each object is analytically distinguished in order to provide a simpler conceptualization of this type of phenomenon (Bygstad 2008).

For example, a socio-technical network of "accounts, clerks, customers, money, and arithmetic machines" is taken to be composed of structure (bank) and agency (financial transactions) dimensions. Following the work of Volkoff, Strong, and Elmes on technologies and organizational change (2007), structures are described in terms of technologies and routines (drawing rights, digital certificates), while actions concern technologies-in-use and performed routines (withdrawal, transfer). Analyzing socio-technical change is then a matter of understanding how the initial structure conditions subsequent interaction, which itself reproduces or transforms the structure (Archer 1995; Volkoff, Strong, and Elmes 2007).

Applied to information infrastructures, this leads to the identification of two socio-technical entities: "the structure as a network of technical and ostensive objects ('structure-as-form'), and agency as a network of performative and material objects ('technology-in-use')", and of the dynamic interplay between them (Bygstad 2008, 7). Hanseth and Lyytinen's design principles and rules (2010) can thus be understood as focusing on the socio-technical structures of information infrastructures, while Star and Ruhleder's guidelines (1996) pertain to the socio-technical activities of the same object of study. These propositions are then complementary, not contradictory.

Designing for Knowledge Infrastructures

These insights provide a strong basis for the understanding and design of knowledge infrastructures. Drawing from previous definitions of information infrastructures (Hanseth and Lyytinen 2010; Star and Ruhleder 1996; Bygstad 2008), a knowledge infrastructure can be analytically separated into two socio-technical aspects: a knowledge base and activities of knowledge transformation (see Figure 8-1). The knowledge base consists of a stabilized (for a time) network of knowledge management tools and documentation, but also people's existing experience, expertise, and relationships. Knowledge transformation activities include information sharing, data production, collaborative problem solving, etc. These activities are shaped by the existing knowledge base, but are also the mechanisms through which the knowledge infrastructure evolves. Observed phenomena such as knowledge creation and innovation are emergent outcomes of the interplay between the knowledge base and knowledge activities within a knowledge infrastructure.

Designing for knowledge infrastructures needs to address structural and agency dimensions, in a way that fosters desirable outcomes such as innovation. Following Hanseth and Lyytinen's recommendations (2010), the structure of the knowledge base could be designed in a modular and incremental fashion that allows for local adaptation and development. This means, for example, to focus on communication protocols allowing network actors to search others' documentation systems, rather than on a centralized database. Following Star and Ruhleder's guidelines (1996), designing for knowledge transformation activities would entail the provision of incentives to collaborate across organizational boundaries and also to feed the knowledge base locally. This could be achieved, for example, through network agreements that reward information sharing through access rights to the resulting intellectual property.

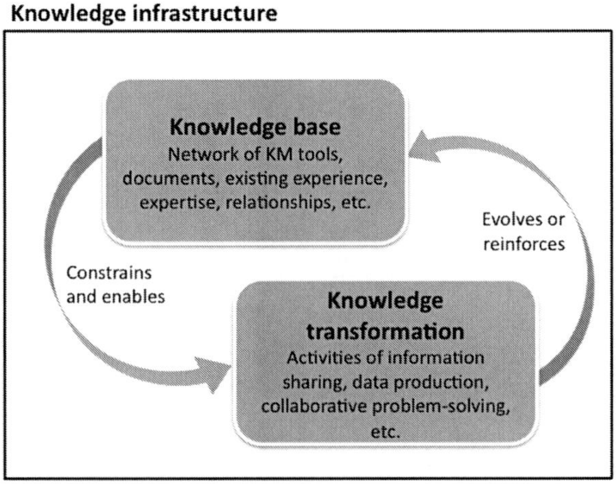

Fig. 8-1. Structure and agency in knowledge infrastructures

Viewing these insights through a Critical Realist perspective is useful because it accounts on one hand for the installed base that both enables and constrains subsequent actions, and on the other for the way in which specific persons' or groups' actions can make the installed base evolve. This helps to guide interventions in the development of a knowledge infrastructure: on one hand toward the development of a structure that is able to grow and adapt, and on the other hand toward the development of policies and reward systems that are aligned with actors' needs while fostering desirable behaviors. This differs from both technological determinist approaches and constructivist ones, which tend to neglect either agency or the specifics of a given technology (Volkoff, Strong, and Elmes 2007).

This approach to designing for knowledge infrastructures does not attempt to draw a line between the "social" and the "technical" – something very difficult to do – , but rather distinguishes between socio-technical structures and socio-technical agency. The latter does not posit an equal ability and willingness to act by humans and technological artifacts, but recognizes the capacity of technologies to produce effects through the delegated intentions of their creators (Kaptelinin and Nardi 2012). This proposition reframes the problem of creating better models of ICTs and of the relationship between ICTs and social actors (Sawyer and

Rosenbaum 2000) as a problem of creating better models of structures and activities and of their dynamic inter-shaping.

Revisiting the Socio-Technical Foundations of Social Informatics

The research area of SI has rested on socio-technical theory since its inception (Sawyer and Rosenbaum 2000). By reminding us about the importance of the context of use, SI has gone beyond a strictly functionalist, or "tool-based" understanding of ICTs to better account for their interaction with the contexts in which they are embedded (Kling 2000). The meaning of "socio-technical" within SI generally refers to the intertwining and inter-shaping of ICTs and the social or organizational setting in which they are embedded (Sawyer and Rosenbaum 2000). But it also concerns a will to improve the lives of the individuals and organizations who design and use ICTs (Sawyer and Tyworth 2006, Sawyer and Rosenbaum 2000). This work is part of a wider effort to critically investigate information technology in its dynamic interaction with people, resources, and other aspects of its social contexts (Orlikowski and Iacono 2001). However, SI pays particular attention to the technologies that process information and enable communication – ICTs (Kling 2000).

The theoretical foundations of SI draw from Social Construction of Technology approaches broadly construed (Bijker 2001). The socio-technical principles articulated by Bijker (1995) are of particular importance (Sawyer and Tyworth 2006). These principles state that conceptual frameworks used to analyze technological development should: 1) account for both change and continuity in technical artifacts; 2) take the working of an artifact as the result rather than the cause of socio-technical development; 3) account for both agency and structural constraints of technical change; and, 4) not make a priori distinctions between dimensions such as social, technical, political, etc. (Bijker 1995). The Actor-Network Theory (ANT) developed by Latour, Law, Callon, and others has also been a marked influence to SI approaches, contributing such concepts as non-human actants, enrolment, and translation (Meyer 2006). These influences are constructivist in the sense that they take the meaning of technical artifacts to be the result of social interactions, not of intrinsic properties of these artifacts; varied social actors can thus interpret them differently (interpretive flexibility) (Bijker 1995).

Two approaches built on these foundations have particularly served to advance socio-technical theorizing within SI (Sawyer and Tyworth 2006):

Socio-Technical Interaction Networks (STIN) (Kling, McKim, and King 2003) and the Social Actor approach (Lamb and Kling 2003). STIN, as a theory and modeling technique, emphasizes the mutual shaping of technologies and social processes by identifying resource dependencies and other relationships that arise between people, people and technology, and technology in socio-technical networks (Kling, McKim, and King 2003). Actors in a STIN model can be human, non-human, or heterogeneous (other STINs) in order to support the understanding of how these entities co-constitute each other. Conceptually, this reminds us that there is not "technology" on one side and "users" on the other, but rather participants of different natures that play multiple roles within a STIN. Such conceptualization draws in part from the Social Actor approach, which aims to move beyond the concept of "users" and provide a stronger conceptual basis for studies of ICTs in use (Lamb and Kling 2003). Social actors are understood to be at once enabled and constrained by their organizational and larger socio-technical affiliations, a perspective that focuses attention on how interactions and inter-actor relationships shape actors' behavior.

Each approach leads to different types of insights. STIN brings a better understanding of how socio-technical networks are developed at a system level, while the Social Actor approach focuses on social processes where actors are constrained but nevertheless have the agency to change their context (Sawyer and Rosenbaum 2000). Yet, they both help to understand how organizational agency and technological infrastructures are intertwined and mutually shape each other in varied ways. However, both theories reflect Sawyer and Rosenbaum's critique (2000) in that they provide little analytical grip on the technical dimensions of ICTs and on the relationship between those dimensions and social action. This weakness can be traced to the underlying philosophical perspective from which these approaches have been developed; indeed, theories developed from a constructivist perspective tend to focus on agency while ignoring the distinctive, material characteristics of particular technologies (Volkoff, Strong, and Elmes 2007). Moreover, while the varying insights afforded by STIN and the Social Actor approach show an attention to structure and agency, they do not clearly articulate how these dimensions relate to each other.

A Critical Realist perspective helps to overcome these limitations by addressing the material and temporal aspects of ICT development and use (Volkoff, Strong, and Elmes 2007). By attributing an ontological status to structures, the configuration of a given technical system can be described as part of the wider socio-technical structure that conditions action through the way in which interests, roles, routines, and more are inscribed within it (Volkoff, Strong, and Elmes 2007; Henfridsson and Bygstad 2013). This understanding is particularly important for the many ICTs that are developed from an existing product or an installed base such as knowledge infrastructures. The temporal aspect of change is addressed through the notion that an initial socio-technical structure conditions – without determining – subsequent actions and interactions, which can change or reinforce that structure (Archer 1995). While this process is iterative, it is not necessarily continuous: cycles of Structure at $Time_1$ – Structure at $Time_2$, both involving transformative social actions and interactions, can be identified (Volkoff, Strong, and Elmes 2007). Such cycles are not monolithic however; different actors react differently to structural conditioning, leading to potentially conflicting efforts of evolution and reinforcement in the same context.

Critical Realism is not at odds with the socio-technical principles at the heart of SI. Revisiting Bijker (1995), we can see that Critical Realism accounts for both change and continuity; can look at the socio-technical process leading to the development of artifacts; pays attention to both agency and structure, and how they interrelate; and, can draw in the many dimensions of social life. Moreover, such a perspective does not reject concepts from STIN (Kling, McKim, and King 2003) and the Social Actor approach (Lamb and Kling 2003); it simply argues for an analytical differentiation between a socio-technical network as described by STIN and what social actors can and are willing to do to evolve or reinforce them. It does differ however by stating that there is *always* an initial socio-technical structure that needs to be brought into the analysis, that actors are not completely free to create new structures or systems but that they can only transform existing ones. This does not deny the idea that social structures are created through intentional and unintentional human agency, but states that past agency results in structures that both enable and constrain agency at a later time (Archer 1995).

These insights can help to extend current SI approaches. For example, STIN (Kling, McKim, and King 2003) can be used to depict a knowledge infrastructure at its initial stage before development is formally undertaken, and again afterward to see how the network has changed. To account for the materiality of ICTs, specific technical actors could be further analyzed to understand how their components and configuration shape their role in the network (Henfridsson and Bygstad Forthcoming; Volkoff, Strong, and Elmes 2007). Furthermore, concepts of agent-oriented modeling (Yu 2009) could be used to integrate explicitly dimensions of Social Actors approach into STIN diagrams; doing so would help to "open up" actors to show how their interests and need for resources shape their actions.

Critical Realism also helps us to move beyond description and create explanatory process theories, identifying the generative mechanisms through which an initial structure shapes agency, and in turn how agency shapes the (re) emerging structure (Volkoff, Strong, and Elmes 2007). Such theorizing is ideally created through empirical studies that account for specific contexts, leading to midrange theories whose generalizability is limited to similar contexts. Midrange theories help to support design efforts, leading to heuristic design rules that practitioners can use to think though potential outcomes of interventions, and choose accordingly (van Aken 2004).

Conclusion

This chapter has argued for the use of Critical Realism as a philosophical perspective from which to reframe the socio-technical problem in SI. Rather than focusing on the development of improved models of technologies and of their mutual relationship with social actors (Sawyer and Rosenbaum 2000; Sawyer and Tyworth 2006), a Critical Realist perspective moves us to develop a better understanding of socio-technical structures, actions, and their dynamic inter-shaping (Bygstad 2008). Doing so helps to extend current SI approaches in a way that accounts for the materiality of specific ICTs, as well as for the temporality of changes to the socio-technical networks that they are a part of (Volkoff, Strong, and Elmes 2007). Exploring the use of Critical Realism as a research perspective could thus facilitate the development of midrange explanatory theories of ICT development and use that are aligned with the socio-technical principles underlying SI, in particular those of Bijker (1995).

This approach is particularly relevant for current objects of studies within ICTs such as social media, information infrastructures, or knowledge infrastructures. Indeed, while these ICTs have a configurational nature (Sawyer and Tyworth 2006), their "interpretive flexibility" (Bijker 1995) is not boundless; the reality of the socio-technical "installed base" from which they are developed and used shows that subsequent transformation – and reinforcement – is structurally conditioned by that base. Critical Realism helps to understand and conceptualize this kind of phenomenon by attributing an ontological status to the initial structure and by positing an analytical dualism between that structure and subsequent actions (Archer 1995). Developing better theories and analytical approaches able to guide the choice, design, and development of ICTs that are developed from existing components, systems, and networks would be greatly needed and fully within the scope of SI as a research area. This paper has outlined the direction that such work could take for knowledge infrastructures, but future theorizing efforts need to be grounded in empirical studies and further conceptualized.

Reframing the socio-technical problem as one concerning the interplay between structural and agentic dimensions of socio-technical networks helps to clarify the scope and focus of design guidelines for these networks. It also points more directly to design opportunities from SI's "installed base" of concepts and approaches. Finally, doing so opens up new avenues for SI and socio-technical approaches in general; indeed, it points to the need to study ICTs at both the structural and agentic levels, in order to understand how these two socio-technical objects of study interact through time to co-constitute observed events.

References

Archer, Margaret S. 1995. *Realist Social Theory: The Morphogenetic Approach*. New York: Cambridge University Press.

Archer, Margaret S., Roy Bhaskar, Andrew Collier, Tony Lawson, and Alan Norrie, eds. 1998. *Critical Realism: Essential Readings*, *Critical Realism – Interventions*. New York: Routledge.

Bhaskar, Roy, and Tony Lawson. 1998. "Introduction: Basic Texts and Development." In *Critical Realism: Essential Readings*, edited by Margaret S. Archer, Roy Bhaskar, Andrew Collier, Tony Lawson and Alan Norrie, 3-15. New York: Routledge.

Bijker, Wiebe E. 1993. "Do Not Despair: There Is Life after Constructivism." *Science, Technology & Human Values* 18 (1):113-138.

—. 1995. *Of Bicycles, Bakelites, and Bulbs: Toward a Theory of Sociotechnical Change*, *Inside Technology*. Cambridge: The MIT Press.

—. 2001. "Technology, Social Construction of." In *International Encyclopedia of the Social & Behavioral Sciences*, edited by Neil J. Smelser and Paul B. Baltes, 15522-15527. Oxford, Amsterdam: Elsevier Science.

Budd, John M. 2012. "Phenomenological Critical Realism: A Practical Method for LIS." *Journal of Education for Library and Information Science* 53 (1):69-80.

Bygstad, Bendik. 2008. Information Infastructure as Organization: A Critical Realist View. *Proceedings of the International Conference on Information Systems*: Paper 190. http://aisel.aisnet.org/icis2008/190.

Ciborra, Claudio U., and Rafael Andreu. 2001. "Sharing Knowledge Across Boundaries." *Journal of Information Technology* 16 (2):73-81.

Collier, Andrew. 1994. *Critical Realism: An Introduction to the Philosophy of Roy Bhaskar*. London: Verso.

Dobson, Phillip, John Myles, and Paul Jackson. 2007. "Making the Case for Critical realism: Examining the Implementation of Automated Performance Management Systems." *Information Resources Management Journal* 20 (2):138-152.

Hanseth, Ole, and Kalle Lyytinen. 2010. "Design Theory for Dynamic Complexity in Information Infrastructures: The Case of Building Internet." *Journal of Information Technology* 25 (1):1-19.

Henfridsson, Ola, and Bendik Bygstad. 2013. "The Generative Mechanisms of Digital Infrastructure Evolution." *MIS Quarterly* (Sp. Issue: Critical Realism in Information Systems Research).) 37 (3): 896-931.

Jones, Matthew, and Wanda J. Orlikowski. 2009. "Information Technology and the Dynamics of Organizational Change." In *The Oxford Handbook of Information and Communication Technologies*, edited by Robin Mansell, Chrisanthi Avgerou, Danny Quah, and Roger Silverstone. Oxford: Oxford University Press.

Kaptelinin, Victor, and Bonnie Nardi. 2012. *Activity Theory in HCI: Fundamentals and Reflections*: Morgan & Claypool.

Kling, Rob. 2000. "Social Informatics: A New Perspective on Social Research about Information and Communication Technologies." *Prometheus* 18 (3):245-264.

Kling, Rob, Geoffrey McKim, and Adam King. 2003. "A Bit More to It: Scholarly Communication Forums as Socio-Technical Interaction Networks." *Journal of the American Society for Information Science and Technology* 54 (1):47-67.

Lamb, Roberta, and Rob Kling. 2003. "Reconceptualizing Users as Social Actors in Information Systems Research." *MIS Quarterly* 27 (2):197-197.

Lessard, Lysanne, and Eric Yu. 2012. "Using Design Science Research to Develop a Modeling Technique for Service Design." In *DESRIST 2012, LNCS*, edited by K. Peffers, M. Rothenberger and Kuechler B., 66-77. Heidelberg: Springer.

Lessard, Lysanne, and Eric Yu. 2013. "Service Systems Design: An Intentional Agent Perspective." *Human Factors and Ergonomics in*

Manufacturing & Service Industries. 23 (1), 68-75. doi:10.1002/hfm.20513.

Maier, Ronald, Thomas Hädrich, and René Peinl. 2009. *Enterprise Knowledge Infrastructures*. Berlin: Springer.

Maxwell, Joseph A. 2012. *A Realist Approach for Qualitative Research*. Thousand Oaks: Sage.

Meyer, Eric T. 2006. "Socio-Technical Interaction Networks: A Discussion of the Strengths, Weaknesses and Future of Kling's STIN Model." In *Social Informatics: An Information Society for all? In Remembrance of Rob Kling*, edited by Jacques Berleur, MarkkuI Nurminen and John Impagliazzo, 37-48. Boston: Springer.

Mingers, J. 2004. "Real-izing Information Systems: Critical Realism as an Underpinning Philosophy for Information Systems." *Information and Organization* 14 (2):87-103.

Orlikowski, Wanda J., and C. Suzanne Iacono. 2001. "Research Commentary: Desperately Seeking the "IT" in IT Research – A Call to Theorizing the IT Artifact." *Information Systems Research* 12 (2):121-134.

Sawyer, Steve, and Howard Rosenbaum. 2000. "Social Informatics in the Information Sciences: Current Activities and Emerging Directions." *Informing Science: the International Journal of an Emerging Transdiscipline* 3 (2):85-95.

Sawyer, Steve, and Michael Tyworth. 2006. "Social Informatics: Principles, Theory, and Practice." In *Social Informatics: An Information Society for all? In Remembrance of Rob Kling*, edited by Jacques Berleur, MarkkuI Nurminen and John Impagliazzo, 49-62. Boston: Springer.

Sayer, Andrew R. 2010. *Method in Social Science: A Realist Approach*. 2nd ed. New York: Routledge.

Star, Susan Leigh, and Karen Ruhleder. 1996. "Steps Toward an Ecology of Infrastructure: Design and Access for Large Information Spaces." *Information Systems Research* 7 (1):111-134.

Strong, Diane M., and Olga Volkoff. 2010. "Understanding Organization-enterprise System Fit: A Path to Theorizing the Information Technology Artifact." *MIS Quarterly: Management Information Systems* 34 (4):731-756.

van Aken, Joan E. 2004. "Management Research Based on the Paradigm of the Design Sciences: The Quest for Field-Tested and Grounded Technological Rules." *Journal of Management Studies* 41 (2):219-246.

Volkoff, Olga, Diane M. Strong, and Michael B. Elmes. 2007. "Technological embeddedness and organizational change." *Organization Science* 18 (5):832-848.

Yu, Eric. 2009. "Social Modeling and i*." In *Conceptual Modeling: Foundations and Applications – Essays in Honor of John Mylopoulos,* edited by Alex T. Borgida, Vinay Chaudhri, Paolo Giorgini, and Eric S. Yu, 99-121. Berlin Heidelberg: Springer.

CHAPTER NINE

PROJECTS AND OBJECTS: POINTS OF CONTACT BETWEEN TEXTUAL STUDIES AND SOCIOTECHNICAL INVESTIGATIONS

GRANT LEYTON SIMPSON

Technological objects are both cultural artifacts and the products of research (or creative activity) in action. In studying them, it therefore makes sense to employ discourses that engage them in both of these aspects, i.e., as artifacts designed, produced, and situated within cultural and technical contexts, and as objects embedded in assemblages engaged in their use, making, and re-making. No single discourse aligns perfectly with both aspects and so it seems necessary to employ the tools of disparate fields. Yet it is often possible that the tools of fields that have not previously overlapped in any significant way – fields we may expect to have different priorities, goals, purviews, and inquiry objects – can be made to work together. Toward that end, I explore a critical approach to the investigation of sociotechnical production and use that makes use of the material semiotics associated with the actor-network approach (also called Actor-Network Theory, or ANT), elements of the critical and analytical strains of Social Informatics (SI), and insights associated with bibliography and textual criticism, often called textual studies (Kirschenbaum 2008). The present article sketches out one hybrid approach to the study of particular kinds of sociotechnical artifacts. It represents an inclusive multidisciplinarity that allows for the possibility of bringing the humanities, including new media studies and certain forms of digital humanities (DH), into the SI discourse. While SI's adherents – and sociotechnical researchers in general – comprise a wide range of researchers in the physical and social sciences, its purchase into the humanities has been virtually nonexistent. However, if the discourse of SI is to incorporate the lines of thought that Kling sketched out toward the end of his career (Day 2007), the future of SI must provide a space for humanistic inquiry.

The Necessity of a Critical Informatics

SI, in the words of Kling (2000, 218), is the "interdisciplinary study of the design, uses, and consequences of information technologies that takes into account their interaction with institutional and cultural contexts." Particularly in the analysis of consequences, SI attempts to address shortcomings, originating in "oversimplified conceptions of the relationship between technologies and social change," in "the writing about the social changes that … new information and communication technologies (ICTs) will or could catalyze" (Kling 2000, 217). It thus rejects technological determinism in favor of "contingency," "context," and "nuance" (Kling 2000, 217–219).

SI has three modes of operation: normative, analytical, and critical (Kling, Rosenbaum, and Sawyer 2005). The normative approach consists of advocacy for changes to ICT design and implementation, while the analytical approach consists of theory-making and gathering data that lead to the induction of theory. In contrast, "The *critical orientation* refers to examining ICTs from perspectives that do not automatically and uncritically accept the goals and beliefs of the groups that commission, design, or implement specific ICTs" (Kling, Rosenbaum, and Sawyer 2005, 6). Day (2007), in an evaluation of the critical orientation in Kling's work, argues that the concept of "the critical" lies at the heart of the SI program. Indeed, given that Kling's work developed in opposition to the unrestrained hyperbole of early artificial intelligence research (King, Iacono, and Grudin 2007), it is hard to conceive of normative or analytical SI work in the Kling tradition that is not in some respect built upon the kernel of critical opposition to naïve views of sociotechnical dynamics.

Though the adjective "critical" is often understood as synonymous with "negative," it is often more useful to understand criticism as an orientation toward an object-of-inquiry that exercises analysis and informed judgment in the service of description, explanation, and theory-building. Criticism employs value judgments, as Eagleton (1996, 11) argues, but it need not be negative or excessively confrontational. In the context of sociotechnical analysis,

> The importance of a critical analysis is to bring into question established social assumptions and values regarding information and communication technologies (ICTs) and established understandings of "information,"

particularly as they play themselves out and are institutionalized in social and professional discourses and professional training. (Day 2007, 575)

Such "bring[ing] into question" is a principal motive and dominant motif of many acts of criticism. Furthermore, it is the goal of a critically-minded program of SI research: SI, as an intellectual approach, whether normative, analytical, or critical, seeks to defamiliarize[1] the technical object by situating it within its assemblage of sociotechnical actors – both human and nonhuman – who contribute to its meaning, interpretation, and avenues of use. This process of defamiliarization deflates the descriptive potential of the so-called discrete-entity model of technology (the "standard model" as Kling et al. (2003) call it) by demonstrating the numerous interstitial connections between humans and nonhumans surrounding a given entity, all of which mark potential points of interaction, control, and meaning-making.

SI's methodological agnosticism allows for a multitude of potential paths for engaging in such a critical project. One such path may be the exercise of criticism. Though work in the SI vein tends toward data-oriented empirical analyses, Day (2007, 579), in a reading of Kling's oeuvre, argues for the possibility of alternative forms of SI work:

> ... if we are to take all of Kling's writing into account, and to take seriously his – and others' claim – that social informatics is empirically based, we would have to include those nonquantitative, non-problem-driven and non-data-driven, conceptual, interpretative, and historical approaches more commonly found in the humanities and the qualitative social sciences. Such approaches are based on cultural materials (foremost, language), and they involve conceptual, interpretative analyses.

Such an inclusion provides the researcher with a wealth of analytical tools employable in the investigation of the ideological conditions that allow the discrete-entity model to present itself as natural, non-ideological, and uncontroversial. The "non-problem-driven" nature of such work allows for analyses that cannot adequately be problematized under the protocols of observational or (quasi-)experimental research.

---

[1] Defamiliarization is the act of taking the familiar and portraying it in a fashion that allows us to experience or understand it in an unfamiliar way. The term originated in Shklovsky (1991), who held that the purpose of art was to make things seem unfamiliar. Recently Bell et al. (2005) have proposed the use of defamiliarization in Human-Computer Interaction (HCI) research.

Textual Studies: The Challenge of New Forms and the Sociology of Texts

Bibliography and textual criticism "should be recognized as among the most sophisticated branches of media studies we have evolved" (Kirschenbaum 2008, 16). Contemporary theorists, such as McKenzie (1999) and McGann (2004) have argued for the application of these disciplines (together often called "textual studies") to a broad range of electronic artifacts. "Text" and "book" have unstable and capacious definitions, a fact that has been leveraged in the service of widening the inquiry objects toward which textual studies may be directed. As Derrida (2005, 4) points out, the concept of the book is not coextensive with writing, inscription, technologies of print, or particular kinds of material manifestation. "Book" intersects with each of these but cannot be reduced to any of them. Furthermore, contemporary bibliography does not study the book alone. Bibliography, according McKenzie (1999, 12), "is the discipline that studies texts as recorded forms, and the processes of their transmission, including their production and reception." Such a field, as the "biblio" in bibliography implies, might seem to apply only to a very limited subset of items. McKenzie's definition of "texts," however, is quite expansive:

> I define 'texts' to include verbal, visual, oral, and numeric data, in the form of maps, prints, and music, of archives of recorded sound, of films, videos, and any computer-stored information, everything in fact from epigraphy to the latest forms of discography. There is no evading the challenge which those new forms have created. (McKenzie 1999, 13)

Thus, "text" expands to include everything having to do with technologies of inscription, material manifestation, and the social practices that surround them and "book," though including these very things, is not coextensive with them. This accounts for some of the terminological confusion one encounters when making sense of the related scholarly practices known as "bibliography," "textual criticism," "textual bibliography," and "textual studies."

McKenzie's broad definition of bibliography gracefully establishes textual criticism as a form of bibliography, a connection that, if we are to give textual criticism its full due as a field that studies a broad range of historical texts and that has, where needed, connections to philological and technological protocols, must be predicated upon a capacious definition of a sort of artifact studies. This sort of study, for genealogical reasons, is called bibliography. Furthermore, it allows for a connection to the study of meaning and hence to literary criticism:

> [It] frankly accepts that bibliographers should be concerned to show that forms effect meaning. Beyond that, it allows us to describe not only the technical but the social processes of their transmission. In those quite specific ways, it accounts for non-book texts, their physical forms, textual versions, technical transmission, institutional control, their perceived meanings, and social effects. It accounts for a history of the book and, indeed, of all printed forms including all textual ephemera as a record of cultural change, whether in mass civilization or minority culture. ... But such a phrase also accommodates what in recent critical theory is often called text production, and it therefore opens up the application of the discipline to the service of that field too. (McKenzie 1999, 13)

McKenzie calls this approach the sociology of texts. The implication is that bibliographers must recognize the complex relations between books, authors, editors, printers, booksellers, readers, reviewers, fans, detractors, and so forth. Shillingsburg (2011, 17) writes that McKenzie's "insights ... were enormously important in bringing together bibliography and sociology in the new field of book history."

Material Semiotics and the Sociology of Translation

In material semiotics, we find one way to develop an approach to the sociology of texts. Material semiotics (Latour 1988; Latour 1996b; Akrich and Latour 1994) is a form of narrative description that owes its lineage in part to Greimas (1983). That is, it is a narratologically inclined method translated from a version of Greimasian structural semantics.[2] Latour (1988, 11) briefly defines the method of his sociological study, *The Pasteurization of France,* as "simply in following all these translations, drifts, and diversions as they are made by the writers of the period. ... [T]he semiotic method is here limited to the interdefinition of actors and to the chains of translations." The phrase "translations, drifts, and diversions" indicates material semiotics' indebtedness to the sociology of translation, the keys of which are the principles of (Callon 1986, 196)

> ... agnosticism (impartiality between actors engaged in controversy), generalised symmetry (the commitment to explain conflicting viewpoints

[2] It is probably best to regard Latour's version of material semiotics as peculiar to him, as it removes the semantics from Greimas's structural semantics.

in the same terms) and free association (the abandonment of all a priori distinctions between the natural and the social)

ANT, whether identified as material semiotics or the sociology of translation, makes of these three principles a strategy for the explication of networks of human-nonhuman interaction. In fact, Callon (1986, 230) "proposed the concept of the actor-network" precisely to "describe the network of constraints and resources that results from a series of operations of translation."

The principle of generalized symmetry requires that we be able to discuss projects and their objects, in our case, texts, in the same terms. The fact that, for ANT, semiotics is a descriptive but not hermeneutic exercise enables our efforts toward this end. When Latour (1988) remarks of a "limited" use of semiotics, the limits he places on himself refer more to his unwillingness to relegate the act of interpretation to the analysis of meaning, in favor of letting the web of connections in his primary sources make their connections known in their own terms. With regard to what he takes to be the purview of semiotics, the result is expansion rather than limitation. As he remarks in a later essay (Latour 1996b, 10),

> It is only because semioticians studied texts – and literary ones at that – instead of things, that they felt obliged to limit themselves to 'meaning.' … But a semiotics of things is easy, one simply has to drop the meaning bit from semiotics.

The issue becomes one of trajectory rather than meaning, one of "path-building, or order-making, or creation of directions." Semiotics in the vein of Barthes, Latour argues, engages in needless reduction that results in the loss of specificity for the thing reduced.[3] "A follower of Roland Barthes," he says (1988, 163), "tries to turn everything not only into texts but into signifiers alone." His resistance to reduction is indicative of his project to level the playing field between actors (also called "actants," "entelechies," and "weaknesses"), that is, to avoid prejudging the situation by valorizing language or text. (This is an example not only of the principle of generalized symmetry but also of the principle of free association, insofar

[3] Saussure's thinking about linguistics necessarily informed his thinking about semiology (his name for semiotics); linguistics was in many ways Saussure's synecdoche *par excellence* for the new science of signs. Even so, at least according to the "broad view" (Deely 2005 163) of semiology he advanced (he elsewhere takes a "narrow view"), Saussure makes it clear that linguistics is a field within the field of semiology. As Deely notes, Barthes inverted this relationship, turning the linguistic sign into the abstract model for all signs.

as language and text is often understood as *a priori* social.) "What those who use hermeneutics, exegesis, or semiotics say of texts," Latour (1988, 166) says, applies to all actants. There is a great deal of similarity between this move – that of extending the interpretive enterprise to objects – and McKenzie's move to apply bibliography to non-book texts. Latour continues:

> For a long time it has been agreed that the relationship between one text and another is always a matter for interpretation. Why not accept that this is also true between so-called texts and so-called objects, and even between so-called objects themselves?

If "text" and "object" are two different terms and we assume that relationships may be asymmetrical, then there are four interpretable relationships entailed here. Texts relate to texts. Texts relate to objects. Objects relate to texts. Objects relate to objects. The first relationship is by all means uncontroversial insofar as textual scholarship is concerned. The second relationship is made possible by McKenzie's capacious definition of bibliography. The third relationship, object to text, is one we encounter regularly. A cake-object, for example, relates to a recipe-text in a fashion that is interpretable (and, as anyone who has made a cake that does not look like the picture in the recipe knows, this relationship is mediated by a variety of environmental factors). Finally, object-object relationships, among other things, furnish the subject matter of classical mechanics.[4] We would expect material semiotics to account for all four of these types of relationships, from intertextual ones to interobjective ones. In Latour's (1996b, 9) definition, "semiotics is a method to describe the generative path of any narration." It is through this definition that he comes to an application of semiotics to things.

Bibliography, i.e. the sociology of texts as we have construed it here, following McKenzie, and ANT, i.e. the sociology of translation, share a focus in opening up black boxes. A black box is any entity, physical or ideational, that seems for all intents and purposes sealed, that presents a reasonably clear separation between its inside and outside and is thus distinguishable from other entities. These black boxes can of course be opened and examined. Harman (2009, 34) explicates the metaphysical implications of the concept of black boxes, complete with their situational

---

[4] As Harman (2009, 124) remarks, a "Latourian physics is conceivable" thanks to the fact that "his global focus on actors allows for a possible treatment of inanimate bodies by the same set of rules that are used to describe human translations."

solidity and separability, i.e. their use as a tool against interpretive reduction:

> Instead of a privileged layer of pampered natural substances, we now have a world made up of manifold layers, none more unified or natural than any other. Every actant can be viewed either as a black box or as a multitudinous network, depending on the situation. … Even a chaotic or multifarious actant can appear solid under the right circumstances; by the same token, any supposed black box can be unpacked, and its components rearranged or challenged.[5]

We continually (and perhaps *continuously*) negotiate such democratic levels in our daily lives; with a high degree of fluency, we engage with, for example, paper money, currency in the abstract, physical banks, networks of banks, the concept of banking, the discipline of economics, the domestic and global economies, credit cards, the idea of credit, bank tellers, ATMs, and electrons passing through banking infrastructure. But the paper of paper money and the discipline of economics, while both black boxes, inhabit different levels. It is through blackboxing – that is, through bracketing off the complexity of objects and concerning ourselves with inputs and outputs, such as money going in and out of a bank – that we negotiate such levels.

Entities seem simple because we habitually treat them that way. As Harman (2009, 36) notes,

> … actants are not ready-made essences that happen to stumble into relations every now and then. An actant is always born from crisis and controversy; only when it succeeds in establishing a foothold in the world do we forget the tribulations of its birth and eventually treat it as a seamless black box.

This fact is equally true of computers as it is of humans. Just as the computer engineer and programmer can open up the black box (either figuratively or literally) and engage with it in processes of investigation and reconfiguration, so too can the psychologist, the surgeon, the anthropologist, and the tattoo artist open up the human black box (again, either figuratively and literally). It is in the investigation of the black box that what is familiar (the human, the computer) becomes radically

---

[5] Of course, to say this *can* be done does not mean that it is always advisable to do so. As Harman (2009, 36) muses, "Thank God we do not do this for all actants at every moment; thank God we are ignorant of the turbulent details and razor-thin margin of victory in the love story of our parents."

defamiliarized. The computer becomes, among other things, a set of printed circuit board assemblies. The human becomes an object of abjection: among other things, a collection of tissue, blood, and nerves. Yet neither of these things is reducible to what it seems to be when it is investigated (Latour 1988, 158).

The complexity of objects-in-the-world and their indeterminate membership to various democratic levels means that we must cast a wide net when it comes to what we accept to be our inquiry objects. Indeed, Day (2007, 576) notes just such a casting in his discussion of the "inexactness" of the objects Kling studied:

> Over the course of Kling's oeuvre one can witness the morphing of the material objects of his concern from that of computers, per se, to information technologies, and then to information and computer technologies (ICTs). The inexactness of the technical object of what would become the central concern for social informatics not only reflects the morphing of social-technological roles for digital computers during this period, but also suggests two points that Kling's work does not: first, that the empirical objects of social informatics can be as much conceptual constructs as empirical entities, and second, that social informatics's central concern is the examination of the notion of information as a culturally and historically specific conception of knowledge.

Conclusion

There is a sort of project-object duality inherent in what we call technological objects, one akin to the particle-wave duality posited by modern optics. As Latour (1996a, 24) writes,

> In the beginning, there is no distinction between projects and objects. The two circulate from office to office in the form of paper, plans, departmental memos, speeches, scale models, and occasional synopses. Here we're in the realm of signs, language, texts. … The observer of technologies has to be very careful not to differentiate too hastily between signs and things, between projects and objects, between fiction and reality, between a novel about feelings and what is inscribed in the nature of things. In fact, the engineers the observer is studying pass progressively from one of these sets to another.[6]

[6] Though Latour speaks of the situation "in the beginning," this formulation is too limited and does not adequately address the nature of projects that are ongoing or are supported for some time after the production of the object. In these cases, too,

For the observer, like the engineer, to "pass progressively" between project and object is to recognize the productiveness in both approaches and the necessity of considering them both. As with optics, in which favoring either wave or particle results in an incomplete view of the phenomena at hand, favoring either project or object will result in a biased account. SI, ANT, and the sociology of texts are all valuable ways of problematizing discrete entity models. But, as textual studies have aptly demonstrated through numerous studies of artifacts, the "object" is itself a black box whose existence is contingent upon countless conditions. Thus our accounts of sociotechnical assemblages need not shy away from accounts of objects as objects, provided they understand them to be inherently complicated black boxes. Accounts of objects provided by disciplines such as textual studies can provide valuable evidence for SI work and, ultimately, enhance the richness of our descriptions of sociotechnical systems and the social and cultural contexts.

As I hinted at the outset, if SI is to embrace its critical legacy, it would do well to find ways to span the boundaries between its traditional foothold in the sciences and social sciences and its future colleagues in the humanities. This falls under our collective responsibility to share SI work with a variety of audiences. Kling et al. (2005, 133-134) articulate this responsibility in terms of awareness, money, legitimacy, and growing the pool of researchers and ideas:

> Social Informatics research should also be communicated to research communities across a range of academic disciplines that share a focus on the social contexts of computing … Regular and pervasive communication of research is an important component in raising awareness among academic researchers about the themes, insights, and findings of SI. … This effort is necessary to legitimize SI among the wider academic community and bring its concerns to the attention of potential funders of this research. It can also help to grow the SI community, as researchers and teachers outside of SI begin to learn more about the field and to explicitly identify themselves as belonging to the community. Many ICT-oriented disciplines already have researchers who are investigating questions and problems that characterize SI. Strategies are needed to bring their work to the attention of their colleagues and to cross-pollinate their disciplines with relevant research from other disciplines.

Boundary spanning is a difficult endeavor – one that will most likely come about in terms of fits and starts. It is my hope that the present work

---

the sorts of artifacts Latour describes passing between offices continue to be created and disseminated.

contributes in a small way toward both the fields of SI and textual studies, as well as to the fits and starts of tying together two conversations about ICT.

To be sure, there has never been a better time for such cross-pollination with the humanities. With the advent of DH, there has been widespread debate – healthy and productive debate to be sure – about just what technology means to the disciplines involved in humanistic inquiry.[7] Latour's appearance as the keynote speaker for DH 2014 in Lausanne demonstrates just how important this conversation has become. DH, especially in the forms practiced by Kirschenbaum (2008), Liu (2004; 2013), Jones (2013), and Hayles (2012), and new media studies, typified by Gitelman (2008), Kittler (1999), and Parikka (2012), have primed scholars in fields as varied as English, art history, cultural studies, and philosophy, to name a few, for thinking about the use and making of technologies as a human activity. They have shown that, if we are to take the term "humanities" at face value, then we must take seriously the technical artifacts made and used by humans. But this line of inquiry must be pushed further. We cannot construe the human-technology relationship as a strict dichotomy between a human subject and a technological object. Those boundaries are rather more porous for, as Haraway (1991) and Clark (1998) have demonstrated, technology is a critical part of the functioning human apparatus. The pacemakers we gain are no less a part of us than were the baby teeth we lost. Technology lives with us, within us, and it mediates our connections to each other and ourselves. The critical strain of SI, which takes for granted a complex, non-deterministic relationship between culture, institutions, people, and technologies, can help provide empirical and theoretical support for a nuanced humanistic approach to the study of technology, just as humanities disciplines can add to the plethora of methodologies and theoretical orientations available to sociotechnical researchers.

References

Akrich, Madeleine, and Bruno Latour. 1994. "A Summary of a convenient Vocabulary for the Semiotics of Human and Nonhuman Assemblies." In *Shaping Technology/Building Society: Studies in Sociotechnical Change*, edited by Wiebe E. Bijker and John Law, 259–264. Cambridge, MA: MIT Press.

[7] See, for example, Gold (2012), *Debates in the Digital Humanities.*

Bell, Genevieve, Mark Blythe, and Phoebe Sengers. 2005. "Making by Making Strange: Defamiliarization and the Design of Domestic Technologies." *ACM Transactions on Human-Computer Interaction.* 12 (2): 149–173. doi:10.1145/1067860.1067862.

Callon, Michel. 1986. "Some Elements of a Sociology of Translation." In *Power, Action, and Belief: A New Sociology of Knowledge?*, edited by John Law, 196–233. London: Routledge & Kegan Paul.

Day, Ronald E. 2007. "Kling and the 'Critical': Social Informatics and Critical Informatics." *Journal of the American Society for Information Science and Technology.* 58 (4): 575–582. doi:10.1002/asi.v58:4.

Deely, John N. 2005. *Basics of semiotics/Semiootika alused.* Tartu: Tartu University Press.

Derrida, Jacques. 2005. *Paper Machine.* Stanford: Stanford University Press.

Eagleton, Terry. 1996. *Literary Theory: An Introduction.* University of Minnesota Press.

Gitelman, L. (2008). *Always already new: media, history and the data of culture.* Cambridge, MA: MIT.

Gold, Matthew K., ed. 2012. *Debates in the Digital Humanities.* University of Minnesota Press.

Greimas, Algirdas. 1983. *Structural Semantics : an Attempt at a Method.* Lincoln: University of Nebraska Press.

Harman, Graham. 2009. *Prince of Networks: Bruno Latour and Metaphysics.* Melbourne: re.press. http://www.re-press.org/book-files/OA_Version_780980544060_Prince_of_Networks.pdf.

Hayles, K. (2012). *How we think: digital media and contemporary technogenesis.* Chicago ; London: The University of Chicago Press.

Jones, S. E. (2013). *The emergence of the digital humanities.* London: Routledge.

King, John Leslie, Suzanne Iacono, and Jonathan Grudin. 2007. "Going Critical: Perspective and Proportion in the Epistemology of Rob Kling 1." *The Information Society* 23 (4): 251–262. doi: 10.1080/01972240701444170.

Kirschenbaum, Matthew. 2008. *Mechanisms : New Media and the Forensic Imagination.* Cambridge, MA.: MIT Press.

Kittler, F. (1999). *Gramophone, film, typewriter.* (G. Winthrop-Young & M. Wutz, Trans.). Stanford Calif.: Stanford University Press.

Kling, Rob. 2000. "Learning About Information Technologies and Social Change: The Contribution of Social Informatics." *The Information Society* 16: 217–232. doi:10.1080/01972240050133661.

Kling, Rob, Geoffrey McKim, and Adam King. 2003. "A Bit More to It: Scholarly Communication Forums as Socio-Technical Interaction Networks." *Journal of the American Society for Information Science and Technology* 54 (1): 47–67. doi:10.1002/asi.10154.

Kling, Rob, Howard Rosenbaum, and Steve Sawyer, ed. 2005. *Understanding and Communicating Social Informatics : a Framework for Studying and Teaching the Human Contexts of Information and Communication Technologies*. Medford N.J.: Information Today Inc.

Latour, Bruno. 1988. *The pasteurization of France*. Cambridge, MA.: Harvard University Press.

—. 1996a. *Aramis, or, The Love of Technology*. Cambridge, MA.: Harvard University Press.

—. 1996b. "The Trouble with Actor-Network Theory".

Liu, A. (2004). *The laws of cool : knowledge work and the culture of information*. Chicago: University of Chicago Press.

—. (2013). The Meaning of the Digital Humanities. *PMLA*, *128*(2), 409–423.

McGann, Jerome. 2004. *Radiant Textuality : Literature After the World Wide Web*. New York: Palgrave.

McKenzie, D. F. 1999. *Bibliography and the Sociology of Texts*. Cambridge University Press.

Parikka, J. (2012). *What is media archaeology?* Cambridge, UK; Malden, MA: Polity Press.

Shillingsburg, Peter. 2011. "The Semiotics of Bibliography." *Textual Cultures: Texts, Contexts, Interpretation* 6 (1): 1125.

Shklovsky, Victor. 1991. *Theory of Prose*. Translated by Benjamin Sher. Dalkey Archive Press.

CHAPTER TEN

TURNING TO THE PRACTICE APPROACH IN SOCIAL INFORMATICS

ANDREW COX

Abstract

This theoretical chapter explores the potential of a turn to the practice approach for Social Informatics (SI). It begins by exploring the character of the practice approach as social theory and its influence on information science to date. The practice approach's theoretical preoccupations are then explored under the headings of materiality and embodiment; process, routine, and change; social construction and social identity; and knowing. A case study of food blogging illustrates these themes with particular reference to the use of computers. An evaluation of the approach for SI considers how it potentially aligns with other social sciences and reflects contemporary trends in the character of computer use. However, the paper also recognizes a problem shared with SI in terms of criticality.

Introduction

SI is a widely accepted term within information science for the study of the "design, uses, and consequences" of IT use in context (Kling 1999; Sawyer and Rosenbaum 2000). Its strengths lie in its sensitivity to the unexpected and unplanned aspects of the introduction and use of computers, combined with a strong awareness of the way that the meanings of technologies are discursively constructed. It is critical in challenging taken for granted assumptions, but is also practical and empirical. Particularly because of its interdisciplinary or transdisciplinary character, SI should be open to new wider currents in social science, e.g. in social theory.

At the beginning of the new century, Schatzki, Cetina, and Savigny (2001) identified a turn to practice across the social sciences. The turn seems to be accelerating in organization studies (Gherardi 2012; Niciolini 2013), media studies (Postill 2010), consumption studies (Shove, Pantzar, and Watson 2012) and education (Trowler, Saunders, and Bamber 2012). Much of this work parallels the interest of SI in the adoption and use of ICTs. There is also now a range of work in information science that employs the latest practice thinking, often drawing on Schatzki's own work for a philosophical foundation. The purpose of this theoretical paper is to explore the relation and potential synergies between the practice approach and SI. It begins by summarizing the past origin and current influences of the practice approach, then, through an exploration of its main preoccupations as a body of theory and an extended application to an example from social media (food blogging), the paper develops the basis for a forward looking evaluation of its use in SI.

Historical Overview

The intellectual sources for the practice approach are commonly regarded to be Wittgenstein, Giddens, and Bourdieu (Postill 2010; Reckwitz 2002). For Reckwitz (2002) at a philosophical level the practice approach is a form of cultural theory, as opposed to other social theories that privilege either individual purposes (micro) or social norms (macro). Among cultural theories it is distinguished by its focus on practices as blocks of bodily actions and conventionalized ways of understanding, knowing, and desiring, rather than on minds, texts, conversation, or interaction. The turn (Schatzki, Cetina, and Savigny 2001) or re-turn to practice (Huizing and Cavanagh 2010) by a second generation of theorists increasingly has the work of the philosopher Schatzki (2001; 2002) at its core. Schatzki (2002) offers a clear philosophical positioning of the practice approach relative to alternative philosophies, an explicit definition of practice and the concept of the site as a way to conceptualize how the same practice can take on a different character in different contexts.

Originating prior to Schatzki, Cetina, and Savigny's (2001) recognition of the practice turn, the community of practice concept has been one of the more influential ideas to come from the practice approach (Lave and Wenger 1991; Wenger 1998). As well as being popular as a practical management tool or strategy, this concept was probably the context within which information science first encountered second generation practice thinking, though it has been much criticized at a theoretical level (Contu and Willmott 2003; Cox 2005; Østerlund and Carlile 2005; Roberts 2006). For those in information science working in the knowledge management area Lave's earlier situated learning theory (Talja 2010), Lave and Wenger

(1991), with Brown and Duguid (2001) remain key reference points. Gherardi's writing through the last decade has developed the practice approach while moving away from the community concept (2008; 2009a; 2009b; 2009c; Corradi, Gherardi, and Verzelloni 2010; 2012). While Nicolini's (2009; 2011) writing has also recently offered a convincing methodological framework for exploring a social site.

For some of those working in the "information behavior" field, the term "scholarly information practice" has come into favor to reflect a shift, influenced by Science and Technology Studies, away from a narrower focus on the study of seeking for secondary literature, to a wider understanding of information activities throughout the research process (Palmer and Cragin 2008). Some writers in this area explicitly reference Schatzki's definition of practice (e.g., Pilerot and Limberg 2011). Prior to this, Mckenzie (2003) used the term "practice," with a stress on the discursive construction of the meaning of information. Savolainen (2007) was the first to propose "information practice" as a preferred umbrella term to "information behavior", though his full development of the concept has its problems as a realization of the practice approach (Savolainen 2008). Lloyd (2009; 2010a; 2010b) has whole-heartedly engaged with Schatzki (2002) to develop her conceptualization of information literacy as an information practice that is quite different on different sites. A growing trickle of other empirical work references the theoretical resources of the practice approach (e.g., Veinot 2007; Haider 2011; 2012; Cox 2012).

Also in the new century, in the field of information systems and socio-technical studies, Orlikowski (2000; 2007; 2009; Feldman and Orlikowski 2011) has used the practice approach to rethink the longstanding debate in information systems and organizational thinking around the rival conceptions of technological determinism and the social shaping of technology. Orlikowski (2000) examines how the meaning and impact of a technology is not pre-given. Rather, how users establish conventions of its use is central to how a technology's affordances are enacted, and in turn these conventions embedded in the technology-in-practice then shape human behavior. This subtle understanding of the ongoing interplay of technology and action is further developed in the concept of sociomateriality (Orlikowski 2007; 2009). Through this concept Orlikowski seeks, by adopting a relational conceptualization of the nature of entities from practice theory, to avoid the weaknesses of seeing technology as an exogenous force but also the weaknesses of seeing technologies' meaning emerging from the interplay of human interpretation. In sociomateriality it is recognized that technologies, like all entities, take their meanings from a nexus of relations to other entities, so it makes no sense either to see technology as pre-given reshaping action (tending to technological determinism) or to see technology as shaped more by humans (which underplays the independence of the technology). The meanings of technology, but also of any object or entity, including people, all arise from their mutual relations. For several authors relational thinking in practice theory is a central feature of its potential value (Osterlund and Carlile 2005; Huizing and Cavanagh 2011).

Taken together, this literature constitutes a significant body of work in information science to mirror turns to practice in cognate social scientific disciplines. In order to understand how the practice approach might be used within SI, the following sections outline its main preoccupations and develop an exemplary analysis in some depth.

The Four Preoccupations of the Practice Approach

A number of characterizations of the second generation practice approach are available (e.g. Geiger 2009; Huizing and Cavanagh 2010: Niciolini 2009; Shove, Pantzar, and Watson 2012), but this paper will explore its main themes through identifying four inter-connected preoccupations that suffuse practice approach thinking (Cox 2012).

Materiality and Embodiment

Schatzki (2002, 72) defines the basic unit of activity in social practice as "bodily doings and sayings". His reference to "doings" reflects the practice approach's focus on concrete activity in the material world, while the definition also recognizes the performative nature of saying or not saying things. The importance of the human body in the practice approach is reflected in Reckwitz's definition of practice as "the regular, skilful 'performance' of (human) bodies" (2002, 251) and Postill's description of practice theories as "a body of work about the work of the body" (2010, 11). The turn to practice is away from privileging mental, especially cognitive states, including rationally driven behavior, and towards a concern with bodily action, skills, and habits. Furthermore, practices shape how we use our bodies and in so doing have a role in defining our sense of our own bodies, hence the theory's concern with "the socialized, inscribed, trained, habituated, and conditioned sentient human body" (Nicolini, Gherardi, and Yanow 2003, 13). Lloyd (2010b) points to the way that the role of the body in information seeking and literacy has been neglected in much previous work in information science, which tends to privilege textual and other encoded knowledge. In the practice approach the activities of the human body in a material world of objects (including ICTs) in physical space is central. The influence of Actor Network Theory is also felt in a recognition of the agentic or at least agent-like capabilities of non-human things (Huizing and Cavanagh 2011).

Process, Routine, and Change

The activities that make up the performance of a practice are played out in time and space. Thus process is a central concern of the practice approach (Geiger 2009). A practice commonly implies a temporal rhythm of activities of bodies and uses of objects in particular spaces. In first generation practice thinking there is a concern with mundane and everyday activity. Reckwitz (2002) emphasizes routines and routinization as aspects of practice. When practices are tied up in objects and habits, they disappear into the background, having a powerful invisible effect to shape future action or (in)action (Haider 2012). Bourdieu's concept of habitus extends this idea to recognize that ways of thinking and acting may be so ingrained that they constitute the often unremarked expectations that shape responses to new and different contexts.

Second generation practice theory tends to place a stronger emphasis on the open-ended rather than routine quality of practice. Although there is a pre-given recipe for a practice, this only has a reality when it is "enacted" (Orlikowski 2000) or actively accomplished. In looking at how routines do themselves contain the material for change and adaptation, Feldman and Pentland (2003) refer to ostensive and performative aspects. The ostensive routine is the recipe for action, but adapting to circumstances is built into such rules, so that actual performances may be quite different. In Schatzki (2002) the complexity of the nexus of elements of practices and social order lead to constant mutation. A preoccupation with the gap between theory and practice, between espoused theory and theory-in-use (Argyris and Schön 1974), between what it is possible to document and the improvised reality of practice (Brown and Duguid 2001; Nicolini 2009) are recurrent concerns of the practice approach.

Social Construction and Social Identity

Practices constitute pre-given social conventions within which we learn and operate. Social actors have latitude within the pre-given recipe and can renegotiate the practice. Further it is in carrying through practices that we encounter and interact with others, though Schatzki stresses that practices are social not merely in the sense implied by interactivity. It seems agreed now that the problem with the "community of practice" concept lay in the overtones of warmth, consensus and self-consciousness associated with the word "community". Yet Wenger's (1998) stress on social identity may be useful. His exploration of our active negotiation of identity within the practice, our trajectory of involvement, our participation in multiple practices is one way to conceive of how subjects are constituted. Hodges (1998) offers a complementary theorization of the more dis-identificatory experiences of an encounter with a practice.

Knowing

The practice approach's view of knowing is anti-positivist, anti-cognitivist and anti-rationalist (Geiger 2009). Rather than seeing knowledge as of truth and facts it recognizes knowing as shaped through given practice arrangements and actively negotiated within the social conventions and material arrangements and activities of practices and sites. It does not privilege the reasoning mind over the body, senses, values, or aesthetics or rational decision making over culturally shaped ways of doing things. In keeping with its other preoccupations, knowing is not merely embrained or encoded in texts but can also be encultured through active social negotiation, embedded in routines, and embodied in people and in things (Blackler 1995). "Objects, tools and artifacts embody knowledge; they anchor practice in their materiality; they interrogate humans and are extensions of their memory" (Gherardi 2009b, 354). Knowing is local and, therefore, is also situated, historically contingent, a temporary accomplishment, and always being reshaped.

The other preoccupations of the practice approach are reflected in its conceptualization of knowing. Thus Nicolini summarizes knowing as "processual in nature, it is emergent and always in the making, it is inherently relational and dependent on a host of connections in time and space, it has as much to do with the body as it does with the 'mind', it is necessarily provisional and contestable, and it is mediated by artefacts and dependent on specific discursive and material conditions" (2011, 605).

Case Study: Food Blogging

The character of these theoretical preoccupations and their implications for the "design, uses, and consequences" of ICTs could be illustrated through any number of everyday activities. In this section of the chapter, food blogging (Cox and Blake 2010) will be used to give more of a flavor of how the practice approach could contribute to SI's focus on the design and uses of computers and the consequences of computer use.

A good way into this is through thinking about the process aspect of the practice approach. Each of the chains of activities assembled into food blogging has a complex composition. Thus Hartel (2006) describes the cycle of steps in a "gourmet cooking episode", as "exploring, planning, provisioning, prepping, assembling, cooking, serving, eating and evaluating". Probably the process is often less linear than this abstract model implies. Each step in the process is associated with different locations and material arrangements (the bookshelves, the shops, the kitchen, the dining room), many having an information aspect, e.g., combing for inspiration through one's collection of recipe books or bookmarks or combining ideas from a number of recipes when cooking. Foodies often have large collections of food related information, both material objects, like books and recipes, and digital material (Hartel 2010b; Elliot Sept 23, 2009). Thus at certain points the computer will be consulted.

The human body is central to these processes, in terms of the bodily movements involved in flicking through books of recipes or typing in Google, leaning over a simmering dish in a steamy kitchen or the decorous enjoyment of the final meal.

When the gourmet cook also has a food blog, there is an additional chain of activity and material arrangements specifically related to writing about food and maintaining and promoting the blog. For example, one interviewee in the Cox and Blake (2010) study talked about drafting a blog entry when planning the cooking, then editing the entry and adding a photo of the final dish (while curled up in front of the TV with their laptop), then publishing the page on Monday morning on their PC at work when they judged that the audience is most likely to notice a release, and finally responding to comments and reading other blogs to reciprocate commenters' interest. Twitter was popular among food bloggers, so this commenting activity might be picked up on a mobile device. Temporally, blog writing has a more extended character than the cooking episode itself (though making a meal is part of exploration of a particular subject and ultimately of a foodie career (Hartel 2010a)). Hartel represents the gourmet cooking episode as a cycle, but it is not so easy to see how evaluating leads back to exploring. In contrast, blogging naturally leads to exploration through responding to comments and looking at commenters' blogs, so blogging reinforces the cycle by bringing one naturally back to sources of inspiration for more "exploring."

Much food blogging includes photography as an integral element. Lorraine Elliot, on her blog *Not Quite Nigella* (Elliot 2009a), tells us "10 things you should know about food bloggers", among which are:

- Food bloggers need light for their food photos, so they must dine early and sit near a window;
- They may let the food get cold while taking photos;
- They may even want to photograph the bread and butter;
- When watching TV, the food blogger is puzzled by why soap opera characters do not take photos of their food.

In other such entries it is revealed that food blogging reshapes what pictures one takes on vacation and implies carrying extra lenses for the camera in the car to avoid the risk of missing a key photo (Elliot Sept. 23, 2009; Apr. 19, 2010). Researching food, taking notes during meals, and collecting recipe books are also unexpected aspects of food blogging, according to *Not Quite Nigella*.

Thus digital photography has certain very particular requirements itself which reshape the process of gourmet food activity, both temporally and spatially, such as when to dine and where to sit. Chalfren (1987) provides a more general framework for thinking about the different elements in the process of photographic practice. He identifies stages of planning, shooting, editing and exhibiting. Kirk et al. (2006), in their investigations of digital photo work, model the elaboration of organization and sharing activities arising from use of digital cameras and networking of computers. In food blogging, photos are taken, photos are selected and edited and added. There is a further element of trying to direct traffic from the photo sharing site to the blog. Complex personal information management challenges are involved in organizing the digital photo collection.

Thus each activity chain for cooking, blogging, and photography is complex. In food blogging the chaining is even more complex, since all these elements are being interwoven. Combining these activity chains can act as reinforcement, as with blogging bringing the foodie back to exploring. It can also be problematic at times, e.g., a kitchen is not a good place to have a computer and the light might be unsuitable for photography. So coordinating the elements of the process is a complex accomplishment that might fall apart if effort is not exerted. While much of food blogging (including computer use) is routinized, each particular episode is rather unique, and unfolds in a slightly different way, if only because of the complexity of the elements being assembled – just as, even following a recipe, dishes turn out subtly differently each time. Individuals practice food blogging differently (Warde 2005), and have an experience of creativity and self-actualization through the choices they make.

As well as observing the meshing of practices, we can zoom out to see how food blogging subtly reshapes other practices, such as what one does when traveling, what one carries with one in the car, interactions with friends, use of ICTs and experiences of the media (Elliot July 13, 2009; Sept. 23, 2009; Apr. 19, 2010).

Food blogging is social in the sense of being a place where we encounter others, e.g., sharing food with friends and family then connecting to fellow bloggers and wider audiences through the blog. It is also social in the sense that all the activity relies on social understandings such as the cultural significance of certain food practices or widely understood conventions of writing for blogs or of food writing and photographic conventions. Gourmet cooking may have slightly snobbish associations. Yet at least one interviewee in the Cox and Blake (2010) study actively contested this image, by the choice of eateries he reviewed and defiantly not checking grammar and spelling, concerns which he associated with social snobbery. There is always considerable play in how practices are performed making the material and activities a vehicle for negotiating social identity.

Understanding of the social conventions of writing about food is part of the knowing required to be a food blogger; as well as a vast range of practical knowing about ingredients, cooking processes, specialist language of menus (Elliot Apr. 19, 2010) basic computer use, social media conventions and taking or editing photos.

To reflect on the central aspect for SI – the design, uses, and consequences of ICTs – computers do play a complex and important part in the shaping and reshaping of a practice like food blogging. However, it would be misleading to think in terms of a process of "computerization", because it is not a process of a pre-existing practice being transferred to computers, rather there are manifold and subtle reconfigurations of an existing activity through computers being incorporated at different stages. Computers are also to be understood as physical objects with their own needs and characteristics. They are often the glue for coordination of activities (Christensen and Ropke 2010) and the web is the place where the multiple activities are connected together. The blog seems to play such a role in connecting different groups of people, places, and activities together. In food blogging people assemble multiple, participatory technologies (Blogger, Facebook, Flickr, Twitter etc.), so that any inscription of routine into those technologies may be accomplished by themselves and experienced as itself a form of empowerment, self-expression, and self-actualization.

Computers quickly come to be used in taken for granted ways. It is also the case that IT generates exogenous change. As new technologies appear, actors seem to have to work hard to understand how to go on doing what they used to do with the new technology and then only later to discover how to do new useful things (Shove, Pantzar, and Watson 2007). Computer uses are social both in the sense that they connect people in more or less interactive ways, but also that they are governed by social conventions of use.

Thus, in summary, the practice approach focuses on how people pursue valued activities, which often include using computers. Food bloggers operate across multiple sites, and use multiple devices. The "systems" in use like social networking or photosharing sites are open ended about how they are used. Computers are used as tools within personally significant projects; information use and ICT adoption is incidental to the wider process of the practice. Through the multiplication and mobility of devices, use of computers is intertwined with real world processes using objects in physical spaces over time. It becomes more difficult to think in terms of "users" of a particular ICT system, since people use multiple sites in complex, interconnected ways, as well as flitting across many other web sites, in infrequent visits but ways reflecting the very particular demands of a complex practice. There is a convergence of consumption, media, and information activities. Indeed it is difficult to understand any Internet activity without considering it both as supporting personal communication and also as a search for audiences and the emulation of media practices. Interviewees talk about boosting "traffic" and tracking statistics among their audience, as well as the hugely personal significance of certain dishes or meals as events. It is often a mediatized experience. It is also a form of craft consumption, where the consumer personalizes and actively appropriates mass produced items as a creative act of self-expression (Campbell 2005). Increasingly, the study of organizational uses of computers, arguably the traditional focus of SI, needs to reflect the wider use of computers in leisure and consumption experiences, partly because of the way such social practices are then commonly taken up and reapplied within organizations.

Evaluation

The elaboration in the discussion of the four preoccupations of the practice approach and the case study of food blogging reveal its ability to sensitize SI research to often neglected aspects of the context of information activity: the body, materiality, space, social identity, and the aesthetic and normative aspects of knowing. The stress on materiality seems to be in keeping with the increasing integration of computers into everyday life, and declining plausibility of seeing the "virtual" as a separate sphere. It is highly relevant to the study of information activities and computer uses in contexts outside rationalized and work place contexts, particularly leisure, consumption, and media use; to contexts where information is not the central purpose being pursued and computers are merely a resource along with many others, not the center of attention. The practice approach has a good sense of the "fleeting, fragile and fragmented" and "ephemerality, multiplicity, dispersion and mobility" (Orlikowski 2011, 1445). This reflects a reality where global socio-technical complexes like the Internet supersede discrete, dedicated computer systems that had correct ways they should be used to achieve predefined ends.

Because it is a rich set of theoretical resources, shared with cognate disciplines such as sociology, Science and Technology Studies (STS), and media studies, the practice approach has potential to strengthen SI as social science. It has been developed philosophically as a distinctive tradition within social theory (Reckwitz 2002). It has its own language (Nicolini, Gherardi, and Yanow 2003) and methodologies (Nicolini 2009; 2013). Yet it is not a theoretical panacea. Postill (2010) (unlike some other authors in his edited book) rejects the notion that it can be a new paradigm for media studies, because it performs less well than existing theories in some areas.

It is at the same time both a strength and problem that no single theorist encapsulates the broad church of the practice approach. Schatzki's work provides one potential philosophical base. Yet often existing concepts such as "affordances" of technology seem to already offer richer ways of conceptualizing particular problems. Nicolini's (2009; 2013) methodology is a convincing approach to zooming in on different aspects of practice and zooming out to wider connections. However, the relatively fragmented body of theory requires a depth of theoretical engagement to deploy.

When compared to much past work in information science as a whole, the practice approach offers a relatively unfamiliar way of thinking, researching, and writing. Much previous information science work is influenced by the cognitivism, individualism, empiricism, and positivism of psychological science and the pragmatism and technophilia of computer science. The practice approach is sociological, rather than focusing on the individual and their motivations, choices, and behaviors. It is theoretical and philosophical more than strongly empirical. The methodological starting point is ethnography rather than the experiment or quantitative techniques.

Indeed, it may be that in some contexts the institutional underpinnings of information science are an obstacle to the adoption of the practice approach more broadly. The profession's association with management of textual knowledge is at odds with the practice approach's recognition of other forms of knowing. It could also be argued that much of the research across information science responds to the profession's need for an evidence base for policy that historically has been seen as most convincing when provided in quantitative form. Studies influenced by practice thinking are unlikely to supply such immediately convincing material, because they do not lend themselves to quantification.

The Practice Approach and Social Informatics

Thus the practice approach offers a refreshing and challenging source of ideas for information science as a whole (Cox 2012). Yet it is a perspective that is close to that of SI. The key empirical findings of SI (Sawyer and Rosenbaum 2000) are very much in tune with the sensibilities of the practice approach. Both bodies of work share a sense of the gap between plans and expectations for use of ICTs and the post-implementation reality. The importance of context is apparent both in Sawyer's statement that "Context dependency is a core principle" (2005, 10) and, at a much more abstract level, in Schatzki's site ontology. Indeed, when Sawyer (2005, 10) writes "Social informatics sees computing as a web-like arrangement of material artifacts such as computers and software, and the rules, norms and practices of people," the echoes of the language of the practice approach are readily apparent. This points to the way that, at least in a general way, the influence of the practice approach has already been felt in SI, e.g. in works that use the community of practice concept. Yet both Postill (2010) and Savolainen (2008) caution that scholars in many fields have come to use the term practice rather loosely and argue that more rigorous and theoretically driven understandings of practice should be developed.

More explicit drawing on practice writing by SI would have a number of benefits. SI is strongly linked to the name of Rob Kling, yet Kling's work is not widely known outside the information world. Socio-technical studies are also fragmented (Davenport 2005). The turn to a practice approach, in contrast, is across much of social science, and so therefore offers an opportunity to bring perspectives from many disciplines together, resting as it does on a body of well-developed social theory from Bourdieu through to Schatzki. Taking a common turn with other social sciences (indeed with some strands of information behavior research) towards a practice approach, therefore, seems promising. The move would align with SI's interdisciplinary or transdisciplinary nature (Sawyer 2005; Davenport 2008). In studying the most important example of an ICT based system, the Internet, it is hard to disentangle information, media, and consumption. The perspectives of the disciplines of media studies and consumption studies are highly relevant. A turn in SI towards the practice approach would encourage research to move beyond purely organizational contexts (as SI has arguably done) acknowledging the degree to which non-work and media uses of technologies are quickly taken up within organizations.

Yet this turn is not necessarily straightforward. Practice theory is rather theoretical and often a little obscure (perhaps because of its foundation in relational thinking); SI is pragmatic and accessible. Furthermore, there may also be common limitation on both approaches in their treatment of power. Day (2007) has explored the multiple meaning of criticality in SI. It is commonly understood as about the need to "challenge taken for granted assumptions" (Sawyer 2005, 10). At other times it goes beyond this towards specifically questioning the priorities and values of those who are in power over computerization. In fact, criticality as concerned with power and the point of view of those without power, may be an area where the practice approach is rather under-developed. One of the weaknesses of the seminal community of practice work was not to follow through on the promise to understand practices within a much wider social context (Contu and Willmott 2003). When tied to an integrative (as opposed to combinative) ethnographic approach exploring discrete, bounded subcultures, the danger is that a sense of the way practice is shaped by wider social structures is lost. This echoes criticisms of socio-technical studies reported by Davenport (2008). Although Schatzki provides a strong sense that the meaning of a practice derives from its place in a site a nexus of other practices, he avoids generalizations about how this site could be ordered. The coda to his 2002 book acknowledges that he has not addressed issues around power directly (Schatzki 2002, 267). There do seem to be some weaknesses in the criticality of practice theory, at times. However, the resources do exist to construct a more critical practice approach. Practice level investigations do show how power structures like androcentric gender relations are instantiated. We could turn to Bourdieu for a more power suffused view of a field (or site). Actor Network Theory as an influence on the practice approach does say much about the operation of power in a political sense, through the sociology of translation (Rivera, Gonzalez, and Cox 2012).

Conclusion

This chapter has sought to contribute to the book by offering a concise overview of the past and present of the practice approach with a view to its future value for SI and questions about the design, uses and consequences of computers. Given existing influences and common ground there is a good potential for the practice approach to contribute to SI's thinking, especially in the context of the ubiquitous use of computers in many aspects of everyday life, as well as work contexts. The wide-ranging influence of the practice approach across the social sciences aligns with SI's interdisciplinary character.

References

Argyris, Chris, and Donald A. Schön. 1974. *Theory in Practice: Increasing Professional Effectiveness*. San Francisco: Jossey-Bass.

Blackler, Frank. 1995. "Knowledge, Knowledge Work and Organizations: An Overview and Interpretation." *Organization Studies* 16 (6): 1021-1046.

Brown, John S., and Paul Duguid. 2001. "Knowledge and Organization: A Social Practice Perspective." *Organization Science* 12(2): 198-213.

Campbell, Colin. 2005. "The Craft Consumer." *Journal of Consumer Culture*, 5 (1): 23-42.

Christensen, Toke H., and Inge Røpke. 2010. "Can Practice Theory Inspire Studies of ICTs in Everyday Life?" In *Theorising Media and Practice*, edited by Birgit Bräuchler, and John Postill, 233-258. Oxford: Berghahn Books.

Contu, Alessia, and Hugh Willmott. 2003. "Re-Embedding Situatedness: The Importance of Power Relations in Learning Theory." *Organization Science* 14 (3): 283-296.

Corradi, Gessica, Silvia Gherardi, and Luca Verzelloni. 2010. "Through the Practice Lens: Where is the Bandwagon of Practice-Based Studies Heading?" *Management Learning* 41 (3): 265-283.

Cox, Andrew M., and Megan K. Blake. 2011. "Information and Food Blogging as Serious Leisure." *Aslib Proceedings* 63 (2/3): 204-220.

Cox, Andrew M. 2005. "What Are Communities of Practice? A Comparative Review of Four Seminal Works." *Journal of Information Science* 31 (6): 527-540.

—. 2012. "An Exploration of the Practice Approach and its Place in Information Science." *Journal of Information Science* 38 (2): 176-188.

Davenport, Elisabeth. 2005. "Social Informatics in Practice: A Guide for the Perplexed." *Bulletin of the American Society for Information Science and Technology* 31 (5): 17-20. http://www.asis.org/Bulletin/Jun-05/davenport.html.

—. 2008. "Social Informatics and Sociotechnical Research – a View from the UK." *Journal of Information Science* 34 (4): 519-530.

Elliot, Lorraine. "10 Things You Should Know about Food Bloggers," *Not Quite Nigella* (blog), July 13, 2009. http://www.notquitenigella.com/2009/07/13/10-things-you-should-know-about-food-bloggers/.

—. "12 More Things You Should Know about Food Bloggers," *Not Quite Nigella* (blog), September 23, 2009. http://www.notquitenigella.com/2009/09/23/12-more-things-you-should-know-about-food-bloggers/.

—. "10 More Things You Should Know about Food Bloggers," *Not Quite Nigella* (blog), April 19, 2010. http://www.notquitenigella.com/2010/04/19/10-more-things-you-should-know-about-food-bloggers/.

Feldman, Martha S., and Brian T. Pentland. 2003. "Reconceptualizing Organizational Routines as a Source of Flexibility and Change." *Administrative Science Quarterly* 48: 94-118.

Feldman, Martha S., and Wanda J. Orlikowski. 2011. "Theorizing Practice and Practicing Theory." *Organization Science* 22 (5): 1240-1253.

Geiger, Daniel. 2009. "Revisiting the Concept of Practice: Toward an Argumentative Understanding of Practicing." *Management Learning* 40 (2): 129-144.

Gherardi, Silvia. 2008. "Situated Knowledge and Situated Action: What do Practice-Based Studies Promise?" In *The SAGE Handbook of New Approaches in Management and Organization*, edited by Daved Barry, and Hans Hansen, part III 516-525. London: SAGE.

—. 2009a. "Introduction: the Critical Power of the 'Practice Lens'." *Management Learning* 40 (2): 115-128.

—. 2009b. "Knowing and Learning in Practice-Based Studies: an Introduction." *The Learning Organization* 16 (5): 352-359.

—. 2009c. "Practice? It's a Matter of Taste!" *Management Learning* 40 (5): 535-550.

—. 2012. *How to Conduct a Practice-Based Study: Problems and Methods*. Cheltenham: Edward Elgar.

Haider, Jutta. 2011. "The Environment on Holidays or How a Recycling Bin Informs Us on the Environment." *Journal of Documentation* 67 (5): 823-839.

—. 2012. “Interrupting Practices that Want to Matter: The Making, Shaping and Reproduction of Environmental Information Online.” *Journal of Documentation* 68 (5): 639-658.

Hartel, Jenna. 2006. “Information Activities and Resources in an Episode of Gourmet Cooking.” *Information Research* 12 (1). http://informationr.net/ir/12-1/paper282.html.

—. 2010a. “Time as a Framework for Information Science: Insights from the Hobby of Gourmet Cooking.” *Information Research* 15 (4). http://informationr.net/ir/15-4/colis715.html.

—. 2010b. “Managing Documents at Home for Serious Leisure: A Case Study of the Hobby of Gourmet Cooking.” *Journal of Documentation* 66 (6): 847-874.

Hobart, Mark. 2010. “What do We Mean by ‘Media Practices’?” In *Theorising Media and Practice*, edited by Birgit Bräuchler, and John Postill, 55-76. Oxford: Berghahn Books.

Hodges, Diane C. 1998. “Participation as Dis-Identificaton With/in a Community of Practice.” *Mind, Culture and Activity* 5 (4): 272-290.

Huizing, Ard, and Mary Cavanagh. 2011. “Planting Contemporary Practice Theory in the Garden of Information Science.” *Information Research* 16 (4). http://informationr.net/ir/16-4/paper497.html.

Kirk, David, Sellen, Abigail, Rother, Carsten, & Wood, Ken. 2006. Understanding photowork. In *Proceedings of the SIGCHI conference on Human Factors in computing systems* (pp. 761-770). ACM.

Kling, Rob. 1999. “What is Social Informatics and Why Does it Matter?” *D-Lib Magazine* 5 (1). http://www.dlib.org/dlib/january99/kling/01kling.html.

Lave, Jean, and Etienne Wenger. 1991. *Situated Learning: Legitimate Peripheral Participation*. Cambridge: Cambridge University Press.

Lloyd, Annemaree. 2009. “Informing Practice: Information Experience of Ambulance Officers in Training and On-Road Practice.” *Journal of Documentation* 65 (3): 396-419.

—. 2010a. “Framing Information Literacy as Information Practice: Site Ontology and Practice Theory.” *Journal of Documentation* 66 (2): 245-258.

—. 2010b. “Corporeality and Practice Theory: Exploring Emerging Research Agendas for Information Literacy.” *Information Research* 15 (3). http://informationr.net/ir/15-3/colis7/colis704.html.

McKenzie, Pamela J. 2003. “A Model of Information Practices in Accounts of Everyday-Life Information Seeking.” *Journal of Documentation* 59 (1): 19-40.

Nicolini, Davide, Silvia Gherardi, and Dvora Yanow. 2003. "Introduction: Toward a Practice-Based View of Knowing and Learning in Organizations." In *Knowing in Organizations: A Practice-Based Approach*, edited by Davide Nicolini, Silvia Gherardi, and Dvora Yanow, 3-31. London: ME Sharpe.

Nicolini, Davide. 2009. "Zooming In and Out: Studying Practices by Switching Theoretical Lenses and Trailing Connections." *Organization Studies* 30 (12): 1391-1418.

—. 2011. "Practice as the Site of Knowing: Insights from the Field of Telemedicine." *Organization Science* 22 (3): 602-620.

—. 2013. *Practice Theory, Work, and Organization: An Introduction*. Oxford: Oxford University Press.

Orlikowski, Wanda J. 2000. "Using Technology and Constituting Structures: A Practice Lens for Studying Technology in Organizations." *Organization Science* 11 (4): 404-428.

—. 2007. "Sociomaterial Practices: Exploring Technology at Work." *Organization Studies* 28 (9): 1435-1448.

—. 2009. "The Sociomateriality of Organisational Life: Considering Technology Management Research." *Cambridge Journal of Economics* 34 (1): 125-141.

Østerlund, Carsten, and Paul Carlile. 2005. "Relations in Practice: Sorting Through Practice Theories on Knowledge Sharing in Complex Organizations." *The Information Society* 21 (2): 91-107.

Postill, J. 2010. Introduction to *Theorising Media and Practice*, edited by Birgit Bräuchler, and John Postill, 1-34. Oxford: Berghahn Books.

Reckwitz, Andreas. 2002. "Toward a Theory of Social Practices." *European Journal of Social Theory* 5 (2): 243-263.

Rivera González, Gibrán, and Cox, Andrew M. 2012. "Using ANT and Practice Theory to Explore the Shaping of Participation and Non-Use of Social Media." Paper presented at Co-production of Knowledge: Social Media, STS and … Symposium, July 18-20 at The University of York, York.

Roberts, Joanne. 2006. "Limits to Communities of Practice." *Journal of Management Studies* 43 (3): 623-639.

Savolianen, Reijo. 2005. "Everyday Life Information Seeking." In *Theories of Information Behaviour,* edited by Karen E. Fisher, Sanda Erdelez, and Lynne McKechnie, 143-148. Medford, NJ: Information Today.

—. 2007. "Information Behaviour and Information Practice: Reviewing the Umbrella Concepts of Information Seeking Studies." *Library Quarterly* 77 (2): 109-32.

—. 2008. *Everyday Information Practices: A Social Phenomenological Perspective*. Plymouth: Scarecrow Press.

Sawyer, Steve. and Howard Rosenbaum. 2000. "Social Informatics in the Information Sciences: Current Activities and Emerging Directions." *Informing Science* 3 (2). http://www.inform.nu/Articles/Vol3/v3n2p89-96r.pdf.

Sawyer, Steve. 2005. "Social Informatics: Overview, Principles and Opportunities." *Bulletin of the American Society for Information Science and Technology* 31 (5). http://www.asis.org/Bulletin/Jun-05/sawyer.html.

Schatzki, Theodore R. 2001. "Introduction: Practice Theory." In *The Practice Turn in Contemporary Theory*, edited by Theodore R. Schatzki, Karin K. Cetina, and Eike von Savigny, 1-14. London: Routledge.

Schatzki, Theodore R., Karin K. Cetina, and Eike von Savigny, eds. 2001. *The Practice Turn in Contemporary Theory*. London: Routledge.

Schatzki, Theodore R. 2002. *The Site of the Social*. University Park, PA: Pennsylvania State University Press.

Shove, Elizabeth, and Mika Pantzar. 2005. "Consumers, Producers and Practices: Understanding the Invention and Reinvention of Nordic Walking." *Journal of Consumer Culture* 5 (1): 43-64.

Shove, Elizabeth, and Mika Pantzar. 2007. "Recruitment and Reproduction: The Careers and Carriers of Digital Photography and Floorball." *Human Affairs* 17 (2): 154-167.

Shove, Elizabeth, Mika Pantzar, and Matt Watson. 2012. *The Dynamics of Social Practice: Everyday Life and how it Changes*. London: SAGE.

Talja, Sanna. 2010. "Jean Lave's Practice Theory." In *Critical Theory for Library and Information Science*, edited by Gloria J. Leckie, Lisa M. Given, and John E. Buschman, 205-220. Oxford: Libraries Unlimited.

Trowler, Paul, Murray Saunders, and Veronica Bamber. 2012. *Tribes and Territories in the 21st Century: Rethinking the Significance of Disciplines in Higher Education*. London: Routledge.

Veinot, Tiffany C. 2007. "The Eyes of the Power Company: Workplace Information Practices of a Vault Inspector." *The Library Quarterly* 77 (2): 157-179.

Warde, Alan. 2005. "Consumption and Theories of Practice." *Journal of Consumer Culture* 5 (2): 131-153.

Wenger, E. 1998. *Communities of Practice: Learning, Meaning and Identity*. Cambridge: Cambridge University Press.

CHAPTER ELEVEN

SOCIAL INFORMATICS AND BUSINESS REFORM

J.P. ALLEN

Introduction: The "Prosperity Paradox"

Social Informatics (SI) argues at its core that an understanding of computerization requires a deep understanding of its institutional and cultural context. As the increasing number of informatics programs (e.g., Groth and MacKie-Mason 2010) and research outlets attest, the argument is winning its followers. Though the contexts of today's informatics work are varied–health informatics, government informatics, and entertainment informatics among many–early SI research focused on the cultural and institutional context of formal organizations, and in particular business organizations. In this chapter, we will suggest that SI research in a business context still has much to contribute, especially as the impact of global business continues to raise important social and economic questions.

One of the main justifications for early SI research in a business context was as a way of explaining the "productivity paradox", or the difficulty of finding productivity and efficiency gains from technology investments. These productivity gains were promised by the "vivid punditry" and utopian visions of computerization offered by media experts and technology vendors (e.g., Kling 2007; Kling 1996). SI research was able to systematically identify how context affected whether these presumably universal organizational values of efficiency and productivity were realized.

In this chapter, we argue that a promising future direction for SI is to embrace the increasing complexity of the cultural and institutional context of business. Modern business is more global, and more thoroughly infused with digital technology, but it is also more contested in its purpose and its larger social and economic effects. While the "productivity paradox" might have spoken to the concerns of socially oriented technology research a few decades ago, we propose an analogous "prosperity paradox" as a way of framing future research. The "prosperity paradox" asks: *why is an increasingly digital economy and society not able to provide broadly shared prosperity and opportunity in an environmentally sustainable way*? Just as early information technology seemed to provide obvious tools for organizational productivity and efficiency, the new digital economy might seem to provide obvious tools for using fewer natural resources, and for creating "frictionless" markets that would provide new opportunities and "level the playing field" for different economic actors. If SI research can systematically identify ways that institutional and cultural contexts prevent the new digital economy from realizing widely shared prosperity, its future as an intellectual movement should be assured. The long SI tradition of critical research in business contexts would not only continue, but perhaps even increase in relevance.

The remainder of this chapter will explore some of the implications and challenges of pursuing explanations of the "prosperity paradox". A major challenge is the increased complexity of the business context. Instead of critiquing a simple managerialist orientation–for example, a belief that information technology can and should lead to more organizational efficiency–SI would need to critique business as an institution, and question the extent to which businesses, along with their socio-technical foundations, serve the common good. SI would need to engage with current discussions of business reform, which are broader and more complex than arguments about organizational productivity. The systems and technologies we choose to study in the future might tend more toward complex socio-technical ensembles that affect entire industries or economies, such as the example of "internet gatekeepers" that stand between businesses and customers in digital economies we will explore later in the chapter. And just as these "internet gatekeepers", such as search engines, social media, review sites, or app stores, necessarily rely on secrecy and hidden algorithms for their effective functioning, so our SI critiques might shift from deconstructing utopian visions that openly promote technology, towards surfacing the value conflicts and social choices built into our digital economy that certain actors might prefer to remain hidden.

An Opportunity: Business Reform and Social Informatics Research

Is business, as an institution, a reliable generator of prosperity, opportunity, and social benefits? Since the recent global financial crises began in 2008, prominent observers have argued that the answer is no, and have renewed calls for reform of the global economic system.

The institution of modern business, particularly in the form of large global corporations, has been accused of causing or encouraging destructive outcomes in many ways. According to these critiques, modern corporate governance encourages short-term thinking (e.g., Bogle and Levitt 2012), the extraction of wealth by managers and shareholders (e.g., Stiglitz 2012), and the capture of the political and legal process, if not outright criminality (e.g., Bakan 2005; Ferguson 2012). These actions by businesses as a whole–not simply by individual unethical firms–have resulted in banking crises, publicly funded bailouts, unprecedented economic and social inequality, corruption, massive tax evasion, and environmental degradation, according to these critics (e.g., Korten 1995; Hawken, Lovins, and Lovins 2010; Hardy 2012).

Almost all of these critiques recognize that the modern economic system fundamentally runs on digital technology. They differ, however, in the role they assign to information and communication technologies (ICTs). Commentators such as Ferguson (2012) mention ICTs as one of the three main drivers of global inequality–primarily through globalization of the labor pool–along with poor education and corruption in politics. Other experts such as Stiglitz (2012) acknowledge the necessity of ICT for the new global order, but place more importance on the political manipulation of rules and regulations by business than on new technology and globalization per se. What is difficult to find is a vision of the role ICTs might play in counteracting these negative aspects of modern business, and bringing about a reformed economic system.

The opportunity for SI research is to better identify and critique the role of ICT in the existing economic order, and to articulate new possible roles that could either reform business, or help develop alternatives.

SI research is particularly well positioned to fulfill this role, with its tradition of challenging utopian claims about technology and economic productivity, for example in the original "productivity paradox" debates mentioned earlier (e.g., Kling 1996). The critical tradition within SI (Kling 2007; Day 2007) has a history of challenging utopian visions of ICT in the workplace, when those visions were based on prevailing ideology rather than empirical reality. More importantly, however, SI has arguably made the most progress of any academic movement in detailing the relationship between digital technology and its cultural and institutional contexts (Kling 2007). We argue that successful research on ICT and business reform will require deep theorizing about the institutional and cultural context of business itself.

As a starting point for an SI analysis of business reform, we suggest focusing on the utopian vision of a seamless, frictionless digital economy that naturally and automatically results in perfect markets for goods and services. We review this utopian vision in the next section.

Early Predictions of the "New Economy"

One classic strategy of SI analysis has been to identify and critique utopian visions of the role of ICT in social and economic life (e.g., Kling 1996). Comparing the predictions about ICT and the "New Economy" made before the dot com boom in 2000, and the current state of the global economy as put forward by those calling for business reform, we see a stark contrast.

Predictions of ICT and economic change from the previous millennium proclaimed that digital markets would work more effectively with more information available, easier searches for buyers and sellers, and lower transaction costs (e.g., Smith, Bailey, and Brynjolfsson 2002). New technology was said to have created a crisis for large corporations and more opportunity for smaller, newer entrants, as more flexibility and nimbleness were required to compete in this new era (e.g., Piore and Sabel 1984). Organizations would be forced to shift away from vertical hierarchies (e.g., Castells 1996) and become more "virtual" through decentralized networks and cooperative teams (e.g., Dutton 1999). A culture of "accelerated creative destruction" would force firms to compete harder for customers, in turn forcing businesses to become constantly experimental and ever changing (e.g., Zysman 2006). The lesson after the collapse of the Soviet Union was that new digital technology was incompatible with any social arrangements other than an open, democratic society and free market capitalism (e.g., Castells 1996).

Within the Information Systems literature, early studies of the "new economy" argued that digital markets would transform the "engine and steering system of our economy" into more transparent and efficient forms (e.g., Bakos 1998) through unprecedented access to information. The reduction in transaction costs caused by digital technology would encourage companies to favor using electronic markets to coordinate economic activity over the use of "hierarchies", or internally coordinated activity. Electronic markets would progress down a common evolutionary path from biased to unbiased markets (e.g., Malone et al. 1987) due to competitive or regulatory forces that would remove bias.

The main picture we are left with from the vision of the "New Economy" is a digital future with healthy competition, widespread information availability and transparency, with almost frictionless, unbiased markets coordinating economic resource decisions with unprecedented effectiveness.

Business, ICT, and the Current Economic Crisis

If the critics of the post-crisis economy are to be believed, these early "New Economy" predictions of nimble, hyper-competitive firms functioning in hyper-efficient markets were inaccurate. The technology linking global financial markets has instead ushered in an era of massive concentration of power in a few "too big to fail" institutions, with the tight coupling between large institutions causing further destabilization during crises (e.g., Ferguson 2012). Global financial systems driven by technology have enabled offshore tax evasion, to the point where perhaps over $20 trillion is stashed in tax havens on behalf of the wealthiest elites (e.g., Henry 2012).

Rather than providing greater broad-based opportunity through transparent markets, the financial crises have instead created massive transfers of wealth from certain groups, such as the 53% reduction in median U.S. black household wealth during 2005-2009 (Pew Charitable Trusts 2012). High-speed digital trading systems are dominated by speculative trade–over 99.2% of all trading activity, according to Bogle and Levitt (2012)–perpetuating a culture of short-termism at the expense of long-term investment. The critics go even farther, claiming that instead of ICT-based media serving as a more effective watchdog of these activities, modern business has instead been able to dominate new media and even in some cases purchase the services of experts and academics to legitimize their activities (e.g., Ferguson 2012; Bakan 2005).

Where did the utopian vision go wrong? SI research offers a set of analytic tools for understanding the weaknesses of utopian technological visions (e.g., Kling 1996), starting with the lack of institutional and cultural context. The "New Economy" predictions focused on multinational corporate behavior as largely separate from its political contexts, or even as completely separated or liberated from control by national governments in a globalized economy. Missing from the vision were any notions of political capture or corruption–the idea that corporations, particularly financial ones, would attempt to control the political process (e.g., Stiglitz 2012) and the legal system through influencing the writing of business-friendly regulations such as intellectual property rights.

SI research also cautions us to be wary of a pro-social bias in utopians visions, and the simplifying assumption that there are no winners and losers–that everyone uniformly benefits from computerization. In early SI research, "reinforcement politics", or the theory that powerful agents use computerization to further reinforce their own positions, emerged as a competing explanation to the view of computerization as primarily a rational and efficiency-enhancing transformation. In the utopian visions of the digital "New Economy", frictionless commerce and unbiased markets were seen as uniformly pro-social. The possibility of established interests finding a way to reinforce their own positions was left relatively unexplored.

In the next section, we offer an example of how future SI research might tackle one aspect of the problem – the problem of internet gatekeepers that stand between customers and businesses. Rather than unmediated markets with perfect information, we find ourselves in a world of markets mediated by complex online institutions and infused with digital technology.

Mediated Markets: The Internet Gatekeepers

The digital economy is arguably dominated by mediated rather than unbiased markets. Powerful internet gatekeepers, including search engines and social media, use a combination of openly-offered contributions (for example, web pages and links, social media posts, or online reviews) and secret algorithms (for example, Google's relevance algorithm based in part on PageRank, or Facebook's EdgeRank algorithm for news feeds) to mediate the online information relationship between businesses and customers.

The combination of open and secret information mediation is not an accident, but a widely accepted strategy for combining many openly-offered pieces of information into high quality results that are not "gamed" by contributors. Google's "organic" (unpaid) search results are determined by a combination of over 200 different factors. The specific factors that influence search results are not revealed, the weights of the factors are secret, and both the factors and weights can be changed at any time. With the internet now the single most influential source of consumer purchasing information (Vogt and Alldredge 2012), how and why this mediation occurs has significant implications. We briefly discuss below how three examples of market mediation interact with the institutional and cultural context of business to shape the kinds of opportunities offered by the digital economy.

Search Engine Optimization: Google

Google has been described as the "most successful scheme for making money on the Internet that the world had ever seen" (Levy 2011, 83). The product being referred to in this quote is not Google's world famous search engine, but instead its close cousin AdWords. It was the discovery of AdWords, a method for advertisers to bid on keyword phrases, and create their own advertisements that would automatically display next to search results, that turned Google into a highly profitable business.

According to Levy (2011), the founders of Google expected that the money to support their business would come from licensing the technology to larger companies, and by selling hardware appliances. Within the institutional and cultural context of venture capital-backed enterprises in Silicon Valley, however, the search for "monetization", or a business model that would meet the substantial revenue expectations of these investors, became a priority. The importance of "scalability" to millions of customers became paramount, so when an early experiment allowing businesses to create advertisements on their own, using only a credit card and requiring no human sales contact, yielded positive results, AdWords was born.

The Google search results algorithm is opaque by design, for fear that businesses will engage in the dark arts of Search Engine Optimization (SEO) in an attempt to improve their placement within search results. The search engine industry so far has been characterized by monopoly, both in the broader sense that Google serves almost 2/3rds of all web searches in the United States and Western Europe, and in the specific sense that businesses not appearing on the first page of search results are typically only seen by 5% or fewer of consumers (Cornwell 2010).

One of Google's innovations that differentiated it from other early search engines was to separate the "organic" (unpaid) from the "sponsored" (paid) results of a search. Even with this separation, however, AdWords does not automatically display the highest bidder for a search phrase at the top of the "sponsored" results list. Instead, it uses a proprietary calculation designed to maximize Google's advertising revenue. Other Google services, such as Google Shopping, currently use a different algorithm and only include paid placements. At the same time, Google's business depends upon a continuing stream of openly-published web content, meaning that its own business practices must continue to support openly accessible content on the web, and not discourage others from investing in online content due to any perceived unfairness in search results.

A continuing controversy with Google is whether its search results privilege its own services over those of its competitors. This accusation has been leveled at Google's local business searches, its own travel products, its online reviews, its news products, and others (e.g., Edelman and Lockwood 2011). Given its secret algorithms, it is difficult to tell whether these accusations are true, short of investigations by regulatory bodies. Because these algorithms are constantly changing, are sometimes tailored to individuals or geographic areas, and are even sometimes hand-tuned through manual interventions, it is difficult for outside researchers to show consistent patterns (e.g., Evans 2007). Perhaps this is the reason why a topic as important to business as the impact of SEO and search engine placement has been almost entirely ignored by academic research. Specific analytic tools from the SI approach, such as the identification of utopian visions, and the surfacing of the institutional and cultural context of complex organizations such as Google, could be useful for making progress on these important issues of economic opportunity and fairness.

Social Media Ranking: Facebook

In contrast to Google and the search business, much has been written about the larger impacts and meaning of Facebook, the billion-user business that currently captures over half of all social media visits worldwide. Facebook provides a well-known example of the importance of business context in the development of internet mediation.

Facebook famously began as a service devoted to optimizing its benefits for users at the expense of making money (Kirkpatrick 2011). It initially shunned advertising and the selling of personal information; it limited itself to specific schools or audiences in an effort to build critical mass and shut out most outside investors. With the arrival of a new Chief Operating Officer (COO) in preparation for an initial public offering on the equities markets, the business emphasis shifted to highly scalable monetization. According to the new COO, "Facebook represented one of the great advertising environments of all time." (Kirkpatrick 2011, 256). In the search to find new revenue models, Facebook attempted to differentiate itself from the dominant online advertiser, Google, by focusing on "brand awareness" or "demand generation" advertising. In contrast to search advertising, which tries to deliver relevant information for people in the midst of a purchasing decision, Facebook has identified its advertising strength as digital display advertising, tailored to specific demographics and friend networks, that would keep business brands in the mind of consumers. These "brand awareness" ads tend to be dominated by larger consumer companies, such as Coca-Cola and Disney.

After a less than successful initial public offering, however, revenue display advertising may not be meeting the expectations of the financial markets. This has encouraged Facebook to find other revenue sources. An early attempt to create "social ads", where consumer purchases are automatically broadcast to friends, proved to be too much of a perceived privacy violation even by modern internet standards.

A more recent attempt to generate revenue has been controversial in the business community. Over time, the news feed of updates that Facebook users receive has shifted from an unedited list, to a generated list of top results using a secret algorithm called EdgeRank. For businesses that built lists of followers on Facebook, communications with their fans are now largely mediated by this secret algorithm. Facebook offers a service, for a fee, that will promote a business' messages and make them more likely to be seen. What began as a free "viral marketing" service that seemed to favor smaller business and entrepreneurs appears to be shifting toward a more traditional pay-to-play service, given the needs of the larger institutional context of business that Facebook has made itself beholden to. Again, the analysis of the cultural and institutional context of Facebook, as suggested by the SI approach, helps unravel the nature of mediated markets online, and better explain its impact on economic opportunity.

Filtered Reviews: Yelp

Online review sites perhaps offer the purest form of digital market transparency, inviting anyone to evaluate any business, and creating the possibility of smaller or newer entrants earning visibility not through expensive advertising campaigns, but by rising to the top of the rankings. The obvious potential for "gaming" the system by posting fake or paid reviews exists, with potential solutions ranging from automatic fraud detection algorithms, to editorial review, to more reliance on the ability of an ongoing customer conversation to identify and correct flawed reviews (Brown 2012). To the extent that for-profit businesses stand as intermediaries in the online review process, we should not be surprised, from our SI perspective, that the open transparency of online reviews will be strongly affected by the larger institutional and cultural context of business.

In the United States, Yelp has emerged as the leading online review site for businesses. Yelp is also firmly embedded in the institutional and cultural context of Silicon Valley venture capital-funded startups. The pressure to "monetize" with "scalability" is significant, with the simultaneous need to maintain an appearance of objective and fair reviews that will maintain the flow of reviewer contributors, and keep consumers visiting. Yelp currently uses a mixed business model, with most revenue coming from subscriptions. Yelp tries to convince businesses to subscribe, while insisting that subscribing and non-subscribing businesses receive the same treatment in the review results. This position has been met with some skepticism, and even a few lawsuits. At the same time, the presence of Yelp reviews has been shown to help local business by shifting consumer spending away from national chains, towards local restaurants with good review results (Luca 2011).

Yelp does not explicitly discuss its method for deciding which review results appear first in a search. It does, however, use a mechanism called "filtered reviews" to automatically remove reviews its algorithm believes are fraudulent. The controversy arises when a number of reviews with very high or very low ratings are put in the "filtered review" category, thereby moving a business' overall review score up or down significantly. By subscribing to Yelp, a business receives assistance in how to manage the process of avoiding fraudulent reviews, as determined by Yelp itself.

Internet gatekeepers such as Yelp are also in a competitive business landscape, reacting strategically to the moves of other intermediaries. For example, Yelp demanded that Google stop including Yelp reviews and scores in their search results, hoping to force consumers to click through to Yelp. Google agreed, but created its own competing online review service soon afterward. These constantly shifting alliances and conflicts also affect how the business-consumer relationship is mediated online.

In this brief discussion, we found common features in all three examples of mediated markets that differ from the original vision of a digitally unbiased market. The connection between customers and businesses is mediated by for-profit firms facing their own institutional and cultural demands. Searches for differentiation, monetization, and scalability have led to approaches that use combinations of open contributions and secret algorithms, subject to the revenue and strategic demands of business. By examining specific cases of market mediation, and approaching them with an SI lens, we have at least one example of a starting point for asking, and answering, the "prosperity paradox" question.

Conclusion: Social Informatics Thinking and Business Reform

We began our chapter about the future of SI with the question of the "prosperity paradox" – why hasn't a digital economy resulted in broadly shared and environmentally sustainable economic opportunity? According to the critics of the recent global financial crises, an increasingly digital world appears to be headed in the opposite direction (e.g., Ferguson 2012; Stiglitz 2012).

In our discussion, we used SI approaches for understanding complex situations. First, we identified a utopian vision of unbiased, fully transparent markets caused by digital technology. Then, we used concepts such as "reinforcement politics", and the larger institutional and cultural context of business, to begin to explain how digitally mediated markets differ from the utopian vision, and why this came to be.

The utopian story of economic prosperity and opportunity through unbiased digitally mediated markets seemingly did not come to pass. Instead, our digital economy features mediated gatekeepers, connecting businesses and customers through hidden algorithms shaped simultaneously by open community contributions, and the business context of specific for-profit firms.

More attention to the business context might encourage an investigation of how internet gatekeepers satisfy the revenue and stock price demands of financial markets, and the demands of skilled employees being lured to join companies by stock options. The cultural context of high-growth startup firms encourages the search for a proprietary advantage, a "secret sauce" that will be a lasting source of profits. These mediated markets provide answers to these business demands, while at the same time acting as a means of aggregating open contributions. It is in some ways a highly functional combination of open and closed approaches to market innovation, though potentially at the substantial cost of a lack of transparency and accountability.

This brief chapter is not meant to be a set of findings, but a suggested starting point for a type of SI research that embraces the full complexity of global business. SI research might ask how the new digital economy serves specific business interests, rewards certain winners, or perhaps even reinforces the position of the already powerful.

As in the past, technological determinism is a primary competitor to SI thinking. The idea that an increasingly digital economic system would naturally and directly lead to improved market function and transparency, based on a few technological attributes of digital systems, has been challenged by the economic crisis. What SI can provide is an account of business ICT that ties it to its modern cultural and institutional context, showing how the new economic crises are fundamentally socio-technical, and how potential alternatives might be as well.

Potential roles for future SI research include: stimulating demand for alternative economic arrangements through a critique of the current ICT-enabled global economic system, generating alternative economic arrangements or reforms that are ICT-enabled, and subjecting those same alternatives to a rigorous critique. SI research can evaluate the plausibility of new forms of social organizing around ICTs (e.g., Shirky 2008; Benkler 2007) that transcend current business institutions, new kinds of ICT-based radical transparency, and new forms of economic activity that are separated from the demands of the global financial system.

Ultimately, SI could provide the intellectual basis for a new computerization movement around business reform. The logical consequence of this is a renewed focus on the business context, but at the cultural and institutional level (e.g., Fort 1996) rather than the organizational level. This approach is necessarily critical, exposing value conflicts and social choices in situations that are supposedly value-neutral – greater efficiency or productivity, for example, or economic opportunity. The job of SI remains to expose the simple logic of social transformation through technology, and hold it up for scrutiny.

References

Bakan, Joel. 2005. *The Corporation: The Pathological Pursuit of Profit and Power*. New York: Simon & Schuster.

Benkler, Yochai. 2007. *The Wealth of Networks: How Social Production Transforms Markets and Freedom*. New Haven: Yale University Press.

Bogle, John C., and Arthur Levitt Jr. 2012. *The Clash of the Cultures: Investment vs. Speculation*. New York: John Wiley and Sons.

Brown, Barry. 2012. "Beyond Recommendations," *ACM Transactions on Computer-Human Interaction* 19 (4):1-24.

Castells, Manuel. 1996. *The Rise of the Network Society.* Oxford: Blackwell.

Cornwell, Collin. 2010. "The Importance of Page-One Visibility," accessed March 15, 2013. http://www.icrossing.com/icrossing-page-one-visibility.

Day, Ronald E. 2007. "Kling and the "Critical": Social Informatics and Critical Informatics," *Journal of the American Society for Information Science and Technology* 58 (4):575-582.

Dutton, William. H. 1999. *Society on the Line: Information Politics in the Digital Age*. Oxford: Oxford University Press.

Edelman, Benjamin, and Benjamin Lockwood. 2011. "Measuring Bias in "Organic" Web Search," accessed March 15, 2013. http://www.benedelman.org/searchbias/.

Evans, Michael P. 2007. "Analysing Google Rankings through Search Engine Optimization Data," *Internet Research* 17 (1):21–37.

Ferguson, Charles H. 2012. *Predator Nation: Corporate Criminals, Political Corruption, and the Hijacking of America*. New York: Crown Business.

Fort, Timothy L. 1996. "Business as Mediating Institution," *Business Ethics Quarterly* 6 (2):149-163.

Groth, Dennis P., and Jeffrey K. MacKie-Mason. 2010. "Why an Informatics Degree?" *Communications of the ACM* 53 (2):26-28.

Hawken, Paul, Amory Lovins, and L. Hunter Lovins. 2010. *Natural Capitalism: Creating the Next Industrial Revolution* (10th Anniversary edition). London: Earthscan.

Henry, James S. 2012. "The Price of Offshore Revisited: New Estimates for "Missing" Global Private Wealth, Income, Inequality, and Lost Taxes," accessed August 14, 2012. http://www.taxjustice.net/cms/upload/pdf/Price_of_Offshore_Revisited_26072012.pdf.

Kirkpatrick, David. 2011. *The Facebook Effect: The Inside Story of the Company That Is Connecting the World*, New Hork: Simon and Schuster.

Kling, Rob. 2007. "What is Social Informatics and Why Does It Matter?" *The Information Society* 23 (4):205-220.

—. ed. 1996. *Computerization and Controversy: Value Conflicts and Social Choices* (2nd ed.). San Diego: Academic Press.

Korten, David C. 1995. *When Corporations Rule the World*. San Francisco: Berrett-Koehler.

Levy, Steven. 2011. *In The Plex: How Google Thinks, Works, and Shapes Our Lives*. New York: Simon and Schuster.

Luca, Michael. 2011. "Reviews, Reputation, and Revenue: The Case of Yelp.com," accessed March 9, 2013. http://papers.ssrn.com/sol3/papers.cfm?abstract_id=1928601.

Pew Charitable Trusts. 2012. "Pursuing the American Dream: Economic Mobility Across Generations," accessed August 14, 2012. http://www.pewstates.org/projects/economic-mobility-project-328061.

Piore, Michael J., and Charles F. Sabel. 1984. *The Second Industrial Divide: Possibilities for Prosperity*. New York: Basic Books.

Shirky, Clay. 2008. *Here Comes Everybody: The Power of Organizing Without Organizations*. New York: Penguin Press.

Smith, Michael D., Joseph Bailey, and Erik Brynjolfsson. 2002. "Understanding Digital Markets: Review and Assessment," in *Understanding the Digital Economy: Data, Tools, and Research*, edited by Erik Brynjolfsson and Brian Kahin. Cambridge: MIT Press.

Stiglitz, Joseph E. 2012. *The Price of Inequality: How Today's Divided Society Endangers Our Future*. New York: W. W. Norton & Company.

Vogt, Colby, and Ken Alldredge. 2012. "2012 Digital Influence Index Annual Global Study," accessed March 15, 2013. http://push.fleishmanhillard.netdna-cdn.com/dii/2012-DII-White-Paper.pdf.

Zysman, John. 2006. "Creating Value in a Digital Era: How do Wealthy Nations Stay Wealthy?" in *How Revolutionary Was the Digital Revolution? National Responses, Market Transitions, and Global Technology*, edited by John Zysman and Abraham Newman. Palo Alto: Stanford University Press.

CHAPTER TWELVE

ADVANCING SOCIAL INFORMATICS[1]

STEVE SAWYER AND MARK HARTSWOOD

We focus attention to advancing Social Informatics (SI). We do so because the SI perspective provides important insights regarding the design, take-up, uses, effects and implications of information and communication technologies (ICT) in contemporary society that other common approaches do not. The focal phenomena of interest is what we and others call computerization; other approaches to research on computing do not emphasize sociality or focus on the deeply enmeshed duality of computing and social structures, behaviors and actions (Buriss 1998; Kling 1999). SI is socio-technical in the "weak constructionist" sense (Russell and Williams 2002). That is, social informaticists acknowledge that social action helps shape, in some – often large – part, a technological artifact. This noted, social informaticists also emphasize that the digital artifact can have some – or even substantial – agency. SI research is characterized by attending the dual, or mutually constituted, effects of (1) the social shaping of technological arrangements and (2) the technological shaping of social relations. Advancing what this looks like in conceptual and empirical forms is the core of SI scholarship and an area of profound intellectual need.

Why is the need so profound? From the 1940s into the 1980s, computing was so expensive that only large organizations could afford the resources needed to leverage computing. Consequently, only governments and major corporations computed. This is no longer the case: Innovations in ICT and uses are no longer focused on supporting organizational

---

[1] Portions of this chapter were first presented as keynote address given at the 2009 Pre-ASIST SIG-Social Informatics Workshop on 7 November, 2009 in Vancouver, British Columbia, Canada. This chapter has benefitted from comments and suggestions by Howard Rosenbaum, Kalpana Shankar, Sean Goggins, Fred Stutzman, Bruce Rowlands, Mohammad Hossein Jarrahi, Mike Tyworth, and members of the University of Edinburgh's SI Group.

activity; they have entered social life – broadly and quickly. The rise of mobile devices, social networking platforms, and the growth of the Web are social activities in that they are consumed as part of people's non-work lives. In saying this we know organizations influence ICT-based innovations and their uses. Corporate interests influence design of people's mobile phones and digital assistants. Corporate rules for consumption and production of information are significant forces in shaping access to information on the web.

As the chapters in this book help make clear, there are large-scale social transformations around computerization which are both broad and encompassing; shifts in social structures and behaviors in non-work activities due in part to the take up and uses of ICT are altering work and workplaces. At the same time workplace transformations – based in part on aspects of computerization – are blurring boundaries between our work and non-work lives. Access to, and uses of information are – as Dutton (2005) argues so compellingly – reshaping the ways we relate to one another, what we consider public or personal, how we work, the ways in which we organize for work, the pursuit of governance, the ways in which families and friends interact, and how (and what) we choose to recreate. We are not very far into this transformation, but already the effects are hugely differentiated along pre-existing socio-economic and national divides, and current conceptualizations of these transformations are evolving quickly in the face of new evidence and broader conceptual insights.

SI provides a means to redress the shortcomings of many current approaches to understanding computerization, beginning with the fundamental position that what is social and what is technological are bound up – enmeshed – in trajectories of mutually-reshaping interdependencies. This sociotechnical interdependence transcends the ability of social sciences or technological disciplines to articulate the roles, the effects and – most importantly – the trajectories of change along which ICT are evolving.

To make the case for advancing SI, this chapter continues in three sections. Next we focus on conceptualizing the phenomena – computerization, followed by a section in which we highlight contributions that distinguish SI from social and technological analyses. We close with a discussion on ways to advance the SI perspective.

Conceptualizing Phenomena and the Roles that Scholarly Communities Play

The combination of social and technological change has many names and no common understanding. Like others, we call this computerization[2] (Burris 1998; Kling 1996; Wolff 2003). Developing a shared understanding of computerization should be a defining activity for social informaticists. Scholarly communities are formed and sustained by their ability to conceptualize phenomena and articulate what this means for others. We envy our colleagues in physics for their ability to articulate the importance of the Large Hadron Collider – to the tune of billions of dollars in funding. Colleagues in computer science have advanced a clear agenda for computational science. Economists in the United States, the United Kingdom and many other countries have been able to articulate the need for the national agencies devoted to economic analysis. Given the importance of computing to society, why is it that we have no clear articulation of the issues?

The intellectual communities of physicists, computer scientists and economists are not single-minded monoliths. These are raucous spaces defined by differences of theory, methods, and the ways in which researchers view the same phenomena (e.g. Prasad 2006; Pickering 1984; Kornfeld and Hewitt 1981; Merton 1973). So, what makes them more coherent than, say, information scientists, at garnering resources and attention? We submit it is discipline which provides this coherence. Discipline here does not mean "having some common degree." For us discipline means "having a strong sense of what to do and how to do it." Scholars in physics, economics, and computer science have developed a means to pass on the core of their perspective to new scholars in these domains. These scholars seem to be able to communicate this core to others who are not in their domain. That is, part of being disciplined is how to communicate what it is that they see and do.

Coming from an intellectual tradition that does not have this discipline, it is possible to confuse the value of being disciplined with the structure of intellectual communities as a "discipline." Those who study science refer to concepts such as "epistemic communities" and not "disciplines" (Knorr Cetina 1999). They do so to emphasize that a group of scholars can be "disciplined," without having to be in a "discipline."

---

[2] Schmiede (2006) calls this combination of large-scale social transformation, increasing uses of ICT, and digitization of data "informatization." Informatization and computerization are interchangeable concepts for the purposes of this chapter.

One example of being disciplined is the intellectual community, the epistemic community, whose members study computers and humans interacting: CHI (Grudin 2004). Those who know CHI are aware it is a vibrant and growing intellectual space that attracts scholars trained in computer science, cognitive science, anthropology, psychology, and information science. What seems to bring CHI scholars together is a set of generally-agreed-upon characterizations of the phenomena of interest. This does not mean CHI scholars are of one mind: the phenomena of central interest for CHI scholars continues to expand and be hotly debated because the space is partly defined by the characteristics and affordances of the digital technologies with and through which humans interact[3].

The concern raised here is the disciplined coherence of physicists, economists, and computer scientists – and what they say about computing – are drowning out SI work on the sociotechnical nature of computing. While some might see SI as some sort of sociological analysis of computing, it is distinguished by its emphasis on the material and performative nature of the computing[4]. SI scholarship is premised on the ICT as having some limited form of agency, of contributing to structure, and to standing in some way as distinct from (but not independent of) the social efforts that made it and shape it. ICT has a voice and it participates. SI research tends to emphasize the form and functions of ICT artifacts more than do other approaches to the social analyses of computing (cf. Avgerou, Ciborra, and Land 2004; Loader 2007; Halavais 2006). In turn, social analyses of computing can be distinguished from economic analyses of computing (and the techno-economic determinism that often arises in this work) by the attention to social structure, the nature and importance of social relationships, and to collective action as a distinct, central, and fundamental activity. As such, social analyses of ICT reject the

---

[3] We note appreciatively that CHI scholars are often social informaticists' closest colleagues. Some participate as intellectual partners in SI scholarship and in doing so showcase the ways in which kindred intellectual communities can join together to pursue impactful scholarship. Many more CHI scholars see the overlaps between what we do and what they do as useful for both and this strengthens both communities' scholarship.

[4] The social analysis of computing emphasizes the socially embedded nature of ICT's design, development, implementation and uses, leaving the technological elements "black-boxed" or indeterminate. This perspective has many variants. Scholars who pursue the social analysis of computing are trained in sociology, communications, organizational studies, education, library science, and information science, among others. This is a hugely varied set of academic training grounds, to which we can add history, English and textual studies, rhetoric and cultural studies, and political science.

neoclassical economic assumption of a "*homo-economicus*," the rationalized, self-interested human (as do many economists, cf. Sen 1977; Swedberg 1994).

SI will never be a discipline in the noun sense. And, there is no intent here to argue for creating one. What we want is for SI researchers to be more disciplined (adjective); more coherent about our perspective and more articulate about our contributions. And, in doing this, to be more like economists or physicists in the ability to garner attention and resources.

Our Contributions and the Attention of Others

The large-scale phenomena of interest – computerization, informatization, re-shaped social and organizational arrangements, pervasive computing, large-scale digital networks, complex human-computer systems – deserve more of our attention. We admire the dreams of computer scientists and their pursuit of big ideas: naïve or not, these are inspirational. We stand in awe of the audacity of economists: they are often wrong about the effects of ICT but are confident and vocal.

In the face of dreams and audacity, SI scholars tend to offer situated details and tentative insights. Many who pursue sociotechnical analyses of computing do so through careful field-based studies that situate, contextualize, and problematize the idiosyncratic character and localized effects of larger-scale digital and social transformations. Law's (2004) wonderful essay "And if the Global Were Small and Non-Coherent? Method, Complexity and the Baroque" captures the essence of this focus. In this essay, he outlines two general forms of science: the first is theorizing as the search for simple and over-arching truths – what Law sees as Romantic notions of how the world works: a common view of science. In contrast to the Romantic notion is a Baroque approach to science that is localized, small, and infinitely detailed. This latter view provides powerful insights that often stand against Romantic notions, but are not as easily communicated.

The thousands of case studies, detailed ethnographies, and micro-studies offer up to the engaged scholar an amazingly rich and detailed view into the issues and the workings of changes due in part to computerization. We know so much about the mangle of practice, the configurational nature of socio-technical change, and the complexities of producing and consuming digital information (e.g., Fleck 1994). What we struggle to do is package this and communicate it to others.

Developing Some Discipline

We need to be a bit louder – and certainly louder than the comfortable quiet which is what scholars often prefer – in articulating and explaining the value of SI scholarship. Beyond a louder voice, we need to speak with more discipline. One way to do so is to be clear about the starting points of SI work: commonalities and the recurring findings. Three common insights that arise from the work of SI, building on many empirical studies, are (see also Kling, Rosenbaum, and Sawyer 2005; Lamb and Sawyer 2005; Sawyer and Tapia 2007):

1. **Computers are social technologies.** The profound simplicity of this point needs constant re-iteration. Technologies, and particularly for us, ICT, are products of human thought and action. Individuals use ICT and contribute to their creation. However, the design, development, take-up, and uses of ICTs reflect collective action. That is, individuals exist in larger social worlds – they are social actors (Lamb and Kling 2003). The ICTs people use are socially constructed, socially shaped, and socially enacted (Russell and Williams 2002). These ICTs serve as forms of social structure, provide for agency, and cannot be seen independently from the people who made them (e.g., Barley 1986; Winner 1986; Hughes 2004). Computer networks are – as Wellman, his students, and colleagues make clear – social networks (Wellman 2001).

2. **There are munificent variations in the uses and effects of ICT.** Any use of an ICT *may* have intended effects, but *will* have un-intended effects. The effects – intended and unintended – will have differential impacts based on the nature, roles, and goals of the people involved. These effects and uses may be both positive and negative. These effects are situated: while situations may share commonalities, each has unique local aspects that moderate prediction. These variations with using ICTs and the effects of their use reflect much of what we know about social organization. But these also are helping to reshape social and technological structures that we often take for granted (such as the differences in public and private communication, the boundaries of work and home, and the location of personal data).

3. **Effects of the uses of ICT are often indeterminate and multivalent.** New ICT-based systems are not solutions, they are interventions (and often with few post-take-up controls in place). The outcomes of the take up on any ICT-based system will take time to assess, will often have differential impacts – benefitting some more than others. Likewise, the take up and uses of new ICT-based systems raise the specter of negative outcomes for some.

Developing some discipline means that we should be clear that the common principles and underlying conceptual perspective are the starting point of our work. The basic tenets of SI must frame our studies, guide our analysis, structure our discussions, and signpost what needs attention. This consistency of expression is how we communicate to others the core of the SI approach. SI can be a large and heterogeneous intellectual space – tolerant of multiple theories, accepting a wide range of methods – and span intellectual communities. However, value comes from the clarity of core principles.

More than informing our scholarship, being disciplined means that SI must also be part of our pedagogy. If these principles are common, if these are core to what we do, then they deserve to be made more explicit to students and others. SI is not a canon of particular readings or particularly dogmatic, beyond core principles. The commonly re-found insights make clear that these are enduring and useful concepts that our future designers, policy analysts and institutional leaders should know.

Advancing Social Informatics

While these commonalities serve as the basis for SI, we see a need to go beyond acknowledging the situated and tentative nature of findings to identify recurring themes and to connect these to the larger-scale phenomena which frame our studies. To do this, to advance SI beyond being disciplined, we offer four paths. These are not mutually exclusive or exhaustive, simply opportunities for our scholarship. That is, each of these opportunities may be combined with others, and certainly there are multiple possible trajectories. In advancing these, our goal is to encourage innovation by building from core SI principles and pursuing opportunity.

Use Macro-Micro Framing to Advantage

To balance our approach with these goals of advocacy, we suggest framing our work as a macro-micro effort. This builds on Dutton (1999) who advocated for more clearly and carefully connecting our detailed micro-studies with larger macro-issues studies. Seen this way, situating a study has two meanings: the first and most common is to situate the study in a larger social milieu. The second meaning, and the one we advance here, is to use a carefully situated study to shift or reframe a larger conceptual debate.

For example, Rob Kling was a master at framing a micro-study relative to a macro-debate, then showcasing the alternative insights an SI analysis provides relative to techno-economic views (e.g., Kling and McKim 2000; Kling 1996). Other exemplars include recent work on women in computing (Cohoon and Aspray 2006), e-science (Meyer and Dutton 2009; Ribes and Lee 2010), online education (Haythornthwaite 2006), and distributed collaboration (Goggins and Jahnke 2012)[5].

Collaborate

A powerful way to advance SI is to work with others. Doing so will help to raise the scale and scope of the research being done. However, this requires multiple faculty, post-doctoral scholars and graduate students to work together as teams – perhaps across different physical locations. Developing the skills to fund, organize and sustain larger collaborations will require that SI scholars gain additional training. Collaboration is a potentially difficult trajectory to pursue because much of social science education and training is based on the concept of independent scholarship. Why can our colleagues in computing or physics have dozens, if not thousands, of co-authors and we must pursue our work in semi-isolation? Perhaps this is an aspect of discipline we must change. As Leonardi and Barley (2008) have argued so well, we must become more involved in the pursuit of common findings across settings relative to the design, take up, and uses of ICT. This means focusing less on the unique and idiosyncratic elements that are common in all field studies. So, we can be more strategic about organizing case studies and selecting our field sites. One example of this is Elliot and Kraemer's (2008) compilation of work on computerization movements. And, funding is typically needed to support larger-scale work, which means SI scholars must be more active in pursuing grants to support this larger-scale, collaborative work.

Innovate through Methods

A third path for advancing SI is methodological innovation. Innovations in methods often define fields (such as operations research) and often reflect important epistemological commitments (e.g., actor network theory). We can identify at least two fruitful paths for method innovations. The first is expanded uses of various forms of trace digital data; the second is new ways to combine data sets.

---

[5] More broadly, please to visit http://sociotech.net to learn about the community of scholars pursuing studies of sociotechnical systems.

Trace digital data such as email records, web logs, digital document logs and folders, digital images, and even activity-tracing software provide social informaticists with opportunities to gain additional forms of evidence that were not available to scholars just a few years ago. Combining trace data and fieldwork provides for new approaches to doing field work that is being called "trace ethnography" (Bowker et al. 2010). Likewise, Pollock and Williams (2008) have been advancing the "biographies of artifacts" (BoA) approach – one focusing attention to multi-site ethnographic study tied to an intensive analysis of software functionality and form. A third example is the attention being paid to multi-modal networks – combinations of people and digital technologies that act as some sort of ensemble or assemblage (Contractor, Monge, and Leonardi 2011). More broadly, we conceive SI as an intellectual space that encourages methodological plurality, innovation, extension, and recombination with greater freedom and responsiveness than is often allowable when working closer in to a method's disciplinary roots.

Think Bigger

A fourth path to advancing SI is to "think bigger." For example, computer scientists seek to invent the future. Economists seek to shape our economy and explain how we should thrive in such a thing. Our colleagues in CHI seek to make interacting with computers seamless – to have the interface "disappear." Too often, SI scholarship is grounded in small thinking: What is happening at this place? Why did this technological arrangement unfold in this place in this way? We emphasize the micro, the situated, and fail to make the larger importance clear. Seen this way, thinking bigger might be interpreted simply as being more macro. We see thinking bigger as more. As Dutton (1999) articulated, we should set our sights on advancing a socially-rich – or at least a socially-grounded – picture of a future where digital devices are far more interactive and involved in our work and non-work lives. A compelling version of this big thinking can be found in a report from the European Union's Institute for Prospective Technological Studies (2009). Thinking bigger is a call to SI scholars to be more actively involved in agenda-setting: something Sherry Turkle (e.g., Turkle 2011) has consistently sought to do.

Opportunities to Action

We began this chapter by noting that SI provides an approach to studying the sociotechnical arrangements to computing that other contemporary approaches do not. Given the more social, more pervasive, and more visible presence of ICT, we also argued there is profound need for just the types of insights and guidance that SI scholars are most adept at providing. To advance SI, we encouraged scholars to assert the common principles, findings and insights as the basis of their work going forward, and to consider pursuing one or more paths to elevate SI scholarship. We did so because SI scholarship is well suited for the challenges of understanding the interactional arrangements among ICT and the personal, organisational, and societal structures in which we live. Where these have often been seen and studied as layered concerns, with different disciplinary emphasis on each, SI views them as (increasingly) interpenetrating concerns. It is this breadth of opportunity that draws us to action.

References

Avgerou, Chrisanthi, Claudio Ciborra, and Frank Land, eds. 2004. *The Social Study of ICT: Innovation, Actors and Contexts*. Oxford: Oxford University Press.

Barley, Stephen R. 1986. "CT Scanners and the Social Order of Radiology Departments." *Administrative Science Quarterly* 31 (1): 78-108.

Bowker, Geoffrey C., Karen Baker, Florence Millerand, and David Ribes. 2010. "Towards Information Infrastructure Studies: Ways of Knowing in a Networked Environment." In *International Handbook of Internet Research*, edited by JJeremy Hunsinger, Lisbeth Klastrup, and Allen Matthew. Berlin: Springer.

Burris, Beverly H. 1998. "Computerization of the Workplace." *Annual Review of Sociology* 24: 141-157.

Cohoon, Joanne, and William Aspray, eds. 2006. *Women and Information Technology: Research on Underrepresentation*. Cambridge, MA: MIT Press.

Contractor, Noshir S., Peter R. Monge, and Paul M. Leonardi. 2011. "Multidimensional Networks and the Dynamics of Sociomateriality: Bringing Technology Inside the Network." *International Journal of Communication 5*, 682-720.

Dutton, William H. 1999. "The Web of Technology and People: Challenges for Economic and Social Research." *Prometheus* 17 (1): 5-20.

—. 2005. "The Internet and Social Transformation: Reconfiguring Access." In *Transforming Enterprise: Economic and Social Implications of Information Technology,* edited by William H. Dutton, Brian Kahin, Ramon O'Callaghan, and Andrew W. Wyckoff, 375-394. Cambridge, MA: MIT Press.

Elliot, Margaret S. and Kenneth L. Kraemer, eds. 2008. *Computerization Movements and Technology Diffusion: From Mainframes to Ubiquitous Computing*, Medford, NJ: Information Today.

Fleck, James. 1994. "Learning by Trying: The Implementation of Configurational Technology." *Research Policy* 23 (6): 637- 651.

Goggins, Sean, and Isa Jahnke. 2012. "CSCL@Work: Computer-Supported Collaborative Learning at the Workplace – Making Learning Visible in Unexpected Online Places Across Established Boundaries." *International Journal of Sociotechnology and Knowledge Development* 4 (3): 17-37.

Grudin, Jonathan. 2004. "Crossing the Divide." *ACM Transactions on Computer-Human Interaction* 11(1), 1-25.

Halavais, Alex. 2006. *Cyberporn and Society.* Dubuque, Iowa: Kendall/Hunt Publishing.

Haythornthwaite, Caroline. 2006. "Articulating Divides in Distributed Knowledge Practice." *Information, Communication & Society* 9 (6): 761-780.

Hughes, Thomas P. 2004. *Human-Built World: How to Think about Technology and Culture*. Chicago: University of Chicago Press.

Institute for Prospective Technological Studies. 2009. *The Impact of Social Computing on the EU Information Society and Economy*, The European Union Joint Research Centre, Seville, Spain. http://ipts.jrc.ec.europa.eu.

Kling, Rob, ed. 1996. *Computerization and Controversy: Value Conflicts and Social Choices (2nd edition).* San Diego: Academic Press.

Kling, Rob. 1999. "What is Social Informatics and Why Does it Matter?" *DLIB Magazine* 5 (1). http://www.dlib.org/dlib/january99/kling/01kling.html.

Kling, Rob, and Geoffrey McKim. 2000. "Not Just a Matter of Time: Field Differences and the Shaping of Electronic in Supporting Scientific Communication." *Journal of the American Society for Information Science and Technology* 51 (14): 1306–20.

Kling, Rob, Howard Rosenbaum, and Steve Sawyer. 2005. *Understanding and Communicating Social Informatics: A Framework for Studying and Teaching the Human Contexts of Information and Communication Technologies*. Medford, NJ: Information Today.

Knorr Cetina, K. 1999. *Epistemic Cultures. How the Sciences Make Knowledge*. Cambridge: Harvard University Press.

Kornfeld, William A., and Carl Hewitt. 1981. "The Scientific Community Metaphor." *IEEE Transactions on Systems, Man and Cybernetics*, SMC-11, Number 1: 24-33.

Lamb, Roberta, and Rob Kling. 2003. "Reconceptualizing Users as Social Actors in Information Systems Research." *MIS Quarterly* 27 (2): 197-235.

Lamb, Roberta, and Steve Sawyer. 2005. "Social informatics: Legacy and next steps." *Information Technology & People* 18 (1): 9-20.

Law, John. 2004. "And if the Global Were Small and Non-Coherent? Method, Complexity and the Baroque." *Environment and Planning D: Society and Space* 22 (1): 13-26.

Leonardi, Paul M., and Stephen R. Barley. 2008. "Materiality and Change: Challenges to Building Better Theory about Technology and Organizing." *Information and Organization* 18 (3): 159-176.

Loader, Brian D., ed. 2007. *Young Citizens in the Digital Age*. London, Routledge.

Merton, Robert K. 1973. *The Sociology of Science: Theoretical and Empirical Investigations*. Chicago: University of Chicago Press.

Meyer, Eric T., and William H. Dutton. 2009. "Top-Down e-Infrastructure Meets Bottom-Up Research Innovation: The Social Shaping of e-Research." *Prometheus,* 27 (3): 239-250.

Pickering, Andrew. 1984. *Constructing Quarks: A Sociological History of Particle Physics*. Chicago: University of Chicago Press.

Pollock, Neil, and Robin Williams. 2008. *Software and Organisations: The Biography of the Enterprise-wide System or How SAP Conquered the World*. London: Routledge.

Prasad, Monica. 2006. *The Politics of Free Markets: The Rise of Neoliberal Economic Policies in Britain, France, Germany, and the United States*. Chicago: University of Chicago Press.

Ribes, David, and Charlotte P. Lee. 2010. "Sociotechnical Studies of Cyberinfrastructure and e-Research: Current Themes and Future Trajectories." *Computer Supported Cooperative Work.* doi: 10.1007/s10606-010-9120-0.

Russell, Stewart, and Robin Williams. 2002. "Social Shaping of Technology: Frameworks, Findings and Implications for Policy with Glossary of Social Shaping Concepts." In *Shaping Technology, Guiding Policy: Concepts, Spaces and Tools*, edited by Knut H. Sorensen, and Robin Williams, 37-132.

Sawyer, Steve, and Andrea Tapia. 2007. "From Findings to Theories: Speculating on the Future of Social Informatics." *The Information Society* 23 (4): 263-275.

Schmiede, Rudi. 2006. "Knowledge, Work and Subject in Informational Capitalism." In *Social Informatics: An Information Society for All? In Remembrance of Rob Kling*, edited by Jacques Berleur, Markku I. Nurminen, and John Impagliazzo, 333-354. New York: IFIP International Federation for Information Processing.

Sen, Amartya K. 1977. "Rational Fools: A Critique of the Behavioral Foundations of Economic Theory." *Philosophy and Public Affairs* 6 (4): 317-341.

Swedberg, Richard. 1994. "Markets as Social Structures." In *Handbook of Economic Sociology*, edited by Neil J. Smelser, and Richard Swedberg, 255-282. New York and Princeton: Russell Sage Foundation and Princeton University Press.

Turkle, Sherry. 2011. *Alone Together: Why We Expect More from Technology and Less from Each Other*. New York: Basic Books.

Wellman, Barry. 2001. "Computer Networks As Social Networks." *Science 293*: 2031-2034.

Winner, Langdon. 1986. *The Whale and the Reactor: A Search for Limits in an Age of High Technology*. Chicago: University of Chicago Press.

Wolff, Edward N. 2003. "Productivity, Computerization, and Skill Change," In *Technology, Growth, and the Labour Market,* edited by Donna K. Ginther, Madeline Zavodny, and Lynn H. Foley, 197-234.